Using Bibliotherapy

A Guide to Theory and Practice

Rhea Joyce Rubin

A Neal-Schuman
Professional Book

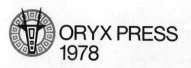
ORYX PRESS
1978

Operation Oryx, started more than 10 years ago at the Phoenix Zoo to save the rare white antelope—believed to have inspired the unicorn of mythology—has apparently succeeded.

An original herd of nine, put together through Operation Oryx by five world organizations, now numbers 34 in Phoenix with another 22 farmed out to the San Diego Wild Game Farm.

The operation was launched in 1962 when it became evident that the animals were facing extinction in their native habitat of the Arabian peninsula.

Copyright © 1978 by Rhea Joyce Rubin
Published by the Oryx Press
3930 E. Camelback Road
Phoenix, AZ 85018

Published simultaneously in Canada

Printed and Bound in the United States of America

Distributed outside North America by
Mansell Information/Publishing Limited
3 Bloomsbury Place
London WC1A 2QA, England
ISBN 0-7201-0804-7

Library of Congress Cataloging in Publication Data

Rubin, Rhea Joyce.
    Using Bibliotherapy.

    (A Neal-Schuman professional book)
    Bibliography: p.
    Includes index.
    1. Bibliotherapy. 2. Bibliotherapy—Study and teaching. 3. Bibliotherapists—Certification.
I. Title.
RC489.B48B8   616.8'916'6   78-9349
ISBN 0-912700-07-6

To my husband, Larry Berman

ERRATA SHEET

1) On the following pages the footnotes should read as follows:
   Page 14—*The Human Mind*[12]
   Page 15—. . . a sense of humanity in human relations. [12]

   . . . categorized by event or situation, related to specific emotional needs.[11]

   Reading Ladders for Human Relations, [18]

   . . . Shrodes laid the groundwork for much of the current theory of bibliotherapy.[24]

   Facilitating Human Development Through Reading: The Use of Bibliotherapy in Teaching and Counseling[32]

   Page 16—In 1971, the University of Wisconsin published a series of lectures on reading guidance and bibliotherapy[15] and the American Library Association published *Bibliotherapy: Methods and Materials.*[16] In 1975, Brown authored a survey of the literature and the ALA Bibliotherapy Committee edited an issue of the *Health and Rehabilitative Library Services Quarterly*[22] on this topic.

2) Page 20—Figure 3 is designed by Phillip Rubin.

3) Page 85—Figure 7 is by Dr. Franklin Berry.

4) The sentence on page 115 should read as follows: These requirements are: 1) M.L.S. or B.A. in education, counseling or behavioral science.

Using Bibliotherapy: A Guide to Theory and Practice

Contents

Appendix III D

Foreword

The power of books for life enhancement is a widespread factor in human cultures, and those cultures which lack this element are distinctively different from those which possess it. In *The High Valley*, Kenneth E. Read, an anthropologist, was wracked by the request of a young boy in the primitive highlands of Indonesia that he learn to read: would Asemo be isolated from his village by this new knowledge? How could he adjust to this wholly different culture which the use of books represents?

The use of literature for its therapeutic effect is instinctive in poets, dramatists, novelists. Ancient Greek tragedy's structure to produce catharsis in the audiences of the day was self-conscious and is widely understood. Emily Dickenson's "There is no frigate like a book . . ." is a cherished sentiment shared by many. At the common reader's level of understanding, the benign effects of literature are understood and purposefully utilized.

Bibliotherapy, however, as the more precisely directed reading to assist in the resolution of specific human ills, is a more recently emerging use of literature. As yet it has not won a widespread recognition, nor has it yet demonstrated the precision to which it aspires. This volume is an important addition to a series of publications that aim at giving form to the practice and a substantial theoretical base to the field.

Rhea Rubin comes to the authorship of this volume with as comprehensive a knowledge of both the literature of bibliotherapy and of the programs and activities in the field as any librarian in the United States at this time. Despite her youth, she has devoted a number of years—as an undergraduate, then as a graduate student, and now as a practicing librarian—to the understanding and the formulation of the field. She personally knows and has conferred with the major exponents of bibliotherapy and is acknowledged generally to be an able spokeswoman for the field.

This volume uniquely contributes a history of this interdisciplinary field, a shaping of the theoretical framework of the field, as well as a detailed analysis of the process of the bibliotherapeutic service in the context of librarianship. Finally, Rubin offers a detailed record of the evolution of training for the practice of bibliotherapy, with recommendations.

Rubin contributes a variety of concepts that will help to shape the development of bibliotherapy. For example, she identifies three types of bibliotherapy: institutional, clinical, and developmental, each of which differ in setting, leaders, participants, techniques, and goals. These categories make possible a clarification of roles in the field of bibliotherapy, and provide a sound base for interpreting the work of the bibliotherapist as librarianship.

The concept of "contract" between the therapist and the client is one which Rubin elaborates usefully from the root perception that therapy "is a political activity" in which persons who use the therapy subject themselves to the influence of the therapist in a "power-structured relationship." Rubin goes on to point out that the therapy process often, as Dr. Seymour Halleck explained, "encourages the patient to try to change himself rather than his environment." Aware that bibliotherapy, like all other therapies, could be used for social control, Rubin emphasizes the ethics inherent in providing bibliotherapy and the implicit "contract" between the client and the librarian, or between society for the client and the therapist.

The concept of social contract or individual contract under a set of ethical principles leads Rubin directly to a detailed discussion of the educational preparation of bibliotherapists and the standards for legal certification. Such standards are set in terms of degrees, internships, and courses in such areas as abnormal psychology and group dynamics. She recognizes that such standards do not command a consensus. It might be important, however, to raise the question as to whether they are premature.

Bibliotherapy in the 1970's is an attractive, growing field of practice. It is an adjuvant therapy, insofar as it is a true therapy, and in institutions it is always related to other therapies administered by licensed therapists. The guarantees of ethical practice in institutionalized or clinical settings are thus secure. Bibliotherapy as practiced by librarians in group settings without relationship to a more formal therapy staff are guided by the ethical principles of librarianship, developed in the context of reading guidance. It is clear that librarians are highly sensitive to these ethical considerations, even to the point of avoidance of an important service if the ethical issue is in doubt.

One can conclude reasonably, therefore, that the licensing issue for the control of practitioners of bibliotherapy is a concern related primarily, at this time, to the independent practitioners of bibliotherapy, and the related literature and poetry therapies, for whom there is no reasonably established body of practice under professional control. And indeed it is among this group that the movement for licensing has responsibly begun.

Perhaps it is appropriate to place the emphasis for bibliotherapy in the 1980's more lightly on the licensing and more heavily on education and research, two topics that Rhea Rubin has dealt with in considerable detail. There is real need for research to establish the validity of the controlled use of books as therapy; the work of Alexander,

McClaskey, and Burt is competent, substantive but still only introductory to the elucidation of the therapeutic process that uses books, films or recordings as the basis for cure of illness or the solution of personal problems. Only when such processes are clearly set forth can truly adequate standards for education be established and a basis for legal certification be soundly assured.

This volume will provide a basis for important clarification of thinking and debate of issues. Hopefully it will lead the alert, prepared librarian-bibliotherapist to undertake the research needed to move bibliotherapy from its status as an activity to its desired status of an art and a controlled science.

Margaret E. Monroe
Professor of Library Science
University of Wisconsin-Madison

Madison, Wisconsin
July 1977

Acknowledgments

Many people have helped me with this book during the two years I have been working on it. Only a few can be mentioned for their indirect contributions. I would like to thank Ruth Tews for keeping my age a secret when I visited the Mayo Clinic in 1969; Margaret Monroe, under whom I studied at the University of Wisconsin Library School, for helping me understand, among other things, the outgrowth of bibliotherapy from traditional library services; and Kathleen Weibel for providing me with an opportunity to work as a jail librarian, using bibliotherapy and testing my ideas. All three of these women have had a great effect on my philosophies which are evident in this book.

For their direct attention to this work, I am especially grateful to Clara Lack and Arleen Hynes for the wealth of experience they shared and for their constant encouragement. Clara also provided Appendix II, A Bibliography of Adult Materials for Group Bibliotherapy. Arleen's training program served as an example in Chapter Four and her description of it is included in Appendix III. Elizabeth Huntoon consulted with me and contributed many ideas to Appendix I, A Bibliography of Juvenile Materials for Bibliotherapy. Rikki Horne and Audrey Powers helped locate obscure materials; Phillip Rubin designed the time line in Chapter One; and Susan Stein did the index. Marcie Rickun, Rikki Horne, Arleen Hynes, and Clara Lack read my rough drafts and made valuable comments and criticisms. Special thanks to Phyllis Steckler and Kaye Reed of Oryx Press, and Pat Schuman of Neal-Schuman Publishers.

I also send thanks to the other friends and family who gave me support, and to the many colleagues who sent me clippings, reported articles, and showed an interest. My husband, Larry Berman, who acted as resident editor, reading and marking each chapter, deserves a lot of credit for the final version of this volume.

Rhea Joyce Rubin

Introduction

In the darkest hour of my sorrow, my only comfort came from the habit of reading, which Gibbon declared he 'would not exchange for the wealth of the Indies'. . . Even the Sphinx is not so enduring as a great book, written in the heart's blood of a man or woman who has sounded the deeps of sorrow only to rise up full of courage and faith in human nature.

—George Hamilton, *Comfort Found in Good Old Books* (1911)

There are many testimonials to the power of literature. Most are emotional, personal statements about its merits. Censorship is the age-old rebuttal to these testimonials, the evidence of a strong belief in the harmful effects of literature. Both the love and the fear of literature have produced authors, critics, teachers, librarians, and readers.

Bibliotherapy is a means of directing this potency. It is an activity which utilizes the strength of literature for the purposes of understanding, insight, and self-growth. This book attempts to clarify the definition and history of bibliotherapy and to offer information on the dynamics and mechanics of the field. To this end, included also are a discussion of education and certification for bibliotherapists, an appendix on certification and job description, and two bibliographies of suggested materials for use in bibliotherapy sessions.

DEFINITIONS

The term "bibliotherapy" is derived from the Greek *biblion* (book) plus *oepatteid* (healing). Samuel McChord Crothers coined the word in a 1916 *Atlantic Monthly* article, and there has been confusion about the terminology ever since. The first definition of the term appears in *Dorland's Illustrated Medical Dictionary:* (1941) "the employment of books and the reading of them in the treatment of nervous disease."

In 1961, *Webster's Third New International Dictionary* included a definition which was officially accepted in 1966 by the American Library Association: "the use of selected reading materials as therapeutic adjuvants in medicine and psychiatry; also, guidance in the solution of personal problems through directed reading." During that same year, the *Random House Dictionary* defined bibliotherapy as "the use of reading as an ameliorative adjunct to therapy." Although this definition is vague, it does avoid associating bibliotherapy directly with medicine.

For the purposes of this book, the following definition of bibliotherapy is used:

> A program of activity based on the interactive processes of media and the people who experience it. Print or nonprint material, either imaginative or informational is experienced and discussed with the aid of a facilitator.

This concept of the field includes the application of bibliotherapy in institutional or community settings, via print as well as other media, using didactic or imaginative literature in programs under the direction of one or more professionals. Its goal is either insight into normal development or changes in emotionally disturbed behavior. Primarily, it applies to group bibliotherapy. Individual bibliotherapy is a refinement of reader guidance, while group bibliotherapy is a hybrid field of psychology and library science using media and discussion of it as a therapeutic modality.

Each of the above delineations represents a point of conflict among people involved in bibliotherapy. For example, bibliotherapy in the 1930's was centered in hospitals with physically ill individual patients who needed information about their illnesses and its implications; didactic literature as used by a team of physician and librarian was the therapy tool. Today there is a renewed interest in "patient education" which fits this general mode. Later the use of bibliotherapy became widespread in educational contexts; groups of normal children participated in sessions using creative literature which were often run by a teacher or librarian. Bibliotherapy is now used by public libraries with both groups of normal and disturbed adults such as those served by community mental health centers. All of these applications are bibliotherapy. But, self-motivated individual reading, personal interaction of a librarian or therapist with a user or client, and the concept of the library as a neutral and comforting center—while they may be therapeutic—are *not* bibliotherapy.

CATEGORIES OF BIBLIOTHERAPY

In 1939, Alice Bryan wrote an article, "Can There Be a Science of Bibliotherapy?"[3] She answered her own question in the affirmative—yes, there can be. However, she added that the field needed a body of experimental data and scientifically trained workers before it could be considered a science. Since that time, there has been a continuing debate as to whether bibliotherapy is an art or a science. One way to deal with this question is to separate the concept of bibliotherapy into two parts and to call one aspect the science and one the art. Eleanor Brown uses this approach when she suggests that:

> . . . the prescription of reading in the treatment of actual mental or physical illness may well be regarded as the science of bibliotherapy; whereas the attempt to remedy personality defects or help an individual solve personal problems through the proper reading suggestions given by a librarian or other individual outside the medical field, can be regarded as the art of bibliotherapy.[2]

This division is consistent with the Webster's Dictionary definition: "the use of selected reading materials as therapeutic adjuvants in medicine and in psychiatry; also, guidance in the solution of personal problems through directed reading."

Another librarian categorizes bibliotherapy as either explicit or implicit. These terms were originally used to distinguish other therapies, but Evalene P. Jackson has adapted them to bibliotherapy.[10] Implicit therapy is a "resource of culture" well used by the reader's advisor, whereas explicit therapy is done only by a trained therapist.

Arleen Hynes proposes yet another dichotomy: bibliotherapy and clinical bibliotherapy. The latter can be practiced only by a mental health professional who has had special training in bibliotherapy. This person uses bibliotherapy diagnostically and evaluatively, in addition to using it as part of the therapy program. A bibliotherapist, in Hynes view, is an individual with specific training who uses bibliotherapy to "address the healthy aspects of the personality."[9]

Diagnostic, clinical, developmental, and protective are the four types of bibliotherapy delineated by Pauline Opler. Protective bibliotherapy is "reading . . . by a patient recovering from a mental breakdown in order to shield his thoughts from the external world while recovery is progressing." Most present-day practitioners do not consider this bibliotherapy. Opler's developmental bibliotherapy and clinical bibliotherapy are similar to Hynes' concepts, general and clinical bibliotherapy. "Clinical bibliotherapy," states Opler, is "done by doctors, psychiatrists, and psychologists for purposes of modifying the attitudes of patients."[15] Diagnostic bibliotherapy is similar to "bibliodiagnostics," which, defined by Lore Hirsch, is the use of reading materials to assess a person's needs and personality. This concept is similar to Sofie Lazarsfeld's "fiction test" in which she asked clients to name books which had impressed them and then analyzed those books to better understand the client's personality.[12]

Distinctions between art and science do not particularly help to delineate medical and nonmedical bibliotherapy. Whether or not bibliotherapy is used in a medical context, the field must continue to strive toward more scientific research and evaluation. Too little is known about the specific effects of reading on individuals in specific situations, the role of intuition in book selection, the importance of the therapist's knowledge and personality, and the interaction of those variables.

Because of these lacks, it may be helpful to adopt a three-pronged approach to bibliotherapy through classification according to settings, leaders, participants, techniques, and goals. The three types of bibliotherapy are institutional, clinical, and developmental. (See figure no. 1 for a schematic illustration).

Institutional bibliotherapy refers to the use of literature—primarily didactic—with individual institutionalized clients. It includes the traditional medical uses of bibliotherapy in which mental hygiene texts are recommended to mental patients. Since this is a one-to-one situation in an institutional setting, Ralph Ball's term, the "prescription of books for specific ills,"[1] applies. This type of bibliotherapy is performed by a librarian only in conjunction with a physician or medical team. The goal is primarily informational and recreational, although some insight materials may be offered. The early (1932-1937) bibliotherapy program in the Menninger Clinic, as reported by William Menninger, is a good example:

> The purpose . . . is three fold: one of these purposes is education . . . the second purpose would seem to be to provide a form of recreation or amusement . . . the third purpose is to help the individual identify with his social group (resocialization as a hospital patient) . . . In the development of our program, we have evolved a plan by which certain responsibilities are delegated to the librarian. It is the established attitude that reading is a treatment method and as such, must be directed by the physician. The librarian is the tool who carries out the mechanics and reports the observations.[14]

This type of bibliotherapy is not prevalent today, but some programs still exist. Institutional bibliotherapy also includes the use of media by doctors with individual patients in private practice.

Clinical bibliotherapy refers to the use of literature — primarily imaginative — with groups of clients with emotional or behavioral problems. These clients may or may not participate voluntarily. Groups can be led either by a doctor or a librarian, but are usually led by both in consultation with each other. The setting can be in an institution or in the community; goals range from insight to change in behavior. Librarian Arleen Hynes offers an example while describing the St. Elizabeths Hospital program with hospitalized mental patients in her *Libri* article:

> Team leadership consisting of a bibliotherapist and a mental health worker has proved to be a mutually supportive mode of cooperative bibliotherapy. In the last year, the librarian has had the privilege of working with two psychologists and a clinical nurse specialist in three on-going weekly groups. The group members were chosen by the staff who knew the patients. The librarian chooses the literary materials and reads aloud to the group which is furnished with copies of the selections. The co-leaders work together to ask appropriate questions or to make statements which enable the members to delve as deeply as possible into their reactions. The goals, the mode of procedure, the balance between personal aesthetic enrichment and the depth of psychological insight are the products of mutual cooperation of the co-leaders as well as the overall mental states of the patients in the groups.[8]

It is rare that a team participates as fully as in this example. The librarian-bibliotherapist may select the materials and run the groups, and have some consultation with a doctor or a mental health worker either in a regular session or as the need arises. Usually this depends on both the setting and the clients.

The Santa Clara County Library Bibliotherapy Program is an example of another mode of clinical bibliotherapy. Clara Lack, Bibliotherapist II, does all three types of bibliotherapy. She says that an independent living situation is a common goal of the ex-mental patients she works with in a board-and-care home. Shirley Jackson's story, "Like Mother Used to Make," has been successful there in starting discussion on living alone, loneliness, and friendship. The method used in this program is oral group reading followed by discussion led by the bibliotherapist. A staff conference follows in which the bibliotherapist mentions significant individual reactions.

Developmental bibliotherapy refers to the use of both imaginative and didactic literature with groups of "normal" individuals. The bibliotherapy group is designed and led by a librarian, teacher, or other "helping professional" to promote normal development and self-actualization, or to maintain mental health. Closely related is the concept of a developmental task. In his book, *Developmental Tasks and Education,* Robert Havighurst defines this as "a task which arises at or about a certain period in the life of the individual, successful achievement of which leads to his happiness and to success with later tasks, while failure leads to unhappiness in the individual, disapproval by society, and difficulty with future tasks." The origin of these tasks can be physical maturation, cultural pressure, personal values of the individual, or a combination of the sources. He states that the concept of developmental tasks is especially important in education because educational efforts should be properly timed. "When the body is ripe, and society requires, and the self is ready to achieve a certain task, the 'teachable moment' has come." Havighurst examines the developmental tasks of six age categories. In infancy and early childhood, these range from learning to walk, talk, and eat, to learning to imitate and identify, and to distinguish right from wrong. In middle childhood (6-12 years), learning physical skills, learning to get along with peers, developing a conscience, and developing attitudes toward social groups are among those tasks that are especially important. Adolescents (11-18 years) must achieve new relationships with others of both sexes, accept the physical body, achieve emotional independence from parents, and acquire a set of values and ethics, among other tasks. The adult (18-30) must select a mate, start a family, choose an occupation, and find a congenial social group. In middle age (30-55), one must achieve civic and social responsibility, maintain a standard of living, develop leisure-time activities, and accept physiological changes. In late maturity, the individual must adapt to decreasing health, reduced income and the death of friends and spouses, besides continuing some of the earlier tasks. Developmental bibliotherapy can help people with these common tasks besides helping to cope with individual problems such as divorce, pregnancy, death, and prejudice, all of which are refinements of developmental tasks. Examples of this type of bibliotherapy include teacher-led groups in the school system and librarian-led groups of adults in the community and in voluntary institutions.

The distinctions between these three aspects of bibliotherapy have implications for the dynamics and mechanics of bibliotherapy, and are especially important to the discussion of education and certification for bibliotherapy. Note also the common characteristic of all three types: discussion of the material after reading.

SEMANTICS

The term "bibliotherapy" has not been widely accepted. Many have said that it is too broad a designation. They suggest narrower terms such as "bibliodiagnostics" for assessment, or "biblioprophylaxis" for the preventative use of literature. Others claim the nomenclature is too narrow and suggest "biblioguidance," "bibliocounseling," or "library therapeutics." These terms have broader application because they are not limited by the word "therapy." "Tutorial group therapy" and "literatherapy" have also been used to avoid the prefix "biblio." As Dr. Michael Shiryon states:

> The name 'literatherapy'—combining literature and therapy—has been chosen mainly to stress its differentiation from the more popular name 'bibliotherapy' which has become extremely vague and almost meaningless. The use or abuse of the term 'bibliotherapy' embraces any and every combination of book-related materials with patient-resembling populations. Literatherapy attempts to emphasize the literary-imaginative trend rather than the merely informative-didactic approach, and also to present literatherapy as a bona fide first-rate method of psychotherapy, rather than a second-rate adjunct patronizingly relegated to librarians.[16]

Another term closely related to bibliotherapy is "counselor librarianship."[13] In 1951, the University of Illinois/Chicago (UIC) replaced its library's Reference Department with a Department of Library Instruction and Advisement and planned "to implement general education, library instruction, and student counseling bureau objectives." Four librarians were selected to become "counselor librarians" by participating in a training course developed by the UIC Bureau. They were to be "rigorously selected, trained, and experienced librarians with special personality and job qualifications including reference, teaching, and group discussion leadership ability, who (undergo) a carefully planned in-service counselor training program." The goals of the counselor librarians were described in the following manner:

> Counselor trained librarians should be able to do much to encourage readers to 'apply books to themselves,' through extension of existing types of library services. The best reference work sometimes tends in the direction of counseling, but its chief concern mostly is with the transmitting of information, the solution of more or less immediate problems, so that usually it is advisement . . . Readers' advisory work and bibliotherapy, with their attention to longer term individual needs, often come much closer to counseling, although it is believed that application of full counseling attitudes and methods to them might also bring them to fuller development.[13]

CHARACTERISTICS OF THE THREE TYPES OF BIBLIOTHERAPY

	Institutional	Clinical	Developmental
Format	individual or group; usually passive	group—active; voluntary or involuntary	group—active; voluntary
Client	medical or psychiatric patient, prisoner, or client in private practice	person with an emotional or behavioral problem	"normal" person, often in a crisis situation
Contractor	society	society or the individual	individual
Therapist	physician and librarian team	physician, mental health worker, or librarian, often in consultation	librarian, teacher, or other
Material used	traditionally didactic	imaginative literature	imaginative literature and/or didactic
Technique	discussion of material	discussion of material, with emphasis on client's reactions and insights	discussion of material, with emphasis on client's reactions and insights
Setting	institution or private practice	institution, private practice or community	community
Goal	usually informational, with some insight	insight and/or behavior change	normal development and self-actualization

FIGURE I

The counselor librarian's work was done in library use classes and in sessions with individual students; group therapy methods were not used. Unfortunately, the Counselor Librarianship experiment at UIC was discontinued after only a few years.

Nicholas Rubakin, a remarkable Russian writer, created a theory of reading which he called "bibliopsychology" in the early 1900's. He formulated this theory in 1916 and published a two-volume *Introduction to Bibliopsychology* in 1922; in that year, his Institute of Bibliopsychology was moved from Geneva to Lausanne. (These facts are included in a fascinating biography of Rubakin written by his son, which is included in a recent book about bibliopsychology. Rubakin himself wrote seventy articles on bibliopsychology from 1921-1946.) Rubakin pointed out that:

> A book, as a material object, will be differently perceived by different people. In our view, when the book is being read it is a subjective psychological phenomenon based on impressions which the reader's psycho-physical organism receives from it as an external object. Should the reader's organism undergo some change (through illness, ageing, etc.) the same book would seem very different to him. Therefore, the book in itself, as a phenomenon independent of the viewer, is an unknown entity . . . The reader does not attribute the psychological phenomenon evoked by a text to himself; he attributes them to the book which is a material object. He objectifies them and projects them onto the book . . .[17]

He felt that this theory should cause librarians to change their attitudes and methods. They "must turn their attention from the book seen as inert matter to the inner life of the human personality. It is the living being which creates, constructs, and combines; the book is no more than an instrument. The librarian who does not understand this can convert the best library into a cemetery for books."[17]

Rubakin devised tests and formulae to classify readers and to categorize books. Each reader was assigned a numerical score representing the average number of physiological responses made while reading. Each book was also assigned a score related to the average number of such responses it evoked in readers. He felt that a comparison of the reader's average score, his or her score on reading a specific book, and the book's score, would demonstrate the amount of that reader's reaction to the book and that this information would enable librarians to be better readers' advisors.

Many terms have been substituted for "bibliotherapy." Some have been applied to new fields, but most arose because of complaints that the term is too narrow or too vague. This author shares the discontent with the term "bibliotherapy." The prefix "biblio" is far too limiting in this age of multi-media. All types of audio and visual materials can, and should, be used to promote self growth. The suffix "therapy" also seems an unfortunate choice in a time when therapies and therapy techniques are proliferating. Bibliotherapy is not psychotherapy (although it can be used in conjunction with psychotherapy) and is not even therapy *per se*. The English word "therapy" is derived from the

Greek word for "cure" and is currently defined by *Webster's New World Dictionary* as "the treatment of disease or of any physical or mental disorder by medical or physical means." However, bibliotherapy is not restricted to the medical or physical context. More importantly, bibliotherapy does not claim to cure, but to "enlighten" in the truest sense of the word. Webster's defines "enlighten" as "to give the light of fact and knowledge to; reveal truths to; free from ignorance, prejudice, or superstition; to give clarification to a person as to meanings, intentions, etc."

The goal of bibliotherapy should be insight and understanding. To understand is to stand under, to stand away, to stand apart, in order to see something from a different perspective; to learn; to know, and then to integrate that knowledge into the self. Insight is the power of a thinking, feeling person to look within and beneath the surface of things; it is an ability that can be strengthened through bibliotherapy. It is especially important that bibliotherapists be aware of the power they can engender in the client, as opposed to the power that is removed. The only demonstration of power for a helpless person is through a nervous breakdown or through commission of a crime. By "acting out," he or she can command attention and sympathy—this is power over others. When a person in therapy learns about the motives for his or her behavior, that power is often removed. Any effective therapy must replace the destructive power with a new, constructive one—that of insight and understanding. Bibliotherapy and other activity therapies help clients gain an appreciation of their abilities in dance, art, or understanding. These therapies also offer opportunities to try out new behaviors.

The word therapy also has political connotations which are objectionable. The interpersonal politics of traditional therapy revolve around a situation which involves a patient and a therapist—one receiving and one prescribing. Michael Glenn, a "radical therapist" states that "therapy today is a power relationship between people—one up, one down; helper and helped. In a society built on individualism and competition, it embodies the problem, and thus can scarcely be seen as a solution . . ."[5] As Claude Steiner, a psychiatrist adds:

> Psychiatry [read: therapy] is a political activity. Persons who avail themselves of psychiatric aid [therapy] are invariably in the midst of power-structured relationships with one or more other human beings. The psychiatrist [therapist] has an influence in the power arrangements of these relationships. Psychiatrists [therapists] pride themselves on being 'neutral' in their professional dealings. However, when one person dominates or oppresses another, a neutral participant, especially when he is seen as an authority, becomes an enforcer of the domination.[18] . .

Bibliotherapy's great advantage is that to a large extent the book or other material does the work of the therapist. Bibliotherapists or group leaders may choose the material, but individual clients interpret it first as an entity apart from the therapist and from themselves, and then integrate it into themselves. Group bibliotherapy utilizes not only the material but the group itself to facilitate self-growth so the tension of the therapist-client relationship is further eased.

The politics of therapy are evident at societal levels as well as the interpersonal one. Therapy should mean change, not simply adjustment, but as Dr. Seymour Halleck explains it:

> The therapeutic process . . . encourages the patient to try to change himself rather than his environment. In most forms of individual psychotherapy, the patient is usually implored to examine his own feelings and attitudes. Of course he also learns how the environment affects his feelings and attitudes, but the main emphasis is on ways in which he can alter his perception of and reaction to his environment. As the patient concentrates upon what are defined as his own inadequacies, he is in effect called upon to adjust and he may easily become resigned to adjusting to an oppressive environment.[6]

Acceptance can be a means of evading one's responsibility to the self, but it can also be a necessary goal of therapy. A patient learning to accept a physical disability is a good example of the latter case.

Librarians and all others who participate in any activity labelled "therapy" must understand the possible use of therapy for social control. As Jerome Agel states: "Psychology is more than a professional field; it is an ideology, a belief in appropriate normal behavior with coercive power to back up that belief."[5] This political potential is critical in terms of contracting for bibliotherapy services, and in terms of the ethics of bibliotherapy, both of which will be discussed in Chapter Four.

The definition of "therapy" as "cure," the interpersonal power structure of therapy, and the exalted position of medical doctors in our society, cause many librarians to fear any activity called "therapy." Others are concerned about the political ramifications of therapy. In either case, it appears to be the nomenclature which alienates people, not the activity of using literature for insight. Librarians should approach bibliotherapy much as recreational and occupational therapists view their work—as an activity which is therapeutic and can be part of a medical program, or as one possible path toward self-actualization.

REFERENCES

1. Ralph G. Ball, "Prescription: Books," *ALA Bulletin* 48:145-147 (March 1954).

2. Eleanor Brown, *Bibliotherapy and Its Widening Applications* (Metuchen, New Jersey: Scarecrow, 1975).

3. Alice I. Bryan, "Can There Be a Science of Bibliotherapy?" *Library Journal* 64:773-777, (October 15, 1939).

4. Alice I. Bryan, "The Psychology of the Reader," *Library Journal* 64:7-12 (January 1, 1939).

5. Michael Glenn in Jerome Agel, *The Radical Therapist* (New York: Ballantine Books, 1971).

6. Seymour Halleck, *The Politics of Therapy* (New York: Science House Inc., 1971).

7. Robert J. Havighurst, *Developmental Tasks and Education* (New York: Longmans, Green, and Co., 1950).

8. Arleen Hynes, "Bibliotherapy in the Circulating Library at St. Elizabeths Hospital," *Libri* 25:144 (December 1975).

9. Arleen Hynes, "The Function of the Bibliotherapist," unpublished paper (1973).

10. Evalene P. Jackson, "Bibliotherapy and Reading Guidance: A Tentative Approach to Theory," *Library Trends* 11:122 (October 1962).

11. Clara Lack, "Group Bibliotherapy," *HRLS Quarterly* 1:19-20 (October 1975).

12. Sofie Lazarsfeld, "The Use of Fiction in Psychotherapy: A Contribution to Bibliotherapy," *American Journal of Psychotherapy* 3:26 (January 7, 1949).

13. David K. Maxfield, *Counselor Librarianship* (University of Illinois Library School Occasional Papers #38, March 1954).

14. William C. Menninger, M.D., "Bibliotherapy," *Bulletin of the Menninger Clinic* 1:263-274 (November 1937).

15. Pauline Opler, "The Origins and Trends of Bibliotherapy as a Device in Mental Hospital Libraries," (MLS Thesis, San Jose State College, 1969).

16. Michael Shiryon, "From Bibliotherapy to Literatherapy: The Next 25 Years," (unpublished speech presented at the California State Psychological Association Convention, Oakland, California January 26, 1973).

17. Sylva Simsova, ed., *Nicholas Rubakin and Bibliopsychology* (Hamden, CT: Archon Books, 1968).

18. Claude Steiner, "Radical Psychiatry: Principles" in *The Radical Therapist* (New York: Ballantine Books, 1971).

Chapter One

Perspectives

HISTORY

The history of bibliotherapy has often been cited as the history of the use of books in mental hospitals. Both Philip Weimerskirch and Pauline Opler present detailed historical accounts of hospital libraries. The other common approach to the history of bibliotherapy is exemplified by William Beatty's article, "A Historical Review of Bibliotherapy," which presents an excellent survey of the articles written on bibliotherapy.[2] Instead of reiterating either of these approaches here, a brief chronology of important events in bibliotherapy will be presented, followed by an interdisciplinary approach to the roots of bibliotherapy as a separate field.

The earliest association of books with mental health was by the Greeks, who envisioned their libraries as repositories for "medicine for the soul." The Romans felt that orations could be read by patients to improve their mental health. One of the earliest records of the use of books for treatment appeared in the Middle Ages. In 1272 the Al-Mansur Hospital in Cairo provided readings of *The Koran* as part of the medical treatment. This example represents a recurring pattern in the inception of libraries in institutions. Religious dedication was the motivation behind the provision of books in mental hospitals and in prisons until the middle of the nineteenth century.

In the late eighteenth century, a number of humanitarians—notably Pinel in France, Chiarugi in Italy, and Tuke in England—sought to improve the treatment of the insane. One method was to provide recreation such as reading. By the beginning of the nineteenth century, these reforms had spread to America; Benjamin Rush became the first American to recommend reading for the sick (in 1802) and for the mentally ill (in 1810). He also advocated the use of fiction as well as religious materials. Another American physician, John Minson Galt II, wrote the seminal article on bibliotherapy in 1846, but he is best known for his 1853 essay entitled, "On Reading, Recreation, and Amusements for the Insane," which lists five reasons why reading is beneficial to mental patients.

In 1904, when E. Kathleen Jones administered libraries at the McLean Hospital in Waverly, Massachussetts, she was the first qualified and trained librarian to use books in the treatment of the mentally ill. Because of her work, bibliotherapy received its first recognition as an aspect of librarianship.

The development of bibliotherapy received a large impetus during World War I. Librarians and laypersons, notably the Red Cross, helped to quickly build libraries in the Army hospitals. At the end of the War, the U. S. Veterans Bureau became responsible for the Veterans Hospitals and the facilities within them, including libraries. From that time on, the Veterans Administration (VA) played a large role in bibliotherapy. (A scan of the literature in the 1930's and 1940's especially shows a disproportionate amount produced by VA librarians.) In 1923, Sadie P. Delaney instituted bibliotherapy at the VA Hospital in Tuskegee, Alabama.

In 1928, Edwin Starbuck edited a *Guide to Children's Literature for Character Training.* It was the first result of the Institute of Character Research established in 1921 at the University of Iowa. The Institute had been an outcome of a 1919 national prize for character education methodology which was awarded to the Iowa Plan. This plan deleted the preaching of morals from the curriculum and replaced it with a dynamic method in which children would learn morals from art, music, and literature. In order to help teachers with the plan, the guide included a booklist, by grade level, of fairy tales, myths, and legends (a second volume covered fiction); a situations list arranged by "the moral situations involved and the character attitudes which they reinforce . . ." and five indexes. Author, title, title of selection, moral situation (e.g. duty, community), and attitude (e.g. adjustment, responsibility), were listed for each entry. This two-volume work was the first major bibliography categorized by character needs.[25]

It was not until the 1930's that the concept of bibliotherapy began to bloom. According to *We Call It Bibliotherapy,*[5] eighteen articles and reports on bibliotherapy for the adult hospitalized patient were published in the 1920's. Of the sixty articles published in the 1930's, 63 percent were published in fields other than library science. In 1930, Dr. Karl Menninger published *The Human Mind,*[11] a mental hygiene book for laymen which was popularly used by a physician with a patient. He was joined in his interest in the use of mental hygiene literature by his brother, Dr. William Menninger, who presented a paper for the American Psychiatric Association in 1937 and wrote about it in the *Bulletin of the Menninger Clinic.*[13] Dr. Julius Griffin, also in Kansas before he opened his own clinic in California, was a third major proponent of bibliotherapy in the 1930's. Their continuing work is still important in the field. Alice I. Bryan, a librarian who was prominent in bibliotherapy, published two classic articles in 1931. Many other significant articles were published during the decade and a 1938 volume by Louise Rosenblatt, sponsored by the Human Relations

Commission of the Progressive Education Association, encouraged the use of literature for developing a sense of humanity in human relations.[18]

In 1939, the Hospital Division of the American Library Association established the first committee on bibliotherapy. Bibliotherapy had finally achieved "official" status in librarianship. During the past four decades, this committee has been responsible for three surveys of progress in the field, numerous bibliographies, a book, and a number of research proposals.

The 1940's, 1950's, and 1960's produced many more publications and some significant research. Elbert Lenrow in 1940 published a major bibliography, categorized by event or situation, related to specific emotional needs.[10] In 1947, the American Council on Education published the first edition of *Reading Ladders for Human Relations*,[17] a similar bibliography for young people; the fifth edition was published in 1972. (It is interesting to note that such a bibliography currently is being prepared in Germany.)

Perhaps the most important work of this period was Caroline Shrodes' doctoral dissertation entitled "Bibliotherapy: A Theoretical and Clinical-Experimental Study." In her work, Shrodes laid the groundwork for much of the current theory of bibliotherapy.[22]

In 1952, the Veterans' Administration compiled a list of references entitled "Bibliotherapy in Hospitals." This was replaced in 1958 with an annotated bibliography, *We Call It Bibliotherapy*,[5] which was updated and revised in 1967. The Veterans' Administration hospitals still provide an important testing ground for bibliotherapy.

In 1962, *Library Trends* devoted an issue of the journal to bibliotherapy.[2, 7, 27] This collection of papers led to the first national bibliotherapy workshop, which was held in 1964. It was sponsored by the American Library Association, funded with a grant from the National Institutes of Mental Health, and attended by leaders representing many professions. Another important publication in the 1960's was *Facilitating Human Development Through Reading: The Use of Bibliotherapy in Teaching and Counseling*,[30] which remains an excellent guide to the use of bibliotherapy in education.

The Association for Poetry Therapy (APT) was founded in New York in 1969. APT has produced a newsletter and currently sponsors an annual meeting. Its founder Jack Leedy has edited two books on poetry therapy. In 1973, the Poetry Therapy Institute was founded by Art Lerner in California.

In 1974 the International Federation of Library Associations (I.F.L.A.) met in the United States and American librarians were called upon to present papers. At the Libraries in Hospitals Subsection, a large program was devoted to bibliotherapy. Three librarians, one recreational therapist, one nurse, and one physician spoke during the half day of lectures. These papers were published in December 1975 in *Libri*.

In addition to the articles resulting from the conference, four other recent publications are noteworthy. In 1971, the University of Wisconsin published a series of lectures on reading guidance and bibliotherapy and the American Library Association published *Bibliotherapy: Methods and Materials.*[15] In 1975, Brown authored a survey of the literature and the ALA Bibliotherapy Committee edited an issue of the *Health and Rehabilitative Library Services Quarterly*[20] on this topic.

A review of the history of bibliotherapy demonstrates its continuing vitality. But to understand the evolution of bibliotherapy into its present common form—that of directed reading and group discussion—one must trace the roots of bibliotherapy in both library science and in psychology.

ROOTS IN LIBRARY SCIENCE

A prominent library science professor, Margaret Monroe, states in "Reader Services and Bibliotherapy," that bibliotherapy is one service of reading guidance. She views bibliotherapy as part of a continuum of library services. Reference services, reading guidance, and bibliotherapy are closely related in function. All three serve informational, instructional, and/or guidance needs. Reference services are objective, informational, and of short duration while reading guidance is subjective, and more broadly educational. Bibliotherapy is a long-term approach to library services used for therapeutic purposes.[15] This concept of bibliotherapy as a functional outgrowth of readers' services, is noted by Margaret Hannigan in her *Library Trends* article: "This skill [bibliotherapy] is a refined application of his normal librarian's function as reader's advisor."[7] Readers' services, in turn, developed out of other library functions.

In the nineteenth century, academics' attitudes toward the library changed as scholarship itself changed and became professionalized and specialized. Scholars became more dependent on the library and demanded more of its personnel. Justin Winsor, hired by Harvard University in 1877, established a precedent when he opened the stacks to students and allowed books to circulate. This was the beginning of reference services. The first proposal for an actual program of assistance to readers was made in 1876 by Samuel Swett Green of the Worcester Public Library. By 1883, the Boston Public Library, which was the largest public library at that time, had a full-time assistance position. At the same time, Melville Dewey at Columbia College was trying to adopt the "modern library idea" of aid to readers there.

The actual phrase "reference work" was first used to replace "aid to readers" and "assistance to readers" in 1891 in the *Library Journal.* By 1900, reference service was available not only in the public library central building in Detroit, but in its branch libraries as well. In 1905, the Washington, D.C. Public Library established a "library hostess" position to guide its patrons. At that time it was a reference classification, but by 1945 it was considered a readers' guidance position.

In the 1920's and 1930's, the readers' advisor came to the forefront of librarianship. The first adult education department and readers' advisory bureau was established at the Milwaukee Public Library in 1923 under the auspices of Miriam Tompkins. In 1924, when Franklin Hopper, the Chief of Circulation at the New York Public Library, decided to establish a readers' advisory position, he had to convince the Reference Department to fund it. Jennie M. Flexner came from the Louisville Public Library to become the New York Public Library's first readers' advisor. Both Flexner and Tompkins saw their work as an integral part of adult education. Though she stressed individually tailored reading lists, Flexner also emphasized the importance of working with groups. By the late 1930's she was developing programs of reading for many types of groups at both the local and national levels. One such reading course, begun in 1931, is an obvious precursor to bibliotherapy; she developed reading lists for adult probationers after interviewing the individuals involved. Much of the readers' advisory services of the 1930's were integrated into the adult education departments of public libraries. One of the best-known examples of adult education in the 1940's is the Great Books Program developed at the University of Chicago in 1945. This program of book-based discussion paralleled the development of the more therapeutically oriented book service called bibliotherapy.

ROOTS IN PSYCHOLOGY

The history of group therapy has been traced to 1905 when Dr. Joseph Platt of Boston began group classes for tuberculosis patients. But some group therapies find their roots in Greek dramas, medieval plays, and religious revival meetings, as does bibliotherapy. An American psychoanalyst, Trigant Burrow, used the term "group analysis" in 1925 and soon developed it into a separate field called "phyoanalysis." He met with much resistance from Freud and from Jung and eventually left the psychoanalytic community.

Also during the early 1920's, Alfred Adler advocated group therapy on political and economic grounds. As a socialist, he felt that working-class people should have access to therapy and that a group approach would be the only financially feasible format. He opened a number of clinics in Vienna, but his work was less popular there than it was in the United States. In 1926 he became a professor at Columbia University.

Another pioneer in the field was Jacob Moreno who, in 1931, coined the term "group therapy." Moreno claimed that he had used the technique in Vienna since 1910. Eventually his work became the basis for the important Bethel Laboratories sensitivity training in 1946, which in turn led to the modern "T-groups." Louis K. Wender and Paul Schilder were also experimenting in the 1940's with group therapy using hospitalized mental patients. Wender combined the group method with individual therapy for patients who were not intellectually impaired but whose disorders were "borderline"; his results were published in 1935. Schilder worked with fifty patients at Bellevue Hospital in New York City and reported his results in 1936. Meanwhile, the field of group dynamics began to develop in the United States. By the end of the 1930's, Kurt Lewin had popularized the term and made great contributions in the field. Besides the new group psychotherapists, social workers, educators, and administrators were especially interested in the nature of groups and group interactions; many other psychiatrists, including Samuel Slavson and Alexander Wolf in America, and W. R. Bion and S. H. Foulkes in England, used the group method experimentally.

It was not until World War II that group therapy really flourished. Much of the rationale was economic: there were too many patients and not enough medical staff. The number of wounded soldiers and veterans needing therapy was overwhelming. As Maxwell Jones, a psychiatrist, explains: "Group therapy in Great Britain made great strides in World War II because one psychiatrist could handle twenty cases in groups rather than four in psychoanalysis . . . We believe (but cannot prove) that the results described could not have been achieved by psychotherapy and hospitalization alone."[9] All types of adjunctive therapies, both individual and group, flourished after the second world war. The war and its aftermath brought many changes, including new therapies, because individual psychotherapy was not able to cope with the new war-created patients.

Play and Activity Therapy developed out of Slavson's earlier "analytic group therapy." Moreno's theatre of spontaneity developed into psychodrama, which he introduced to the United States in 1925. Dance therapy was started in 1942 by Marian Chace, and in the 1950's, both art therapy and music therapy were established.

It is no coincidence that the World War II era of 1939-1945 also produced much of significance in the field of bibliotherapy. Librarians were busy serving patients in hospitals and veterans on the streets. By 1950, more than 400 journal articles on bibliotherapy had been published. From 1950 to 1960, more than 100 articles were published just dealing with bibliotherapy for adult hospitalized patients. Two-thirds of all the publications in the field during that decade were published in journals outside the library field, and four-fifths were published in nonmedical journals. From 1960-1975, 195 articles plus 32 dissertations and research studies were published. Of the 131 articles published from 1970-1975, 35 percent appeared in library journals and 65 percent in periodicals of other fields such as nursing, occupational therapy, psychiatry, and education. Bibliotherapy clearly is—and should be further developed as—an interdisciplinary field.

SURVEYS OF THE FIELD

For an overview of opinion and practices in bibliotherapy during the past four decades, it is useful to review the surveys. To date, at

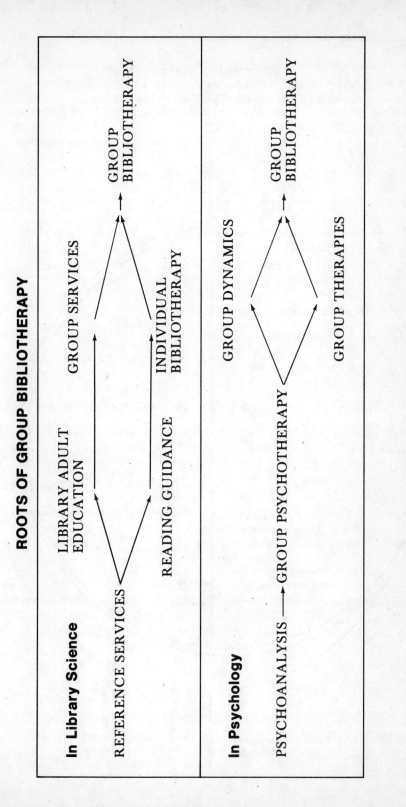

ROOTS OF GROUP BIBLIOTHERAPY

In Library Science

LIBRARY ADULT EDUCATION

GROUP SERVICES

GROUP BIBLIOTHERAPY

REFERENCE SERVICES

INDIVIDUAL BIBLIOTHERAPY

READING GUIDANCE

In Psychology

GROUP DYNAMICS

GROUP BIBLIOTHERAPY

PSYCHOANALYSIS → GROUP PSYCHOTHERAPY

GROUP THERAPIES

FIGURE 2

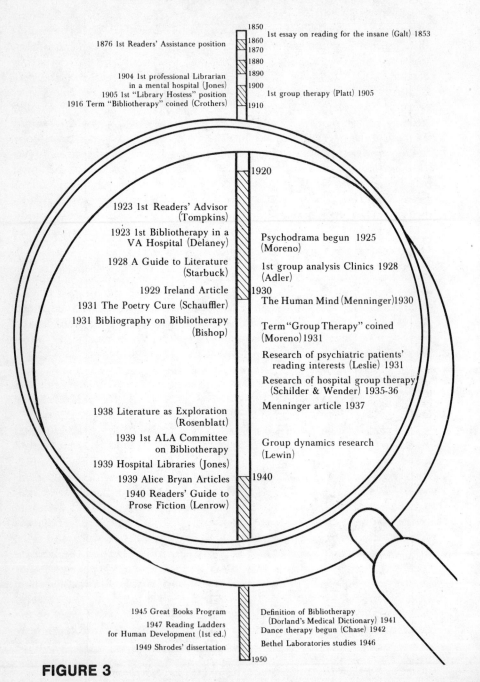

Roots of Bibliotherapy
important dates in Library Science/The Humanities
and in Psychiatry/The Behavioral Sciences

1850
1st essay on reading for the insane (Galt) 1853
1860
1876 1st Readers' Assistance position
1870
1880
1890
1904 1st professional Librarian
in a mental hospital (Jones)
1900
1905 1st "Library Hostess" position
1st group therapy (Platt) 1905
1916 Term "Bibliotherapy" coined (Crothers)
1910

1920

1923 1st Readers' Advisor
(Tompkins)

1923 1st Bibliotherapy in a
VA Hospital (Delaney)   Psychodrama begun 1925
(Moreno)

1928 A Guide to Literature   1st group analysis Clinics 1928
(Starbuck)   (Adler)

1929 Ireland Article   1930
1931 The Poetry Cure (Schauffler) The Human Mind (Menninger)1930

1931 Bibliography on Bibliotherapy Term"Group Therapy" coined
(Bishop)   (Moreno)1931

Research of psychiatric patients'
reading interests (Leslie) 1931

Research of hospital group therapy
(Schilder & Wender) 1935-36

Menninger article 1937

1938 Literature as Exploration
(Rosenblatt)

1939 1st ALA Committee
on Bibliotherapy   Group dynamics research
(Lewin)
1939 Hospital Libraries (Jones)

1939 Alice Bryan Articles   1940

1940 Readers' Guide to
Prose Fiction (Lenrow)

1945 Great Books Program   Definition of Bibliotherapy
(Dorland's Medical Dictionary) 1941
1947 Reading Ladders
for Human Development (1st ed.) Dance therapy begun (Chase) 1942

1949 Shrodes' dissertation   Bethel Laboratories studies 1946

1950

FIGURE 3

least two private surveys and three American Library Association Bibliotherapy Committee surveys have been prepared, used, and
analyzed.

In 1948 Robert Tyson reported on the effects of "mental hygiene
literature," which he defined as "any reading matter designed to maintain, improve, or restore emotional adjustment." He stated that bibliotherapy is an economical approach to the problem of increasing
mental health problems. To evaluate both the efficacy of reading prescribed by a psychiatrist and self-selected reading, he used two different questionnaires. One was used with eight psychoanalysts ("selected
because of the probability that their estimate of bibliotherapy would
be conservative"); the other was sent to one-hundred twenty-four
female undergraduate students. The majority of the psychoanalysts
"almost never" recommended mental hygiene literature for personal
adjustment, but more than half felt it had some value. Some felt it
helped the client most for reassurance, five felt its value was for information. Half felt that bibliotherapy could help in selected cases.
Three-quarters distinguished between neurotics who might misuse the
reading, and "normal" patients who could make good use of it. The
students' responses showed that 13 percent felt that reading about personal adjustment helped them "a great deal," 80 percent felt that it
helped a little to a lot, and 7 percent felt that it had "not helped at all."
Fifty-seven percent named texts as the reading that helped the most,
28 percent said magazine articles, and 15 percent cited popular books.
Fifty-five percent felt the help received was in the category of "information about personality," 25 percent mentioned "ideas on how to get
along better," and 20 percent cited "general reassurance and
encouragement." Tyson looked for—but did not find—any correlation
between "reports of degree of worrying and amount of help obtained
from reading." Unfortunately Tyson did not survey any librarians.[30]

In April 1956, the Bibliotherapy Committee of the then Hospital
Libraries Division of ALA, chaired by Margaret Hannigan, conducted
a survey "to show the nature and extent of bibliotherapy services performed by members of the Hospital Libraries Division." The questionnaire was published in the *ALA Hospital Book Guide* and sixty-four hospital librarians responded. Twelve questions were asked, grouped
under the headings of librarian-patient relationship, doctor-librarian-
patient relationship, planned group activities using library materials,
and maintenance of records. The questions were planned to elicit information about ongoing programs. Respondents emphasized that
their primary use of bibliotherapy lay in individual reading guidance;
in fifty-three cases this was based on direct contact with the patient,
and in nineteen on frequent referral to case histories. One-half of the
respondents reported advice from medical or other staff although only
nine reported frequent conferences. Less than half reported no follow
up by the medical staff. Planned group activities using library materials were limited almost exclusively to neuropsychiatric hospitals.[6]

In June 1961, another ALA Bibliotherapy Committee, chaired by Ruth Tews, conducted a study to "determine current thinking of a selected group of individuals who were actively engaged and interested in bibliotherapy and who possessed knowledge of the potential for the use of reading in a therapeutic way; obtain from the respondents a consensus of what bibliotherapy is and can do; and provide a basis for the formulation of a definition." A five-question survey form was mailed to sixty individuals known to be active in bibliotherapy through their participation in research, publications, etc. Thirty-five of those surveyed were hospital and institution librarians, the others were psychiatrists (9), institutional library consultants (4), library educators (4), other educators (5), one teacher, one chaplain, and one sociologist. Five months later, the questionnaire was sent to sixty other people chosen at random from the members of the Association of Hospital and Institution Libraries; all were librarians. In each group, 14 percent agreed with the statement: "bibliotherapy is any form of library service offered by a librarian to patients"; 38 percent of the expert group disagreed as did 30 percent of the control group. The major concern was that the definition was too vague. Seventeen percent of the expert group and 10 percent of the control group agreed that "bibliotherapy is any form of reading for character formation (in hospital, schools, etc.)." Thirty-five percent and 18 percent, respectively, disagreed, stating that the definition was still too general. The respondents were evenly split on the statement "bibliotherapy is a group reading activity with patients, initiated and conducted by a librarian (or other) in association with a member of the medical staff " (Twenty-two percent of the experts and 12 percent of the control group agreed; 29 percent and 16 percent, respectively, disagreed). The fourth statement, "bibliotherapy is a group reading activity with patients, conducted by a librarian in association with a member of the medical staff " received the most uniform support (Forty-five percent of the first group and 23 percent of the other felt that this was a good definition; 5 percent and 3 percent, respectively, rejected this definition). In the last question, 40 percent of the experts and 27 percent of the control group agreed that "bibliotherapy is a request for a specific title or type of reading for a patient by a medical staff member to the librarian who fills the request and reports back to the physician." Eleven percent and 4 percent, respectively, disagreed. There were many comments and suggestions from the survey's 116 respondents, but statement number four came closest to representing their definition of the field.[29]

As part of an MLS thesis, in July 1967, Pauline Opler sent a twelve-question survey to two-hundred seventeen state mental hospitals throughout the United States. She received a 46 percent response. Eighty percent of the respondents were medical personnel such as doctors, psychologists, and hospital administrators; 20 percent of the respondents were librarians or others doing librarian tasks. The first two questions focused on a definition of bibliotherapy. The majority of the respondents agreed that bibliotherapy is a "group reading activity with patients conducted by a librarian in association with a member of the medical staff"—this is also the definition that Tews found most acceptable in 1961. Respondents from large and small hospitals disagreed (by 45 percent). The majority also agreed that bibliotherapy has a definite place in the therapy of a state hospital although most had no bibliotherapy program at that time and Opler found no correlation between the yearly expenditures of a hospital and whether or not it had a bibliotherapy program. As to where in the state hospital bibliotherapy would be worthwhile, 5 percent felt that it would be especially effective in the children's ward, 45 percent in the geriatrics ward, and only 3 percent in the admitting ward. They were not asked about its potential in continued treatment or intensive care wards. Over 86 percent of the doctors and 65 percent of the librarians felt that a doctor's presence in bibliotherapy groups would not be essential—82 percent of the total felt that the presence of a doctor was not essential. In answer to "Do you believe that reading can be classified from a therapeutic viewpoint, i.e., books suitable for schizophrenics, paranoids, etc.?" Fifty percent of the librarians but only 32.6 percent of the doctors responded affirmatively. Ninety percent of the librarians and 91.3 percent of the doctors agreed that a book might have different meaning for patients having the same diagnosis, depending on their different backgrounds.[17] Obviously, Opler tried to discover both the philosophies and the action of her respondents.

The third survey by the ALA Bibliotherapy Committee conducted in 1975, also used a two-pronged approach. By far the most lengthy and detailed survey, it contained forty-five subdivided questions. The questionnaire was sent to librarians and library consultants in every state, and to all VA Hospital librarians; it was also published in the October 1975 *Health and Rehabilitative Library Services Quarterly.*[22] As of April 1976, thirty-six people had responded to the survey. Fifteen stated that they were not currently using bibliotherapy; one commented that he could not answer the questions because his perception of the field was so unlike that of the survey. Twenty people answered the questionnaire based on current bibliotherapy programs; of these, five worked in VA Hospitals, eleven in mental hopitals, three in correctional facilities, and two in other situations. Fifteen of the respondents were librarians, three were volunteers, one was a mental health technician, and one a reading specialist. Seventeen of the twenty used bibliotherapy in groups only; three used it with individuals. Sixteen respondents used many types of materials, including nonprint; three used only poetry (and called their groups poetry therapy or poetry workshop), and one used only newspaper and magazine articles (and called the group current events). Interestingly, only three respondents called their activity bibliotherapy or bibliocounseling; the rest avoided the term and substituted names as diverse as "reading and discussion

group," "library hour," "the Monday group," and "guides for living."
As for the question of team work, four reported that they always
worked with a co-leader and six more stated that they sometimes
worked with a co-leader. Four worked completely alone, seven led
groups alone and had infrequent consultation with other staff members, and five led groups alone but consulted regularly with others
about the group's progress. The survey results contain much other information which is still in the process of analysis by the committee.

All of these surveys reflect the philosophies and practices of bibliotherapy during the past thirty years. These trends have greatly influenced both the mechanics and dynamics of bibliotherapy.

REFERENCES

1. Jerome Agel, ed., *Rough Times*, (New York: Ballantine Books, 1973).

2. William K. Beatty, "A Historical Review of Bibliotherapy," *Library Trends* 11:106-117 (October 1962).

3. W. J. Coville, "Bibliotherapy: Some Practical Considerations," *Hospital Progress* 41:138-142 (April/May 1960).

4. Sadie Peterson-Delaney, "The Place of Bibliotherapy in a Hospi-tal," *Library Journal* 63:305-308 (April 15, 1938).

5. Rosemary Dolan and others, *Bibliotherapy in Hospitals: An Anno-tated Bibliography* 1900-1957 (Washington, D.C.: Veterans Admin-istration, 1958) and *We Call It Bibliotherapy* (Washington, D.C.: Veterans Administration, February 1967).

6. Margaret C. Hannigan, "Survey of Hospital Library Activities in Reading Guidance and Bibliotherapy," *ALA Hospital Book Guide* (17:65-66, April 1956).

7. Margaret C. Hannigan, "The Librarian in Bibliotherapy: Phar-macist or Bibliotherapist?" *Library Trends* 11:192 (October 1962).

8. Lore Hirsch, "Book Service to Patients," *Wilson Library Bulletin* 27:634 (April 1953).

9. Maxwell Jones and others, *The Therapeutic Community* (New York: Basic Books, 1953).

10. Jack J. Leedy, *Poetry Therapy* (Philadelphia, Pennsylvania: Lippin-cott, 1969) and *Poetry the Healer* (Philadelphia, Pennsylvania: Lip-pincott, 1973).

11. Elbert Lenrow, *Reader's Guide to Prose Fiction* (New York: Appleton-Century-Crofts, 1940).

12. Karl Menninger, *The Human Mind* (New York: Alfred A. Knopf, 1930).

13. William C. Menninger, "Bibliotherapy," *Bulletin of the Menninger Clinic* 1:263-2:74 (November 1937).

14. Margaret E. Monroe, *Library Adult Education* (Metuchen, NJ: Scarecrow Press, 1963).

15. Margaret E. Monroe, *Reading Guidance and Bibliotherapy in the Hospital and Institution Libraries* (Madison, Wisconsin: University of Wisconsin Library School, 1971).

16. Mildred Moody and Hilda K. Limper, eds., *Bibliotherapy: Methods and Materials* (Chicago, Illinois: American Library Association, 1971).

17. Pauline Opler, "The Origins and Trends of Bibliotherapy as a Device in Mental Hospital Libraries," (MLS thesis, San Jose State College, 1969).

18. Virginia M. Reid and others, *Reading Ladders for Human Relations* (Washington, D.C.: American Council on Education, 1972).

19. Louise Rosenblatt, *Literature for Exploration* (New York: Appleton-Century-Crofts, 1938).

20. Louise Rosenblatt, *Literature As Exploration* Rev. ed. (New York: Noble and Noble, 1976).

21. Samuel Rothstein, *The Development of Reference Services,* (ACRL Monographs No. 14, [Chicago, Illinois: ACRL, 1955]).

22. Rhea J. Rubin, ed., "Bibliotherapy," *Health and Rehabilitative Library Services Quarterly* (1:1-27 [entire issue], October, 1975).

23. Rhea J. Rubin, *U.S. Prison Library Services and Their Theoretical Bases,* (University of Illinois Occasional Papers No. 110, December 1973).

24. Caroline Shrodes, "Bibliotherapy: A Theoretical and Clinical-Experimental Study," (Ph.D. dissertation, University of California, 1949).

25. Edwin Starbuck, *A Guide to Literature for Character Training* (vol. 1; New York: Macmillan, 1928).

26. Claude Steiner, "Radical Psychiatry: Principles" in *The Radical Therapist* (New York: Ballantine Books, 1971).

27. Walter Stone, "Adult Education and the Public Library," *Library Journal* 88:437-454 (April 1953).

28. Ruth M. Tews, "Bibliotherapy," in Allen Kent and Harold Lancour, eds., *Encyclopedia of Library and Information Science* (New York: Marcel Dekker, 1969).

29. Ruth M. Tews, "A Questionnaire on Bibliotherapy," *Library Trends* (11:217-227, October 1962).

30. Robert Tyson, "The Validation of Mental Hygiene Literature," *Journal of Clinical Psychology* 4:304 (July 1948).

31. Philip J. Weimerskirch, "Benjamin Rush and John Minson Galt II—Pioneers of Bibliotherapy in America," *Bulletin of the Medical Library Association* 53:510-526 (1965).

32. Joseph S. Zaccaria and Harold A. Moses, *Facilitating Human Development Through Reading: The Use of Bibliotherapy in Teaching and Counseling* (Champaign, Illinois: Stipes Pub. Co., 1968).

Chapter Two

Dynamics

EFFECTS OF READING

He ate and drank the precious words,
His spirit grew robust;
He knew no more that he was poor,
Nor that his frame was dust.

He danced along the dingy days,
And this bequest of wings
Was but a book—what liberty
A loosened spirit brings.

—*Emily Dickinson, "A Book"*

Emily Dickinson reflects the feelings of many readers. People often comment on the changes in their lives that literature has made. "It is really where you can get your mind right, in books . . ." stated an Attica inmate. Why do books affect people so strongly? Louise Rosenblatt offers one explanation in her classic *Literature as Exploration:* "The peculiar power of literature resides in the fact that it can exert an influence upon an emotional level, similar to the kind of influence exerted by people and situations in life."[40] Edwin Alston, a psychoanalyst, feels that literature actually has significant advantages over real life relationships and experiences:

> In the world literature, there is plenty to meet every need and taste. It is easily and widely available, to everyone, at relatively little cost. A helpful or favorite book, unlike a passing conversation, relationship, or experience, can be referred to time and again in the full and original form it had for the reader. The written word, which one can take or leave, is not as intensive as the spoken word, nor is the written word likely to have been as associated with demands and prohibitions and other anxiety-provoking experiences as the spoken word. Accordingly, many people can approach a book with minimal defensiveness and maximal accessibility. For many people, the written word has an exceptional authority and authenticity.[4]

It should be noted that nonprint materials have similar advantage in that they are also nondemanding, nonanxiety-provoking, and available for reconsideration. As access to films, records, and other audio-visual materials improves, both print and nonprint sources will be available for repeated use, whether privately owned or borrowed. In Caroline Shrodes' words: "Literature, being at once a phantasy and yet a realistic portrayal of human behavior, permits the reader, paradoxically, both an illusion of psychic distance and immediacy of experience."[41]

The effects of reading (or listening or viewing) were carefully delineated in 1940 by Douglas Waples, and his associates. They outlined five basic uses of reading: "instrumental, prestige, reinforcement, aesthetic, and respite." Four of these have social aspects—instrumental, prestige, reinforcement, and respite. Instrumental effects include the fuller knowledge of a practical problem and competence in how to deal with it. Prestige or self-esteem effects are defined as the mitigation of guilt and inferiority feelings by increasing self-approval. Reinforcement includes validation of one's personal views and conversion to new attitudes. Respite is often referred to as escape or entertainment and results in a relief of tension. Of these four so-called social effects, two are especially related to bibliotherapy—prestige and reinforcement. The raising of self-esteem and the reinforcement of personal values are important goals of any therapy. Waples stressed that the major factors which produce effects in reading include socioeconomic status, sex, age, occupation, and motives.[43] The importance of the readers' personal makeup is also emphasized by Ruth Strang who states: "What a reader gets out of a passage depends in large measure on what he brought to the passage."[42] It should be apparent that the reader's personal needs greatly affect the results of his reading.

Psychologist Abraham Maslow suggests six types of human needs, noting that people cannot be free to satisfy their higher needs until their lower, and stronger, needs are met.[32] Physiological needs are basic: hunger, thirst, and fatigue. The next most basic needs are safety concerns. After these are the types of needs that reading can help to fulfill. Belonging needs and love, including affiliation and acceptance, are followed by the esteem needs of achievement, strength, and status. When these are responded to, self-actualization and self-fulfillment needs, followed finally by cognitive needs, must be satisfied. The cognitive needs as delineated by Maslow are similar to the instrumental and aesthetic effects of reading described by Waples. His notion of prestige and reinforcement effects correspond to belonging, esteem, and self-actualization needs contained in Maslow's hierarchy.

The myriad of effects of structured reading is summarized by Rosenblatt:

> Through books, the reader may explore his own nature, become aware of potentialities for thought and feeling within himself, acquire clearer perspectives, develop aims, and a sense of direction. He may explore the outer world, other personalities, other ways of life. Liberated from the insularity of time and space,

he may range through the wide gamut of social and temperamental alternatives that men have created or imagined.[40]

OBJECTIVES OF BIBLIOTHERAPY

Many authors have enumerated goals of bibliotherapy. The following is a chronological review of some of the more significant lists.

Dr. William C. Menninger (1937) was one of the first to detail the benefits of bibliotherapy. He divided them into those achieved by identification, stimulation, and narcissistic gratification. Identification of the reader with a character or experience in the book can result in an abreaction of emotion; relief by recognition that others have similar problems; or projection of his traits onto the character. When a reader is stimulated to compare his ideas and values with the author's, attitude change can result. The reader may also achieve narcissistic gratification by escaping his conflict through fantasy, by making contact with reality, or augmenting his knowledge through didactic reading.

Alice I. Bryan (1939) listed six objectives of bibliotherapy: to show the reader he is not the first to have the problem; to permit the reader to see that more than one solution to his problem is possible; to help the reader to see the basic motivations of people (including himself) involved in a particular situation; to help the reader see the values involved in experience in human terms; to provide facts needed for the solution of his problem; and to encourage the reader to face his situation realistically.[10]

Kenneth C. Appel (1944) stated that bibliotherapy may be used

as a means of acquiring information and knowledge about the psychology and physiology of human behavior . . . Reading may be necessary to enable the individual to live up to the injunction 'Know Thyself.' Reading may be advised in an attempt to extravert the patient and arouse his interest in something outside himself. Other purposes may be to arouse interest in and acquaintance with external reality, or to effect a controlled release (abreaction) of unconscious processes, or to offer opportunities for identification and compensation. Of course, it is used to help the patient develop a clarification of his difficulties and contribute to the development of 'insight' into his condition. It is also an attempt to implement the experience of others in effecting a cure . . . Its final aim is to help the patient live more effectively.[5]

Another psychotherapist, Louis A. Gottschalk (1948) stated the purposes of bibliotherapy in this way:

Prescribed reading may help the patient to understand better his own psychological and physiological reactions to frustration and conflict . . . It may help the patient understand some of the terminology used in psychology and psychiatry so that communication between the therapist and patient may be facilitated . . . It may help or stimulate the patient to verbalize problems which he ordinarily finds difficult to discuss 'freely' because of fear, shame or guilt. If, through the reading chosen for him, the patient discovers his own problems in the vicissitudes of others, his frequent feeling of being different from others may

be dispelled . . . It may help stimulate the patient to think constructively between interviews and to analyze and synthesize further his attitudes and behavior
patterns. . . It may reinforce, by precept and example, our social and cultural
patterns and inhibit infantile patterns of behavior . . . It may stimulate imagination, afford enormous satisfaction, or enlarge the patient's area of interest.[22]

Edwin F. Alston (1962) summarized many objectives of bibliotherapy:

Often patients will find courage to enter therapy or discuss a particular problem
after reading about it. Occasionally a patient will be able to discuss something
that he has read when he cannot at the moment talk about the same matter as it
applies directly to himself. Thus, the discussion of a book is sometimes helpful as
an introduction to more personal topics; the non-threatening literature helps to
ease tension. Books may be used to help the patient obtain greater insight into his
problems or to acquire language and ideas with which to communicate his problem. They may help the patient focus attention outside himself and to find new
interests. The reading of books may help the patient in the processes of socialization by providing him with something he can share and talk about with other
people. Often people can find new directions and attitudes in books. The
knowledge that other people have similar problems may give the patient greater
courage to face his own problems, and a lesser sense of isolation and loneliness.
Finally, although too much should not be made of it, there is a therapeutic value
of relaxation and diversion to be found in books.[4]

The authors seem to be in agreement that bibliotherapy can offer
vicarious experiences and situations which the reader may not have
had, or may wish to relive; can help the reader to achieve emotional
and intellectual insights; can provide opportunities for identification,
compensation, and abreaction; can increase self-worth and reinforce
values; can provide a link to the external world and contacts with
reality; can arouse new interests in the readers; can dispel isolation;
and can reinforce cultural and behavioral patterns.

All of these objectives of bibliotherapy assume positive effects of
bibliotherapy; however, some practitioners are concerned about possible negative effects.

POSSIBLE NEGATIVE EFFECTS OF BIBLIOTHERAPY

Although Joseph Zaccaria and Harold Moses optimistically state
that: "not a single study found bibliotherapy to be ineffective . . . No
one has attacked the use of bibliotherapy on theoretical or ethical
grounds either,"[43] some practitioners are concerned with the possible
negative effects of bibliotherapy. In 1937, William Menninger warned
that:

Psychoanalysts usually advise their patients against any psychiatric or psychoanalytic reading during the analysis . . . It is perhaps conservative to avoid
prescribing or recommending mental hygiene reading to any individual whose
situation or understanding is such that he may distort the ideas so gained to meet
his own unconscious aggressive or self-destructive desires . . . In general, we
have found it inadvisable to permit psychotic patients or individuals with obses-

sional neuroses and anxiety states to have such books. It is not advised for psychoanalytic cases under treatment. In the milder neuroses, it is tolerated. We have found it practical . . . for individuals with alcohol addiction . . . for near-recovered psychotic individuals, and occasionally for intelligent neurotic individuals in conjunction with psychotherapy.[8]

It should be noted that Menninger is only suggesting parameters for the use of bibliotherapy and is not denigrating its value. He is referring only to didactic materials, and makes no comments on restriction of literature.

Daniel Brower is also concerned with the use of didactic materials by individuals incapable of reading them correctly:

The reader may simply discover a label for his difficulty and indulge in the most extreme form of the terminology fallacy: feeling relief with a label for his condition and with the illusion that such a label provides an explanation. The very resistance which keeps this individual from seeking active help may well be intensified by protracted and involved attempts at self-analysis.[8]

Brower does not consider bibliotherapy as an "active help." Rather, he subscribes to Menninger's definition of bibliotherapy as prescribed reading of psychological books by patients not necessarily involved in a therapy situation. He continues:

Excessive, compulsive psychological reading may serve to aggravate the emotional disorder and impede the progress of psychotherapy to the extent that unhealthy defense mechanisms are reinforced through purely verbal rationalizations. The aggravation of disorders in this manner is also frequently encountered by students in courses in abnormal psychology and mental hygiene. There is the further question of whether reading can actually provide the basis for any new pattern of defense mechanisms or accustomed channelization of anxiety in the individual . . . Reading may, in certain extreme cases, shatter the structure of defense to such a degree that the individual may be precipitated into a suicide or psychotic reaction pattern or some 'equivalent state. However, this would not argue against the use of bibliotherapy for the general population.[8]

R. W. Medlicott, an Australian librarian, worries about the distortion of "books used as sources of (mis)information."

The pseudo-sophisticated psychological intelligentsia show remarkable readiness in interpreting the unconscious sources of behavior both in themselves and in their friends. This seldom, however, is reflected in mature behavior. Commonly, one finds amongst such psychologically preoccupied individuals highly destructive life patterns and it is often clear that they use their intellectual knowledge to avoid rather than strive for real change.[37]

In perhaps the best-known articles on adverse effects from bibliotherapy, John Briggs similarly concentrates on the use of didactic materials and possible negative effects:

The purpose of bibliotherapy is to instruct the individual, as well as his family, concerning the nature of the specific illness . . . bibliotherapy should not be acute. The therapist should by observation and information received decide the types of reading that are indicated; what types are contra-indicated; how long the patient should be under bibliotherapy; when to stop it successfully; but, above all, to be aware that adverse effects can occur . . .[7]

Briggs describes seven examples of negative reactions to didactic materials: two patients became more insecure and anxious about their diseases; three became depressed; and two became obsessed with their illnesses. Yet, as Briggs himself states:

> The adverse effects usually result from misadventure in the selection or by misunderstanding the material . . . The failure of bibliotherapy may result from a lack of knowledge on the part of the therapist and the physician as to what the patient should read. The therapist and the physician should consult with the patient regarding his interests and his capabilities in accepting this form of treatment. Both the therapist and the physician should be familiar with the material they recommend. They must assure the patient that certain portions of the material are not applicable to his problem. If such seems to appear, the patient should then consult with either the physician or the therapist.[7]

Obviously, Briggs' concept of bibliotherapy does not include discussion of the materials read. Eleanor Brown notes: "Since adverse effects usually result from wrong choices of material or wrong understanding of the material by the patient, the post-discussion between patient and therapist is of the utmost importance."[9] This cannot be over-emphasized—the assignment of reading material is not bibliotherapy. Bibliotherapy, as it is practiced today, requires a discussion component. As Alston says:

> Some people simply do not read; others do not get much out of what they read . . . Reading, without active, critical participation and application can hardly be expected to have any significant effect [with mental patients] . . . There is no book that can possibly substitute for a vital, give-and-take exchange between two people. Unless such a relationship is somewhere in the background, whole libraries of books will be of no avail.[4]

This is why the discussion component of bibliotherapy is considered so important. If the materials are well selected for the individuals involved, and discussion with a sensitive competent leader follows the reading, the negative effects discussed by Briggs and others can be avoided.

Louise M. Rosenblatt addressed herself to the inherent dangers in "cheap escape fiction." She likens it to a drug which temporarily relieves tension. "If there is no psychiatrist at hand to set up the necessary constructive tendencies, repeated indulgence in the drug of escape fiction, without any change in the circumstances that created a need for it, can lead only to an unconscious craving for such escape."[40] She is not referring to books used as part of a professionally controlled therapy. Elaborating, she says:

> In most cases, these writings present a falsified image of life. The obstacles placed in the way of the characters are oversimplified. The ease with which problems are solved, or the absence of any real problems, probably constitutes one appeal of this type of reading. Even more subtly enervating are the emotions undiluted with thought and lacking in individual quality in which the reader shares . . . The reader will return to life from this kind of easy satisfaction and success less capable than before of understanding and coping with the complex situations,

the subtly blended combinations of pain and pleasure, the mixture of frustrations and satisfactions, that life offers.[40]

Alston reiterates the most commonly mentioned adverse effects of bibliotherapy:

Patients may derive from reading some definite therapeutic gains . . . but reading and its results may also be deterrents to therapeutic progress. It is possible to acquire erroneous information and misunderstanding from books. Reading may be used as a way of avoiding the personal issues of therapy or of achieving further withdrawal and isolation. False hopes and expectations may be engendered, or the patient may be discouraged, or depressive trends may be enhanced. In response to reading, the patient may attempt to use ideas and facts that do not apply to him. Some patients become overwhelmed or especially anxious from reading. Obsessive-compulsive tendencies may be enhanced. In short, reading may become a resistance to therapy, especially if the reading is not accompanied by appropriate critical discussion.[4]

Discussion as to why the material upset the person is essential. Dr. Julius Griffin, a proponent of bibliotherapy first at the Menninger Clinic and subsequently in his own clinic, says: "If such an interaction 'hurts' a patient and makes him regress, this is a valuable index as to his ego capacity and function. With several people who were 'hurt' their setback was dealt with by the ward doctor . . . (who) tried to discover with the patient why he was set back and to use the situation to help the patient to deal better with reality."[23]

Brown's review of the possible adverse effects of bibliotherapy includes the following:

Religious patients may brood about real or imagined sins, or may be offended by certain materials; the patient may become depressed or may have his dream world intensified; forcing a non-reader to read may cause a dislike for reading; sedated patients may not be able to read or to understand; too much information can be dangerous; reading may erode the patient-doctor relationship; patients often show increased suggestibility during illness; physical responses to emotions—blood pressure, heart beat, sexual response—may be dangerous for some; laughing could open an incision; small print may cause poor eyesight; some patients may not be able to physically hold books; brain damaged or elderly patients may feel frustration at their difficulty reading; elderly patients may have mental blocs against paperbacks, or may be shocked at obscenity; children's imaginations may run wild; directed reading may imply criticism of the patients' literary tastes; it is harmful for too many staff members to question a patient.[9]

All of these complaints are based on fallacies. They assume incompetent bibliotherapists making improper diagnoses, having no team or consultant to work with, selecting improper materials, working with individuals rather than groups, and having no discussion with the readers about the material. All the critics, with the exception of Rosenblatt, speak of didactic materials only and deal exclusively with print materials in book format. It is apparent that these objections have arisen because of confusion about the nature of bibliotherapy and its practitioners.

A more reasonable drawback to bibliotherapy seems to be the ascription of skills to the client. Even these problems can be overcome by a well-trained, creative therapist. Briggs states "Bibliotherapy means treatment by the use of reading. It implies that the individual has the ability to read, the intelligence to understand the materials he is reading, and can project what he reads to the understanding of the problem."[7] He does not take into account a self-trained, sensitive therapist working with the client, or the availability of audiovisual materials. Fairbanks cautions: "One special feature of bibliotherapy, as compared to most other treatment media in activity therapy, is that verbalization is necessary."[18] Some therapists are working with people who cannot verbalize but can understand carefully selected materials and can respond in other fashions. Although progress is being made in working with many types of people, it is well to keep in mind these words from Zaccaria and Moses: "Bibliotherapy does not replace other techniques; it cannot be used indiscriminately; it cannot be used with all persons, in all settings, and for all purposes. Undoubtedly, bibliotherapy should be used as a technique by only certain [professionals] . . . for as with all educational and therapeutic techniques, it will be adopted, adapted, and utilized effectively by some practitioners and avoided, abhorred, and criticized by others."[43] While this statement has validity, the recognition that bibliotherapy is a technique which has needed refinement is behind the recent efforts to set clearer goals, define basic issues, utilize new media, and more clearly identify the role of the therapist in facilitating the patron's relationship with the material.

THEORIES OF THE AESTHETIC EXPERIENCE

Although Bryan (1939) has been cited as the first to formulate a theory of bibliotherapy because of her adoption of the psycho-physical interactionism concept, not until a decade later did anyone attempt a comprehensive theory.[11] Caroline Shrodes, in a 1950 doctoral dissertation, postulated a theory of the dynamics of the aesthetic experience based upon personality theory and psychoanalysis. Her work remains the psychological basis of bibliotherapy.

Shrodes' theory rests on the common approaches to personality in Gestalt psychology, molar behavior theory, field theory, and Freudian psychoanalysis. She states that there are a few basic concepts common to all of the personality theories which help to explain the relationship between the dynamics of the personality and the dynamics of the aesthetic experience.

> By the dynamics of the personality is meant the inner forces, the drives, urges, or instincts, some of which, inherited or suddenly emerging, may be held accountable for the occurrence of motility without external stimulus . . . The phrase, the dynamics of the aesthetic experience, signifies that the reader, under the impact of imaginative literature, is subject to certain processes of adaptation or growth. The process of reading imaginative literature is a dynamic process, and not a

static one. Inasmuch as reading involves perception, apperception, and cognition as well as attention and conceptualization, the reading process from a dynamic point of view cannot be divorced from the wants and feelings of the reader. One must take account not only of the dynamics of personality but also of the interaction and counteraction between the personality of the reader and literature as a psychological field.[41]

This interaction constitutes Shrodes' definition of bibliotherapy. Borrowed from the theory of molar behavior is the concept that changes taking place in one part of the personality are the direct result of influences in the other parts. The total behavior of an individual is determined by his or her present needs, emotions, and actions; the direction of the behavior is determined by his or her goals. The past experiences of the individual also affect his or her present experiences in that they are part of his or her experienced world. Gestalt psychology adds the idea that what the individual has previously perceived is organized in a specific form (or gestalt) to give certain meanings to individual experience. New perceptions must either fit into or change that structure. Literature may also be considered a gestalt of words and images; their specific structure affects the literature as a whole just as the structures of the human mind affect that which is perceived.

Freudian psychoanalytic theory uses other jargon but basically corroborates the concept. Freud's "pleasure principle" accounts for censorship of ideas unacceptable to the ego. Objects and ideas which are pleasurable are absorbed (introjected), whereas whatever is painful to the ego is projected onto the external world. If this principle did not apply to the human psyche, the human mind would be non-discriminating and all new perceptions would affect the individual.

A similar idea from field theory is the concept of symbolization — personalized, selective perceptions based on the individual's organization of a symbolic world, composed of symbols and signals which evoke positive or negative perceptions. Unless new patterns are learned through an intense emotional experience, or through therapy, the patterns of the symbolic world persist. The individual reacts to perceived, symbolized situations and experiences by identification, introjection, and projection.

Although the psychoanalytic approach emphasizes the genesis of the subject's response and field theory concentrates upon the present experience, both schools recognize that the personality is conditioned by past experience. The former is concerned primarily with the emotional experience whereas the latter is concerned with the immediate effects of past experience upon perception and cognition. Shrodes states that:

In spite of the differences in terminology and emphasis, the two approaches are congruent if looked at from the point of view of the dynamics of personality. Freud, no less than the contemporary field theorist, views the world in dynamic equilibrium, whereby living beings change substance with their environment. Man's proneness toward symbolization, which the field theorists emphasize, is simply his exercise of such familiar Freudian mechanisms as identification, projection, and introjection. What Burrow calls the confusion of the social symbol, and Sullivan, parataxic distortion, Freud calls the transference whereby emotion is directed at a given stimulus in terms of a previous affective experience. Freud's principle of stability, providing for the release of tension and leading to a reconciliation of pleasure and reality, and his principle of surplus energy, providing for a substitutive release of energy acceptable to the ego and super ego, are consistent with dynamic psychology which holds that all behavior is an attempt to preserve the organismic integrity of the personality by homeostatic restorations of equilibrium. While Freud speaks of the executive function of the ego, whereby separated and independent impulses are drawn into integration, creating order out of chaos, the field theorist stresses the possibility of extending the perceptual world of the subject, whereby his cognition of the world will be in conformity to reality, culminating in the re-structuring of the personality.[41]

Concepts drawn from all these theories form the background of Shrodes' theory of the aesthetic experience. Because of her training in both psychology and the humanities, Shrodes was able to understand, and explain, the human response to literature.

Literature becomes a part of the experienced world of the individual . . . [through] the process of symbolization, whereby the symbol becomes interchanged with actual experience by means of a transfer of affect from the total situation to the symbol of it. A portrayal of a personal relationship, a conversation, a reflection of mood, a traumatic experience, an act of aggression, represented in literature may become for the reader a symbolic equivalent of a personal relationship, a conversation, a mood, a traumatic experience, an act of aggression in his own life. As such it must evoke, at least in part, the same affective responses as did the original experience. These situations or characters assume importance for the reader because they reflect his own need, fulfill his own wish, or remind him of his own frustrations which are embedded in similar psychological units. The reader's state of tension, having its origin in his needs, may then readily communicate with a state of tension in the literature. . . .[41]

The processes by which literature is experienced and integrated by the reader correspond to the major phases of psychotherapy. These phases are identification, projection, abreaction and catharsis, and insight. According to Shrodes:

Identification is generally defined as an adaptive mechanism which the human being utilizes, largely unconsciously, to augment his self-regard. It takes the form of a real or imagined affiliation of oneself with another person, a group of persons, or with some institution, or even with a symbol. There is usually involved admiration for the object of one's identification, a tendency to imitate, and a sense of loyalty and belongingness. Projection has two common usages in the literature. It consists of the attribution to others of one's own motives or emotions in order to ascribe blame to another instead of to oneself. The term is also used to describe one's perception, apperception, and cognition of the world and people. Catharsis is used synonymously with abreaction to denote the uncensored and spontaneous release of feelings; in the Aristotelian sense it means the purging of emotions. Insight is commonly used in psychotherapy to indicate emotional awareness of one's motivations, a recognition that proceeds from the re-living of one's early experiences and the subsequent abreaction.[41]

MANIFESTATIONS OF DYNAMIC PROCESSES REFLECTED IN READING LITERATURE ACCORDING TO SHRODES*

I. Identification

    a. expression of affect toward character

    b. expression of agreement or disagreement with character's opinions

    c. evidence of concern about a character's fate

    d. expression of homonymy, of pleasure in being like a character

II. Projection

    a. apperceptive projection

        1. interpretation of relationships between characters

        2. interpretation of character's motives

    b. cognitive projections

        1. inferences re author's meaning

        2. explanation of outcome in terms of theory about life

        3. superimposition of moral upon story

        4. values asserted or erroneously deduced

III. Abreaction and catharsis

    a. evidence of emotion in verbalization (guilt, anxiety, tension)

    b. early memories aroused

    c. expression of aggression toward character or author

    d. evidence of transference; i.e., reacting to symbolic experience as if to a previous total affective experience

IV. Insight

    a. evidence of self-recognition (feeling of belonging, self-understanding)

    b evidence of recognition of others (understanding, tolerance, acceptance)

    c. accuracy and objectivity of analysis of motivations

    d. accuracy of cognitive perceptions (reality testing vs. stereotopy)

    e. incorporation of new concepts (i.e., values, goals)

    f. integration (unconscious becoming conscious)

FIGURE 4

---

*Reprinted with permission from Dr. Shrodes.

Since Shrodes presented her theory of bibliotherapy, only a few new theories have been proposed. In 1962, Evalene P. Jackson suggested that the interpersonal theory of Henry Stack Sullivan applies to bibliotherapy.

> The organism which becomes reader brings into the world little more than a bundle of potentialities. To what extent these potentialities are limited by native endowment is uncertain. The organism will seek satisfaction in ways that are determined by the culture. The self which emerges is the result of approval and disapproval by significant others: mothers, fathers, siblings, etc. . . . One becomes what he is by interaction with the interpersonal situations of which he is a part. Life is a patterned sequence of these. If significant others were not limited by being human, the possibility of the healing acceptance of books might not be such an important means of transcending these limits. In Sullivan's conception, the book itself may be a significant other: "In general, my frame of reference, whether constituted by real people, or imaginary people existing only in books . . . along with one other real person, can make up an interpersonal situation." On this basis, one may propose that the variety and richness of books are means of counteracting the meagerness of the environment and the limits of those who are parts of interpersonal situations.[25]

Another theory, based on learning theory, was advanced in a 1968 dissertation by Frank Fisher. Humans learn primarily by imitation of real and symbolic models. Therefore, the imaginary people and situations in literature provide learning models for the reader. The vicarious experience of the reader is a viable alternative to real-life experiences; reading can provide models the reader would not otherwise have. Similarly, the discussion after reading permits the reader to discuss and experiment with concepts and reactions he or she may not have experienced in daily life.

The opportunity to test emotions and behavior is considered preventative mental health. Zaccaria and Moses have suggested that:

> In terms of the preventative function, bibliotherapy can help to foster adequate positive mental health. In terms of the remediation function, bibliotherapy can provide the practitioner with a useful diagnostic and therapeutic strategy. As education has broadened its focus and extended its goals to become concerned with the whole child, it has become natural to supplement the didactic or instructive use of literature and books with the use of books in a noninstructional manner, i.e. bibliotherapeutically.[43]

Norman Holland, a literary critic and psychoanalyst, who has been studying readers' responses to determine the principles of literary experience, observes that: "all of us live by creating variations on an identity theme that is our essential self. 'Creating' is a key word, for such a view of human nature implies not only sameness but differences that we create. . . . Identity implies, too, that all these creations have a unity, particularly that we meet and create external reality by the same strategies we use to maintain internal reality."[24] He delineates four principles that describe the dynamics of reading. "Style seeks itself " is the first. Readers respond positively to materials which apply to his or her characteristic cluster of needs and wishes. If a reader responds negatively, or has no reaction, he or she has been unable to translate the materials into his or her own lifestyle. His second principle is that "defenses must be matched." In other words, readers must synthesize the material into a characteristic defense or adaptation structure in order to respond favorably to a book. People especially like characters who have the same defense mechanisms that they do. Thirdly, "Fantasy projects fantasy" is Holland's way of stating that the fantasies perceived by the reader to be part of the story are really part of his or her self. As people read, they project their own fantasies onto the story line. Holland's last principle, "character transforms characteristically" means that the reader understands a work by recasting it into his or her own internal language, taking into account upbringing, character, needs, defenses, and fantasies. All of Holland's principles reflect the concept that reading is an active process in which the reader creates a new work which applies to his or her own experience and character.

All theories of bibliotherapy, whether rooted in librarianship, education, mental hygiene, psychology of personality, or psychoanalysis, stress the interaction of a reader with literature as if the literature were another human being. If the literature is selected wisely, the reader reacts to this imaginary "other" through identification and projection, and catharsis may occur. Discussion aided by a skilled therapist can then lead to insight which is a major objective of all therapy. Sometimes, attitudinal and/or behavioral change will also result.

ATTITUDES AND BEHAVIOR

To reiterate, the goals of bibliotherapy include insight into normal development, and changes in disturbed behavior. Both of these processes involve the inception of attitudes, the evolution of attitudes, and—sometimes—change in behavior. Much of the important research in bibliotherapy has reflected an attempt to change attitudes and behavior, yet the literature of the field ignores relevant findings of social psychology. If bibliotherapists continue to cite attitudinal and/or behavioral change as a goal of bibliotherapy, the complex relationship between attitudes and behaviors, and our perception of attitudes and behavior, must be better understood. The works of social scientists in this field provide essential knowledge needed for a scientific approach to bibliotherapy.

Since the 1920's, social psychologists have concentrated on categorizing, quantifying, and determining the characteristics of attitudes. In the 1950's and 1960's, there were many studies of how attitudes are changed. But a single theory on attitudes has yet to be generally accepted.

In 1935, G. W. Allport offered the seminal definition of an attitude: "An attitude is a mental and neural state of readiness, organized through experience, exerting a directive or dynamic influence upon the individual's response to all objects and situations with which it is related."[3] Two psychologists, Bobby Calder and Michael Ross, dissect Allport's definition and comment that an attitude is neither a conscious experience nor a physiological state. "Both the experiential and the physiological side of attitudes are best viewed as indicants of attitudes. Attitude exists only as a theoretical variable, an abstraction that does not imply any necessary phenomenological or physical referent."[13] Calder and Ross stress that attitude is a latent process or, in Allport's words, "a readiness to respond,"[3] rather than a behavior in and of itself. The latter view is that of the positivistic philosophers; the former is the more popular approach. A third characteristic of Allport's definition is that attitudes are organized. Two models corroborate Allport's assumption that attitudes are structured. The cognitive-affective-conative model structures attitude into three components—cognitive or rational, affective or emotional, and conative or behavioral tendencies. Another model of this organization is the expectancy-value model whereby the structure is determined by the expectancy and value of each belief that composes the attitude. The fourth charactertistic of Allport's definition is that attitudes are learned through previous experience. Finally, he states that attitudes are directive and dynamic:

> A directive influence would simply channel behavior while a dynamic one would provide a motivational input to behavior. A directive influence, for example, would determine who a person votes for whereas a dynamic influence would determine whether or not a person votes. It seems likely that this dynamic aspect of attitude is really not a necessary part of the definition of attitude and should remain a question for attitude theory.[3]

Calder and Ross summarize the definition:

> Attitude is an idealized abstraction serving as an intervening variable with no known physical referent. Its only basis is in psychological theory. Attitude is assumed to have experiential and physiological correlates. Some internal organization is generally assumed. An attitude is assumed to be a result of past experience and to exert a directive influence on behavior.[13]

Phillip Zimbardo and Ebbe Ebbesen comment:

> A practical consequence of thinking about attitudes as highly generalized predispositions is that by changing attitudes one should also be able to produce many specific changes in overt behavior. For example, in trying to produce changes in black children's self-conceptions, it is not sufficient to merely get these children to say that they think more highly of themselves as black people, but rather the goal is to have the children behave toward themselves, toward other blacks, and towards other whites in a host of changed ways . . .[46]

The lack of any clear notion of the interdependence of attitudes and behavior is a continuing problem in psychology today.

That attitudes affect behavior appears to be axiomatic given the definition of attitude as having a directive influence. This must be qualified however, for "changes in attitude are not necessarily accompanied by changes in behavior," says Allport. "Furthermore, when changes in behavior do occur, they are rarely, if ever, general or enduring."[3] Empirical studies employing the testing and observational approaches found only minor correlations between attitudes and simple behaviors. Calder and Ross offer a possible reason for low attitude-behavior correlations: ". . . in many instances, a general attitude was measured while the behavior to be predicted was extremely specific . . . It is conceivable, then, that the relationship between verbally expressed attitudes and overt behavior would be stronger if the measured attitudes were specific to the behavior."[13] Another possible explanation is the behavioral threshold theory. "Some indicators of attitude may have low thresholds, in that they will occur even with a weak attitude, while other manifestations may require a strong attitude before they will occur."[13] The third—and more popular— explanation is suggested by Calder and Ross:

> A person's behavior with respect to an object in a situation is determined by at least two interacting attitudes—his attitude toward the object and his attitude toward the situation . . . In summary, observational research indicates that relatively accurate behavioral prediction is obtained when attitude measures are combined with other factors. While an attitude may be related to a behavior, it is not the sole determining factor. Attitudes interact with other attitudes and with situational influences to produce behavior.[13]

Whether or not behavior causes attitudes has also been the subject of much research and debate. Self-perception theory (developed by B. J. Bem) states that behavior should influence attitudes because a person infers his/her attitudes by observing his/her own behavior. Bem cites as an example a person who is asked whether s/he likes brown bread and replies "I suppose I do. I am always eating it."[6] Research has shown that an individual "bases" his/her attitudes only on relevant behavior and that the context of the behavior is also important.

The social learning approach is another theory that supports the contention that behavioral change precedes attitudinal change. It says that most human behavior leads to consequences which affect the probability of similar behavior in the future. The basic idea is that the likelihood of a specific response is determined by what the person expects will follow the response. If the consequences are positive or rewarding, the behavior is likely to occur. If they are negative or punishing, the behavior is not likely to occur.[44] In addition to learning through experiences, a person can learn by observation or vicariously what the result of an action may be. Reading can be the basis of social learning. Social learning theory does not refer to attitudes at all but stresses types of behavior.

One very important theory postulates both that attitudes can change behavior and vice-versa. This is Leon Festinger's theory of cognitive dissonance. In reviewing the literature, Festinger found that three major studies concluded changes in attitude did not result in changed behavior. Although the experimenters altered their subjects' attitudes toward behavior, they did not succeed in changing that behavior.[19] Another experimenter produced behavioral change without the expected attitudinal change. Both of these results contradict the once prevalent assumption that attitudinal change results in behavioral change. It is interesting to note that similar results were obtained in the research on bibliotherapy by McClaskey (1970)[33] and Burt (1972).[12] Researchers are now trying to determine what conditions allow attitude change to affect behavior.

Festinger postulates that attitude change may be unstable, may need commitment in order to stabilize, and will be motivated by cognitive dissonance, or psychological inconsistency.

> The central assumption is that human beings cannot tolerate inconsistency. This means that whenever inconsistency exists in a person, he will try to eliminate it or reduce it . . . When psychological inconsistency exists, it does two things to the organism: it activates him and it directs him. The inconsistency thus pushes (motivates) the organism in a specific direction which, if acted upon, will result in reduction of the unpleasant tension produced by the inconsistency.[19]

Dissonance exists when one cognitive element conflicts with another. An example of cognitive dissonance is a person who has worked toward a goal and failed—the person's self-concept and the actuality are in conflict. Either the self-concept or the perceived value of the goal must be altered to reduce the discomfort.

Four variables determine the amount of cognitive dissonance an individual experiences. The first is requisite for any cognitive dissonance—a cognitive element about oneself. Zimbardo and Ebbesen use this example, "Smokers have the cognition, 'I smoke.' The knowledge (which a smoker may have) of the evidence which ties smoking to lung cancer is dissonant with the knowledge that he smokes. That is, if smoking causes lung cancer, he feels he ought not to smoke . . . If our subject stopped smoking, the cognitive element 'I smoke' would obviously change to 'I don't smoke.' "[19] The importance of each of the cognitive elements also has an effect. "For example, if it weren't important to our hypothetical smoker that he may die of lung cancer (because he was 80 years old and felt he had lived a full life anyway) then there would be little dissonance produced by the two cognitions 'I smoke' and 'smoking is related to lung cancer.' "[19] Another variable is the ratio of dissonant to consonant elements; the greater that ratio, the greater the dissonance. To continue our example, the knowledge that "I smoke low tar cigarettes" and "I only smoke four cigarettes per day" increases the consonant elements and reduces cognitive dissonance. The fourth variable is the amount of commitment to a behavior. Cognitive dissonance is greater the more committed a decision maker is to an action while s/he is aware of his/her volition to do otherwise.

In terms of attitude and behavior change, the primary goal is reduction of dissonance. Zimbardo and Ebbesen explain:

> Once dissonance is aroused, there will be a *need* to reduce dissonance. This need to reduce the psychological tension created by inconsistency motivates a wide variety of behavior. It is only by observing the presence and characteristics of dissonance-reducing behavior that one can infer that dissonance must have been present . . . Dissonance may be reduced in many ways:
>
> a)   by attempting to revoke a decision,
>
> b)   by lowering the importance of the cognitions or the decision,
>
> c)   by increasing the cognitive overlap between cognitive elements [searching for or misperceiving aspects of functional equivalence], and
>
> d)   by adding consonant elements to change the ratio of dissonant to consonant ones . . .
>
> A person can reduce dissonance either by changing his behavior, or by changing his internal environment (attitudes and perceptions), or his external environment.[46]

Cognitive dissonance theory clearly illustrates that behavior can change attitudes and conversely, attitudes (in conflict with behavior) can change behavior.

Although attitude change can lead to behavior change, an additional bit of information can greatly enhance the probability of such occurrences. Howard Leventhal states that behavior compliance follows attitude change when additional information—in the form of action instruction—is presented to the subject.

> These instructions specify the response necessary for compliance . . . and link the responses to particular external cues. Without action instructions, a situation can elicit an image which generates a subjective attitude without action; if the image has been linked to an action plan, action will be likely . . . For example, if one's image of cancer and smoking elicits anxiety, it can produce defensive and avoidant behavior.[31]

Another important point he makes is that "any specific setting may arouse a great number of attitudes and any response that is congruent with one of these attitudes may be incongruent with other attitudes. Because of this, it may be costly or difficult to make an attitudinally congruent response (a new behavior created because of a change in attitude) in a particular setting . . ."[31]

Although behavior induced by attitude change is of obvious importance to bibliotherapy, it is noteworthy that attitudes themselves also affect perceptions. People are more aware of their attitudes' effect on perception than on behavior. In both cases, self-reports are often incorrect.

GROUP PROCESSES

Because this book deals primarily with group bibliotherapy, it is necessary to examine the definition of a group and its dynamics. The group dynamics approach to attitudes and behavior developed by social scientists is also significant for bibliotherapy. Clara Lack, a bibliotherapist, states (in private correspondence, to the author):

> Bibliotherapy is the experiencing of selected literature in a *group situation* for the purpose of providing a non-threatening exploration of a patient's problems. Literature provides models of behavior which can be analyzed to provide self-insight, to break down defenses, to provide a safe way to try out alternative behavior, and can lead to more intensive therapy. Bibliotherapy can assist in self-acceptance by illustrating the commonality of human behavior, aid in socialization in the give and take of a *group,* and can assist in finding meaning and purpose in life tasks at particular times and ages of life . . . The sharing of literature *in a group* with *group processes* and discussion are essential. The leader and material are secondary to *experiencing literature in a group.* [Italics added]

Lack's definition reflects the concern with *group* bibliotherapy that many practitioners currently share. Group therapy of any type has the advantages of economy of time and money, dilution of the therapist's powerful role, and—most importantly—the added dimension of group membership and participation. The group establishes a center of objective gravity for the member, increases self-understanding and other-acceptance, lessens anxiety and isolation feelings, and validates the participant's feelings and experiences.

Jerome D. Frank lists the following advantages of group over individual therapy:

> The patient's anxiety is reduced by the knowledge that others have similar problems; listening to others and talking with them stimulates the patient to recall and relive experiences that affected him; new ways of approaching and solving problems are suggested; the patient can dissipate feelings of guilt and/or hostility; the group gives emotional acceptance and support; the group—representing social reality—gives the patient a chance to test new behaviors and ideas.[21]

A respected textbook in this field, *Group Dynamics: Research and Theory,* defines a group as a "collection of individuals who have relations to one another that makes them interdependent to some significant degree . . . a collection of people who are striving to attain a common goal also constitutes a group."[15] A person's relation to a group is influenced by membership in the group in question and in any other groups, the amount of dependence on the group, attraction to—and acceptance by—the group, the voluntarism of membership, and personal frame of reference.

The approaches of group dynamics are based on field theory which states that people are social beings who need others as a basis of self-knowledge, social knowledge (such as appropriate responses), and behavior (which is modified by the group norm). The group's pressure modifies the individual's attitudes and behavior by expressing a need for uniformity. Under this theory, a person molds him or herself to fit the group demand so as to be accepted in the group.

The field theory orientation of group dynamics was established by Kurt Lewin in the 1930's. When Rogers popularized the client-centered approach to individual therapy in the 1960's, he also greatly affected current group therapies. His "self-theory" assumes that the self's single goal is realizing itself, and that non-directive therapy can help the individual perceive growth and understand his/her interactions with others, thereby modifying self-concept. In Rogerian therapy the emphasis is on the self-direction of the group. The attitude is permissive so that communication is freed; Rogers emphasizes the need for a sensitive, listening approach to reduce threat and reveal the person or people involved. Rogers' principles apply to all varieties of groups.

There are many types of groups which can be classified by function (i.e., educational, task-oriented, therapy) or by method (i.e., lecture, democratic, T-groups). In bibliotherapy, counseling or therapy is used, often with group centered methods. Counseling and therapy groups concentrate on interpersonal interaction for the satisfaction of emotional needs, as opposed to educational and task-oriented groups which work toward a specific goal and focus on ideas. Both counseling and therapy provide an accepting environment for reality testing and new experiences, with group therapy connoting group counseling with troubled patients. Counseling and therapy groups use many methods ranging from authoritarian to completely permissive, and from therapist-centered to group-centered. While psychoanalytic group therapy is authoritarian and is structured so that the therapist is a leader, encounter groups are permissive but remain therapist-centered in that the leader is not a member of the group. In group centered or democratic groups, the leader is a participant in the group and its discussions.

It is crucial that bibliotherapists are aware of the varying roles a group leader can play in therapy. Differing styles of leadership form distinctive aspects of group therapies. As Helen Driver delineates them, the degrees of directivism/nondirectivism in group leaders provides a continuum of leadership styles. The least directive groups are:

a) Leaderless discussions in which the leader physically leaves or becomes occupied with paperwork during the group meeting.

b) The next step is the group in which a counselor is present but silent.

c) A "hmmm" response or any other meaningless verbal response can be used to show that the nondirective therapist is listening.

d) Reflection—or repetition of what a participant said—is a similar but slightly more active response.

e) Clarification of what was said through rewording and questioning, is the most involved response which a nondirective leader gives. Eclectic leaders also use clarification but often supplement it with

f) Interpretation in which the counselor states an opinion as to the meaning of a client's statements and feelings.

g) Information and

h)   Suggestions as to actions or alternatives are sometimes given. The eclectic leader also

i)   Summarizes what has been said. Finally the directive leader goes beyond suggestions to

j)   Advice in the form of strong suggestions and pressure for the client to make a decision.

k)   Orders from the counselor to a participant are not unusual;

l)   Threats and coercion are less common.[16]

The directive style of leadership is most often used by physicians, academic advisors, and personnel managers. Such authoritarian group leaders rely on extrinsic motivations, including reinforcement, pressures, rewards, and punishment. A major problem with directive leadership is that it may cause identification with an authoritarian figure. The opposite type, the nondirective leader, is most common in adjunctive therapies. A combination of both of these techniques is found in the eclectic leader who relies heavily on intrinsic motivation which develops from differences between the client's goals and his or her progress toward them. Eclectic techniques seem best suited for bibliotherapy.

To a great extent, the therapist's style affects the participants' activities. Members' response to a leader and to a group situation can be best observed through their participation. Members can participate positively by showing solidarity and supporting other members, or negatively by showing antagonism or by dominating the situation. Other responses include giving opinions and suggestions, agreeing or disagreeing, asking questions, and refusing to become involved. All of these responses reflect on the individual and on the group's style.

Despite differences in the purposes and methods of groups, styles of leadership and participation, group dynamicists stress that there are many similarities among all groups. Driver explains that group therapies have five common characteristics: they are inductive (i.e., no definite objectives or assignments), short term, restricted in membership, have attitude change as a goal, and place the responsibility for personal growth on the individual.[16] Gratton C. Kemp states that a common element of all groups is the three way process required for group activity.[30] Communication from member to member, member to whole group, and whole group to member are necessary to distinguish group behavior from social behavior.

Another commonality of group behavior pertains to the six phases of group development. Social scientists report that all groups progress through six stages: The first three phases are labelled dependence-power relationships, and the second three are interdependence-personal relations. The first phase is dependence-submission. Group members act as they would at a new social gathering, denigrate authority, and allow the most aggressive members to dominate. In the second or counterdependence stage, members fight among themselves and split into cliques. They unify again during the resolution phase. During the fourth phase, enchantment, a "group mind" is evident and the group members enjoy their sessions and each other; there is a high rate of interaction and participation. But disenchantment follows; the group members react anxiously and once more split into cliques. Absenteeism and tardiness are common. Phase six—consensual validation—shows pairing, understanding, and true communication. This phase is, of course, the goal of group activity. At the final stage, the group experiences *esprit de corps*. As Joseph Luft describes it, "a high-morale group can endure greater conflicts and stress without serious damage, without falling apart. Thus there are two interrelated aspects to a group's morale: the extent to which an individual's personal needs are met and the effectiveness with which the goals of the group are realized."[30] In order to achieve these ends, the group allows for three significant processes: ventilation, validation, and experimentation.

Ventilation, or expressing a problem to others, does not necessarily lead to change, but may be a step in that direction. Though it may only be a ploy to get attention, it is nonetheless valuable in that one may learn that he or she is worthy of attention. It certainly is the important first step in creating a group spirit. The next process available to the group is validation of the member's experiences; group members validate each other's emotions and dispel feelings of isolation. One advantage of bibliotherapy is that validation is accomplished also through imaginary characters and vicarious experiences in literature. Psychologists have found that confirmation by a number of sources is usually necessary for attitude change to result. The literature, other group members, and the group setting in itself can provide input to help determine attitudes and behavior. As psychologists Calder and Ross have demonstrated, "a person's behavior with respect to an object [or person or experience] in a situation is determined by at least two interacting attitudes—his attitude toward the object [person, experience] and his attitude toward the situation."[13] The opportunity for experimentation is the last of the triad of group processes. Because of the acceptance of the other group members and of the therapist, the confidential status of therapy, and the heightened sense of self-worth, a member may try out a new idea or attitude on the others. Or he or she may have what Luft has termed a "corrective emotional experience" through interaction with real and imaginary others.[32] After reality-testing or re-experiencing in the safety of the group, the client may be able to try new approaches in everyday life.

Obviously the group assumes much influence over its members. Some of the ways in which this is felt are summarized by Zimbardo and Ebbesen:

1) A person's opinions and attitudes are strongly influenced by groups to which he belongs and wants to belong.

2) A person is rewarded for conforming to the standards of the group and punished for deviating from them.

3) People who are most attached to the group are probably least influenced by communications which conflict with group norms.

4) Opinions which people make known to others are harder to change than opinions which people hold privately.

5) Audience participation (group discussion and decision-making) help to overcome resistance.

6) Resistance to counternorm communication increases with salience of one's group identification.

7) The support of even one other person weakens the powerful effect of a majority opinion of an individual.

8) A minority of two people can influence the majority if they are consistent in their deviant responses.[46]

While principles of group dynamics are difficult to summarize, the following suggestions collected and condensed from many psychologists and sociologists may be useful:

1) Interaction is physical and not just verbal; it takes energy to hide or deny behaviors which others witness.

2) Forced awareness is usually undesirable.

3) Mutual trust and group acceptance increase awareness.

4) A group generates its own conformity pressures.

5) Conflict and concensus are powerful dynamics in all groups.

6) Groups can and do raise tensions by attacking and confronting members; they lower tensions through support, humor, and affection.

7) A certain level of tension is necessary for learning but too much tension debilitates learning.

8) Peer acceptance is necessary for feelings of self-worth; only other members (and not the leaders) can offer that.

9) Human relationships themselves, both in the group and in literature, can be used as learning instruments. Participants learn about individual differences, defense mechanisms commonly used, the influence of emotions and drives on behavior, and the value of significant others.

10) Group participation is composed of the group dynamics, social interaction, and discussion of content, which in bibliotherapy is the media used.

RESEARCH IN BIBLIOTHERAPY

In this section, only studies on bibliotherapy itself (defined as an activity of reading/viewing/listening and discussion, usually in a group setting) will be surveyed. Because studies on reading interests, characteristics of readers, use of institutional libraries, institutional library programming, etc. are abundantly represented in other texts, they will not be considered here.

The literature of bibliotherapy reveals five types of research. According to Zaccaria and Moses, they are: exhortatory studies, theoretical research, descriptive studies, case studies, and experimental research.[45] Exhortatory articles call for greater use of bibliotherapy and for more research. Theoretical research relates bibliotherapy with other practices and attempts to explain the dynamics of the field and to emphasize its usefulness. Descriptive research does the same thing in that it describes the use of bibliotherapy in a particular setting. Techniques and suggestions are offered to the reader, but little specific detail is given. In case studies, the opposite is true—they are descriptive only about a specific example. Much of the literature is generally descriptive or case studies; unfortunately, neither of these types of research are considered conclusive by scientists. The only two types of experimental research evident in the literature of bibliotherapy are before-and-after studies and controlled studies. In both of these, more than one group of subjects is used and all are tested before and after bibliotherapy. Presumably, the change that occurs between the pre- and post-tests is attributable to the therapy. In before-after studies, one group of subjects is used. In controlled studies, at least two are used; one is given no treatment at all. Therefore it can be determined whether the differences in levels of adjustment, satisfaction, and so forth can be traced to bibliotherapy or to another intervening variable.

Although case studies and descriptive research are interesting and usually support the findings of experimental research, this section will discuss experimental research because its results are by far the most reliable. According to psychologists, experimental methods are the best we have for reaching the conclusion that a particular behavior is caused by some particular event or events. Unfortunately, very few experimental research studies in bibliotherapy have been reported. In an extensive 1958 analysis of the bibliotherapy literature, Artemisia Junier found that five hundred ninety-eight articles on bibliotherapy had been written from 1900-1958. Of these, twenty-seven were research articles; only two were experimental research.[29] Since 1958, approximately four hundred articles have been published but the number of studies remains low.

A significant number of the experimental research projects have been done as Master's or Doctoral theses. The first Master's thesis on bibliotherapy was done by Evalene Jackson in 1944;[28] the first Doctoral dissertation in the field was Shrodes' 1950 study.[41] The theoretical aspects of her work were corroborated by her clinical-case study research on bibliotherapy as a projective technique.

As part of her study, five students were given material carefully tailored to their reading habits, interests, abilities, and modes of adaptation. Their responses were structured by means of directions for reports on readings, analyses of the reading, and personal reactions to the readings. In addition, the five subjects took the Rorschach test,

Maslow's Security-Insecurity test, the California Public Opinion Poll, and the Progressive Education Interest Survey. All gave a preliminary interview and a written statement of problems and goals; four also wrote autobiographies. Although Shrodes selected only one case for a detailed analysis, she stated that the others "have consistently provided corroborative evidence of the general principles involved." She found that a pattern of identification, selective perception, projection, and insight followed the reading of each piece of literature.

Another test of Shrodes' theory of literature as a projective technique came in 1951 when Esther Hartman presented a dissertation. She used 68 unselected college students in psychology and English classes. The subjects read four excerpts from novels and then filled out structured questionnaires and rating scales about the readings. Hartman validated the responses by comparing them with autobiographies the students wrote. Three hypotheses were explored:

1) A questionnaire based on response to certain selections of imaginative literature will tend to elicit self-references which describe the subject's concept of his psychological field.

2) Specific aspects of the field (such as the concept of self in family relationships) may be determined through the use of imaginative literature as a projective device.

3) Responses elicited from imaginative literature contain evidence of therapeutic elements (e.g., identification, catharsis, etc.).[24]

The results of her study were positive in respect to all three hypotheses. In response to hypothesis number one, Hartman states "It would seem from the percentage of responses that in general the stories used in the experiment do elicit self-references in sufficient frequency that imaginative literature as a projective instrument appears to be successful in eliciting information about a subject's psychological field."[24] She notes that the story, the questionnaire, and individual differences in the respondents all affect the number of self-references reported, whereas no relationship to scholastic ability was found. In regards to hypothesis number two, Hartman states "A percentage analysis of the data supports the hypothesis that imaginative literature may be used as a projective device to describe the psychological field within the areas designated."[24] The subject's concept of self in relationships with his or her parents, and his or her concept of home atmosphere, were secured through imaginative literature when the respondent was positive or negative; ambivalent responses were not demonstrated. To test the last hypothesis, evidence of identification and catharsis were examined. However, "since the sample employed was limited, the conclusion (that identification and catharsis were evident) is offered as suggestive rather than conclusive evidence."[24]

In 1946, Henry C. Meckel studied adolescents' responses to a novel. The most important mechanism he isolated was identification which he stated:

. . . was found to be involved as a factor in reading responses which are nonappreciative as well as in reading responses which are appreciative. The data indicated also that identification with the central character may be direct, or indirect through identification with female characters associated with him. Superiority of the central character appeared to be an important mechanism in favorable responses.[36]

Concerning identification, Meckel presented four hypotheses:

1) Identification between reader and character may be repressed and reading content criticized or rejected by unacceptable behavior of the central character or characters closely associated with him; by unacceptable changes in behavior of the character or unacceptable traits which develop as the character is delineated; and by unpleasant experiences which happen to the character and which are uncongenial to the reader.

2) Fear of emotion or desire to avoid emotion may result in repression of identification with a character who gives way to his emotion.

3) Where identification is fairly complete, there are parallel experiences in the life of the central character and the reader of a satisfactory sort. In such case, the book is likely to be enthusiastically accepted.

4) Identification may be encouraged by opportunities to live vicariously through an experience of the central character.[36]

Evalene Jackson investigated the effects of reading upon attitudes toward blacks in her 1944 thesis. The subjects, 12-14 year old residents of Atlanta, Georgia, were split into control and experimental groups which were matched in respect to sex, intelligence, chronological age, and socioeconomic status. An original short story stressing the similarity of needs and personality of black and white children, and avoiding stereotypes and dialect, was written for use in the study. Initially both groups were tested by the Hinckley scale to determine attitudes; then the experimental group read and informally discussed the story while the control group did no reading. The groups were then tested again, and retested two weeks later to see if the changes produced were lasting.

A small but significant shift from a less to a more favorable attitude toward the Negro race, as measured by the Hinckley scale, was indicated . . . This shift was not lasting. A repetition of the experiment in a second school revealed a small but insignificant shift in the same direction on the part of the experimentals . . . The score of the experimental group on the third test indicated that the gain made after reading fiction was lost in two weeks. It should be remembered that the time involved was brief, the reading and two tests all falling within an hour . . .[27]

Three years later, Sister Mary Agnes followed up Jackson's study with an investigation of the influence of reading on racial attitudes of 100 adolescent high school girls. The control and experimental groups were matched according to IQ but they differed in reading history. The group of girls who had read two or more books about Negroes during the year "were more homogenous in outlook, more favorably disposed to the Negro, more cognizant of his rights, and more aware of the problem than the others."[2]

George Carlsen's 1948 dissertation continued the discussion of bibliotherapy and racial attitudes. He felt that the assumption on the part of many educators that "prejudice is primarily emotional rather than intellectual and as such must be attacked emotionally as well as intellectually . . ."[14] leads to an assumption that bibliotherapy should be especially suited to the changing of prejudicial attitudes. Five experimental and five control groups of eleventh grade students were used in his study. Each read three books concerning blacks chosen from an annotated list of twelve books on the topic. Six of the titles were fiction, three biography, and one each of drama, poetry, and prose. Then the student took a simple objective test about the book (to ascertain whether or not it was actually read) and filled out a personal reaction sheet for each book. In addition, a battery of five personality and attitude tests were given pre- and post-reading. The students were given thirteen class hours to read. Unfortunately, Carlsen purposely did not include discussion in his experiment. "The books apparently did foster much discussion among the students, anyway." His results showed:

> . . . a statistically significant gain [on attitudes toward black people] for 75 percent of the experimental group. Only 25 percent of control group scores showed a significant gain. However, the difference between the mean gains of the experimental and control groups was not statistically significant. The greatest gain in scores of the experimental group came from the students who were in the middle fifty percent on initial scores.[14]

Carlsen discovered that discussion should have followed the reading if more substantial changes were to occur.

> Comments of students show the need for constant discussion of their reactions and some help in finding the broadest base of interpretation for the feeling the book aroused in him. The number of students who failed to react positively and of those who failed to react at all might have been minimized through group discussion. The simple reading of books with free reaction, unchallenged by another person, is potentially dangerous.[14]

In 1968, Frank Fisher did a study of the influence of reading and discussion on attitudes toward the American Indian.[20] This study used 15 fifth grade classes from different socioeconomic backgrounds split into three groups, each consisting of two classes from each social stratum. The first group read selections about the American Indian, while the second group read the excerpts and discussed them. The third group acted as a control and neither read nor discussed the literature. Structured attitude scales were used before and after the treatment as the testing measure. The attitudes of groups one and two changed significantly while those of the control group remained static. The group that both read and discussed the literature changed the most in their racial attitudes.

The other significant experimental studies also deal with effects of bibliotherapy on varying types of attitudes and behavior. Earl George Heminghaus tested the effects of bibliotherapy on the attitudes and personal and social adjustment of a group of elementary school children.[23] Two groups of matched eighth grade students in St. Louis, Missouri were studied for an eight-month period. Three measurement instruments — Rosenzweig Picture Frustration Study, Thematic Apperception Test, and the California Test of Personality — were used before and after the experimental period. The experimental group improved significantly in the areas where the most reading and discussion was done. The experimentals also decreased in extra-punitive responses, anti-social aggression responses, and negative themes; they increased in positive themes.

In a 1968 dissertation, Charles M. Whipple studied 104 inmates at the Oklahoma State Reformatory.[42] Eight sets of control and experimental groups each met as biology classes for three hours weekly over a ten-week period. The control groups received regular lecture-demonstration classes while the experimental groups spent one of their three biology hours on mental hygiene and personal problems. The Minnesota Multiphasic Personality Inventory Scales were administered before and after the ten-week period. The experimentals significantly improved on the psychiatric deviate, hysteria, schizophrenia, paranoia and social introversion scales of the MMPI, whereas the control group showed significant negative values (increase) in the psychiatric deviancy and hypomania. The experimental group also showed positive gains in the study of biology.

The 1967 study by Rosa Alexander and Stephen E. Buggie also attempted attitude and behavior change in twenty-four female chronic schizophrenics at Agnews State Hospital. These patients were divided into three groups of eight. One group received maximal librarian-physician contact during bibliotherapy; one had minimal contact; and the control group received no bibliotherapy. Stephenson's self-concept test was administered before and after the experimental period of two sessions per week for 12 weeks. Six short stories and fiction passages were used in ascending order of abstraction. In addition to the Stephenson analyses, a post-therapy psychiatric evaluation was performed.

> It would have been expected that the three groups would have mean scores on the pre- and post-therapy testing nearly equal at the beginning, and that the prescribed bibliotherapy would produce test results in the two experimental groups superior to that of the control. However, according to this test data, treatment effects were negligible, showing no significant differences after therapy. One could conclude that Stephenson's statements were not an adequate measure of improvement due to bibliotherapy. . . . Despite the inadequacies of these measuring devices, in the post-therapy psychiatric interviews most of the patients were rated positively on attitudes, changes in attitudes, task orientation, interaction capacity, and accessibility. Maximal patient interaction with staff had the greatest impact on the characteristics of task orientation. The psychiatrists' evaluations suggest that bibliotherapy did help to effect positive changes in these five categories.[2]

A 1961 study by Gloria Matters concentrated on problem solving rather than attitude change.[35] Two sixth-grade classes, one an experimental group and one a control group, were studied over a six-month period. Books were chosen to help pupils solve personal and social problems which arose during the experimental period. The California Test of Personality, used pre- and post-bibliotherapy, did not show any change, but the Bloomer Identification Figure Test and personal statements indicated that bibliotherapy was effective.

A 1965 poetry therapy experiment by Kenneth Edgar and Richard Hazley tested the effects of literature on personal problems.[17] Eight college students who had applied for individual counseling at the school clinic were used as the experimental group and eight other persons were used as the control group. By the end of the four-month experimental period, the control group had dissipated and comparisons were impossible. The control group met once a week for a two-hour session. Poems chosen by the therapists were "thought to convey symbolically feelings and attitudes being repressed by the members of the group." The students were also encouraged to write poetry. A battery of five tests given before treatment were repeated at the end of 26 hours of treatment, and the results given to an independent panel of three psychologists. They concluded from the pre- and post-tests alone, that seven of the eight subjects had improved psychologically. The results, however, are inconclusive in that the control group was not post-tested and the results show that the females, who happened to have a higher average IQ than the male subjects, also improved more significantly—the confound of IQ and sex is still unexplained.

The effectiveness of bibliotherapy using didactic and imaginative literature, and its dependence on hospital setting, sex, and length of institutionalization was the subject of a 1970 dissertation by Harris McClaskey. The subjects were 73 chronic emotionally ill patients in two state mental hospitals, who participated in six groups (four experimental and two control) which met three times per week over twelve weeks. Two tests (the Wittenborn Psychiatric Rating Scales and a semantic differential test) were administered before and after the experimental period. The control group members met for activities, not including reading, while the experimental groups read and discussed four pieces of didactic literature and four of creative literature. McClaskey tested fourteen hypotheses; the first seven concerned behavioral change and the second seven related to attitudinal change.

McClaskey summarized his results in this manner:

1) Bibliotherapy, using either didactic or creative literature, with chronic emotionally disturbed patients will be effective in bringing about significant behavioral change.

2) Bibliotherapy, using either didactic or creative literature as the basis for reading and discussion, with chronic emotionally disturbed patients will be effective in bringing about significantly improved behavioral change.

3) Bibliotherapy, using either didactic or creative literature, with chronic emo-

tionally disturbed patients will be independent of factors involving setting, sex, and length of institutionalization.

4) Bibliotherapy, using either didactic or creative literature, with chronic emotionally disturbed patients, will not be effective in bringing about significant attitudinal change.[33]

McClaskey's findings appear to directly contradict the results of Jackson and Heminghaus but they do corroborate Alexander's conclusions.

Lesta Burt's 1972 dissertation was designed to further explore the effect of bibliotherapy on attitudes. "The general objective was to test the prediction that bibliotherapy would affect positively the attitudes of inmates in correctional institutions, and would do so for all inmates regardless of age, recidivism, sex, race, achievement, offense, number of months served, or number of months to be served."[12] Burt used 59 volunteer inmates from two state correctional institutions. Each institution had two experimental and two control groups; the experimental groups met two hours weekly for twelve weeks and discussed six books (imaginative and didactic) while the control groups only met three times to participate in a reading-interest survey. The Personal Values Abstract and a Semantic Differential test were administered before and after the experimental period. Three hypotheses were tested. The first, concerning the effects of bibliotherapy on eleven concepts, was supported in part. Burt found significant change in attitudes toward behavior—stealing and drug addiction—but not toward the other concepts. Her second hypothesis dealt with the effect of bibliotherapy on socialization and was not supported. Hypothesis three concentrated on the relative effects of factors such as sex, race, offense, recidivism, etc. The results indicate that some of the factors did interact. For example, race and number of months to be served affected the attitudes toward the black and the white races; the number of months served affected the attitude toward women; differences in race, achievement, and time served affected the attitude toward men. The results of her study are complex. She summarizes them in the following manner:

1) Bibliotherapy may be a helpful adjuvant to the correctional program for improving attitudes related to behavioral concepts for all categories of inmates.

2) Bibliotherapy may be a helpful adjuvant to the correctional program in improving attitudes toward persons for inmates possessing certain background characteristics.

3) Bibliotherapy may be effectively carried out by librarians when working with small inmate groups who meet the criteria for group book discussion leaders described in this study.[12]

Current research, it is obvious, is conflicting and confusing. The field is badly in need of further studies which will investigate the effects of bibliotherapy on attitudes toward people and concepts, on attitudes toward behavior, and on behavior itself.

McCLASKEY STUDY RESULTS

Hypotheses	Behavioral Change	Attitudinal Change
#1 and #8: The use of didactic literature in bibliotherapy will result in	supported	not supported
#2 and #9: The use of creative literature in bibliotherapy will result in	supported	not supported
#3 and #10: Creative literature will produce	not supported	not applicable
#4 and #11: Bibliotherapy will result in more positive than negative gains	supported	not supported
#5 and #12: Relationship of hospital to results		
#6 and #13: Relationship of sex to results	These variables independent of results	
#7 and #14: Relationship of length of hospitalization to results		

FIGURE 5

BURT STUDY RESULTS

Hypotheses		Supported	Not Supported
#1	Bibliotherapy Will Have A Significant Effect On Eleven Concepts		
	1. stealing	x	
	2. drug addiction	x	
	3. white race		x
	4. women		x
	5. men		x
	6. mothers		x
	7. fathers		x
	8. black race		x
	9. parole officer		x
	10. God		x
	11. Myself		x
#2	Bibliotherapy Will Have An Effect On Socialization		x
#3	Relative Effects of Nine Other Factors On Bibliotherapy		Too complex to chart here. See her study for a detailed analysis
	1. sex		
	2. race		
	3. age		
	4. offense		
	5. time served		
	6. time to be served		
	7. treatment		
	8. recidivism		
	9. achievement		

FIGURE 6

REFERENCES

1. Sister Mary Agnes, "The Influence of Reading in the Racial Attitudes of Adolescent Girls," *The Catholic Educational Review* 45: 415-420 (September 1947).

2. Rosa Horn Alexander and Stephen E. Buggie, "Bibliotherapy with Chronic Schizophrenics," *Journal of Rehabilitation* 33:27 (November/December 1967).

3. G. W. Allport, "Attitudes" in C. Murchison, ed., *A Handbook of Social Psychology* (Worcester, Massachusetts: Clark University Press, 1935).

4. Edwin F. Alston, "Bibliotherapy and Psychotherapy," *Library Trends* 11:166-167 (October 1962).

5. Kenneth C. Appel "Psychiatric Therapy," in J. Hunt, ed., *Personality and the Behavior Disorders*, vol. two (New York: Ronald Press, 1944).

6. D. J. Bem, "An Experimental Analysis of Self-Persuasion," *Journal of Experimental Social Psychology* 1:199 (1965).

7. John F. Briggs, "Adverse Effects from Bibliotherapy," *Hospital Progress* 45:123-125 (July 1964).

8. Daniel Brower, "Bibliotherapy" in Daniel Brower and Lawrence E. Abt, *Progress in Clinical Psychology*, vol. two (New York: Grune and Stratton, 1956).

9. Eleanor F. Brown, *Bibliotherapy and Its Widening Applications* (Metuchen, New Jersey: The Scarecrow Press, Inc., 1975).

10. Alice I. Bryan, "Can There Be a Science of Bibliotherapy?" *Library Journal* 64:773-776 (October 15, 1939).

11. Alice I. Bryan, "Personality Adjustment Through Reading," *Library Journal* 64:573-576 (1939).

12. Lesta Norris Burt, "Bibliotherapy: Effect of Group Reading and Discussion on Attitudes of Adult Inmates in Two Correctional Institutions," (Ph.D. dissertation, University of Wisconsin, 1972).

13. Bobby J. Calder and Michael Ross, *Attitudes and Behavior* (Morristown, New Jersey: General Learning Press, 1973).

14. George Robert Carlsen, "A Study of the Effects of Reading Books About the Negro on the Racial Attitudes of a Group of Eleventh Grade Students in Northern Schools," (Ph.D. dissertation, University of Minnesota, 1948).

15. Dorwin Cartwright and Alvin Zander, *Group Dynamics: Research and Theory* 3rd ed. (New York: Harper and Row, 1968).

16. Helen I. Driver, *Counseling and Learning Through Small Group Discussions* (Madison, Wisconsin: Morona Pub., 1958).

17. Kenneth Edgar and Richard Hazley, "Validation of Poetry Therapy as a Group Therapy Technique," in J. J. Leedy, *Poetry Therapy* (Philadelphia: Lippincott, 1969).

18. Lucy F. Fairbanks, "Activity Therapy" in William Beatty, ed., *Proceedings of the ALA Bibliotherapy Workshop St. Louis 1964* in *AHIL QUARTERLY* 4:1-60 (Summer 1964).

19. Leon Festinger, *A Theory of Cognitive Dissonance* (Evanston, Illinois: Row and Peterson, 1957).

20. Frank Fisher, "Influence of Reading and Discussion on Attitudes of Fifth Graders Toward American Indians" *Journal of Educational Research* 62:130-134 (November 1968).

21. Jerome D. Frank, *Group Methods in Therapy* (New York: Public Affairs Pamphlet #284, 1959).

22. L. A. Gottschalk, "Bibliotherapy as an Adjunct in Psychiatry," *American Journal of Psychiatry* 104:632-637 (April 1948).

23. Julius Griffin, "Summary of Bibliotherapy Lectures Presented to the Professional Staff of Patton State Hospital During July and August, 1959," (Encino, California: Griffin Clinic, 1959.)

24. Esther A. Hartman, "Imaginative Literature as a Projective Technique: A Study in Bibliotherapy" (Ph.D. dissertation, Stanford University, 1951).

25. Earl George Heminghaus, "The Effect of Bibliotherapy on the Attitudes and Personal and Social Adjustment of A Group of Elementary School Children," (Ph.D. dissertation, Washington University, 1954).

26. Norman N. Holland, *Five Readers Reading* (New Haven: Yale University Press, 1975).

27. Evalene P. Jackson, "Bibliotherapy and Reading Guidance: A Tentative Approach to Theory," *Library Trends* 11:118-126 (October 1962), p. 119.

28. Evalene P. Jackson, "Effects of Reading Upon Attitudes Toward the Negro Race," *Library Quarterly* 14:47-54 (January 1944).

29. Artemisia J. Junier, "A Subject Index to the Literature of Bibliotherapy 1900-1958," (Master's thesis, Atlanta University, 1959).

30. C. Gratton Kemp, *Small Groups and Self-Renewal* (New York: Seabury Press, 1971).

31. Howard Leventhal, "Attitudes: Their Nature, Growth, and Change" in Charlan Nemeth, ed., *Social Psychology: Classic and Contemporary Integrations* (Chicago: Rand McNally, 1974).

32. Joseph Luft, *Group Processes: An Introduction to Group Dynamics* 2nd ed., (Palo Alto, California: Mayfield Publishing Co., 1970).

33. Harris C. McClaskey, "Bibliotherapy with Emotionally Disturbed Patients: An Experimental Study," (Ph.D. dissertation, University of Washington, 1970).

34. Abraham H. Maslow, *Motivation and Personality* (New York: Harper, 1954).

35. Gloria Matters, "Bibliotherapy in a Sixth Grade," (Ed.D. dissertation, Pennsylvania State University, 1961).

36. H. C. Meckel, "An Exploratory Study of the Responses of Adolescent Pupils to Situations in a Novel" (Ph.D. dissertation, University of Chicago, 1947).

37. R. W. Medlicott, "Bibliotherapy," *New Zealand Libraries,* 38:206-207 (August 1975).

38. William C. Menninger, "Bibliotherapy," *Bulletin of the Menninger Clinic* 1:263-273 (November 1937).

39. Margaret Monroe, ed., *Reading Guidance and Bibliotherapy in Public, Hospital, and Institution Libraries* (Madison, Wisconsin: University of Wisconsin Library School, 1971).

40. Louise M. Rosenblatt, *Literature as Exploration* (New York: Appleton-Century-Crofts, 1938).

41. Caroline Shrodes, "Bibliotherapy: A Theoretical and Clinical-Experimental Study," (Ph.D. dissertation, University of California, 1950).

42. Ruth Strang, *Explorations in Reading Patterns* (Chicago: University of Chicago Press, 1942).

43. Douglas Waples, Bernard Berelson and Franklyn Bradshaw, *What Reading Does to People* (Chicago: University of Chicago Press, 1940).

44. Charles M. Whipple, "The Effect of Short-term Bibliotherapy on the Personality and Academic Achievement of Reformatory Inmate Students," (Ed.D. dissertation, University of Oklahoma, 1968).

45. Joseph S. Zaccaria, and Harold A. Moses, *Facilitating Human Development Through Reading: The Use of Bibliotherapy in Teaching and Counseling* (Champaign, Illinois: Stipes Pub. Co., 1968).

46. Philip Zimbardo and Ebbe B. Ebbesen, *Influencing Attitudes and Changing Behavior: A Basic Introduction to Relevant Methodology, Theory and Applications* (Reading, Massachusetts: Addison-Wesley Pub. Co., 1970).

Chapter Three

Mechanics of Bibliotherapy

Careful planning is essential to the implementation of a bibliotherapy program. The many possible objectives discussed in Chapter Two play an important role in planning. These, and the methods, techniques, and materials of a specific program, depend on the theoretical bias of the therapist, his or her personal attributes, and the needs of the clients. Moreover, the bibliotherapist, and any other professionals involved, must consider the setting in which therapy will take place. Then decisions must be made about procedures, record keeping guidelines, and evaluation techniques. It is essential that all of these decisions be made before the first bibliotherapy session.

SETTINGS

Although bibliotherapy originated in hospitals and has since been considered an institutional library service, teachers and school counselors have also used bibliotherapy extensively, and public librarians have begun to extend bibliotherapy into the community. Each of these settings has specific problems and advantages, which influence the objectives and procedures of the bibliotherapy program. A brief look at some of the more common contexts for bibliotherapy should clarify their differences.

Medical hospitals. The current status of bibliotherapy is due in great part to its use in medical hospitals. The Veterans Administration Hospital librarians, in particular, have fostered bibliotherapy programs. Although the introduction of television sets in hospital rooms has diminished interest in hospital book cart service, bibliotherapy programming has been abundant, varied, and successful. The reasons that hospitals have provided an excellent setting for bibliotherapy include: the large number of hospitalized patients in the United States; the relatively large number of staff in medical institutions as compared to other institutions; the readily available "therapeutic team"; the boredom of long-term patients; the ability of many patients to move or be moved to a central, neutral location such as the library; an atmosphere conducive to all types of therapy; and the philosophy of patient care.

Illness is always unpleasant and often painful for the patient. The hospital stay itself is an unhappy experience, often entailing separation from family, unfamiliar surroundings, a new schedule, and disagreeable medications. For short-term patients, recreation, externalization and some education are often the objectives of bibliotherapy. The situation is different for the chronically ill. Chronic illness can be an emotional trauma for the patient as well as relatives and friends. Both the illness and its concomitant confinement and, in some cases, disabilities and the possibility of death, must be accepted. Self-acceptance and insight, then, become the objectives of bibliotherapy. But while bibliotherapy for the patients themselves is fairly common at this time, there are no hospitals providing bibliotherapy for the patients' families although some hospitals do provide social workers and counselors to help relatives and friends of patients. Bibliotherapy would be an excellent technique to help the concerned people cope with institutionalization, their feelings of helplessness, and the patients' reactions to hospitalization.

Institutional bibliotherapy—defined earlier as individual bibliotherapy in an institutional setting for informational purposes—is most prevalent with short-term patients. This is often in the form of bookcart service which has been discussed in great detail by John H. McFarland and others. Bibliotherapy coincides with bookcart service only when the goals are therapeutic, and discussion follows the patients' readings. Otherwise the service offered is merely reading guidance. Clinical bibliotherapy—group bibliotherapy in an institutional or other setting for the purpose of insight and self-growth—can also apply to the hospital setting, as is described by Sadie Peterson-Delaney and Lore Hirsch among others.

Mental hospitals have been another important setting for bibliotherapy for many of the same reasons as medical hospitals. The major difference is that mental patients are sometimes unable—because of their illnesses or the results of drug therapy—to read aloud and/or to express themselves clearly. Also, the administrators of mental hospitals seem to be more prone to censorship of materials than are medical hospital staffs. These problems are partially offset by the fact that diverse psychotherapies are well accepted in this setting. Many librarians have successfully used clinical bibliotherapy in mental hospitals. Groups of ambulatory patients may meet in the library while others meet on the wards. Patients may be grouped according to diagnosis, interests, or ward. All types of materials may be used. Exemplary bibliotherapy programs in mental hospitals include one led by David McDowell at McLean Hospital in Belmont, Massachusetts and one led by Clara Lack at Agnews State Hospital in Santa Clara, California. The latter was financed from 1968-1970 with a Library Services and Construction Act (LSCA) grant "to demonstrate that beneficial results could be achieved by using books in the general treatment program of a mental hospital." The pilot project was considered successful by all involved and continued until 1973 when the hospital was closed.

Educational settings for bibliotherapy have been popular since the 1940's. A review of the literature shows that most bibliotherapy sessions in schools are led by a teacher or counselor rather than by a librarian, and that the educators have led the field.

Since 1947 when the American Council on Education first published *Reading Ladders for Human Relations*, the literature of education has been replete with references to bibliotherapy. The 1950's resulted in the well-known works of Russell and Shrodes, Witty, and Kircher. Much of their research was done in the context of elementary and secondary classrooms. In the 1960's, both Harold A. Moses and R. Rovin extended the study of bibliotherapy in education to school counseling.

Bibliotherapy is compatible with the goals of contemporary education. As H. M. Lindahl and K. Koch state in *Bibliotherapy in the Middle Grades*, "Inasmuch as the building of a wholesome, self-confident, self-respecting, effective, happy personality is one of the major goals of education, the teacher is seeking constantly to find ways of giving each child the particular guidance that he needs."[41] Joseph S. Zaccaria and Harold A. Moses, in *Facilitating Human Development Through Reading*, a major work on bibliotherapy in education and counseling, observe that the classroom teacher using bibliotherapy can help students both developmentally ("a slow steady growth into a deepened self ") and remedially (as "an immediate first aid").[90]

The advantages of doing bibliotherapy in the educational context include the facts that the students are already in an atmosphere conducive to—and related to—both reading and verbalization; the bibliotherapist can meet with the students as often as five days a week; the therapist has the opportunity to observe the student in other activities and interactions; school records and conferences with the teachers are available to the therapist; bibliotherapy can easily be added to a typically varied program; and a library or media center is usually available.

Correctional institutions present problems for all types of programming, including bibliotherapy. Security is the primary concern of correctional administrators; the introduction of new personnel, movement of residents to and from group meetings at which officers are not present, bringing books and other materials into the institution, and the content of materials, may be considered security risks. There are many problems for the bibliotherapist to consider. These include securing the permission of the administration; establishing the trust of the residents; the presence of security officers; censorship of materials; and confidentiality of the sessions and records. Often residents will not feel that they can speak freely because they fear that what they say will be used against them; they attempt to please the therapist in the hopes that a favorable report will go to the administration and to the parole board. Residents have reasonable grounds for these beliefs; correctional administrators often demand reports on residents from all staff who work with them. Another problem is the availability of materials and audiovisual hardware; more than half the correctional institutions in the country have no libraries. Of those that do, material is often censored and machinery is not allowed.

If these problems can be circumvented, bibliotherapy can be most useful and find grateful acceptance in correctional institutions. Residents are usually eager for any social activity and the opportunity to think about and discuss something new. On the other hand, the administration may be interested in providing programs which keep the residents occupied and which foster the image of the correctional institutions as a rehabilitation center. The bibliotherapist in a correctional institution must be aware of the special problems this environment presents, and must make a concerted effort to see that the program is not used as a reward or punishment.

Other institutional settings for bibliotherapy include: nursing homes, institutions for the retarded, halfway houses, drug addiction and alcohol treatment centers, and homes for the physically disabled. As Genevieve Casey discusses in her 1971 book entitled *Libraries in the Therapeutic Society,* librarians and professional associations have recently written standards for institutional library services; now it is up to librarians to demonstrate their interest by implementing the standard. Because institutions have been lacking in adequate general library services, all library programming, including bibliotherapy, has been rare. An early article by Esther Pomeroy[66] which discussed bibliotherapy in a tuberculosis sanitorium, Peterson-Delaney's 1955 report[14] on bibliotherapy in a drug abuse center and Hannigan and Henderson's 1963 report on bibliotherapy with drug addicts[27] are all classics. More recent projects in this category include Lack's work with the elderly[37] and Hynes' work with drug addicts.[30] Unfortunately, not as much has been done in this field as is warranted.

Community settings are becoming more important for all types of therapies. The current trend in both corrections and mental health is toward reducing institutional populations and increasing parolees or patients out in the community. Margaret Monroe explains: "As the walls between the institution and society are lowered, the special services of hospital and institution libraries [including bibliotherapy] take on a universal meaning in librarianship. What is pioneered in the institutional context will have broader application in public and school libraries . . ."[55] Until now, the public library's involvement with bibliotherapy has generally been limited to its extension librarians working in neighboring institutions. Little has appeared in the library literature about public libraries directly using bibliotherapy in their communities. The one notable exception is the Santa Clara County Library in San Jose, California, which took over the bibliotherapy program of Agnews State Hospital when that institution was closed in 1973; two bibliotherapists lead bibliotherapy sessions in the community and in numerous institutions.

Agencies other than public libraries are beginning to use bibliotherapy in their community endeavors. The National Council on the Aging has an exemplary Senior Center Humanities Program in which eight week units in fields such as history, philosophy and literature are taught in senior citizen centers by volunteers. Because one of the objectives of the program is to "foster the sense of self-esteem and personal possibility among participants" and materials are chosen in accordance with the special interests of older Americans, the program appears to use bibliotherapeutic principles. The future should show an increased interest in bibliotherapy in community settings, sponsored by any of a number of public agencies including the library.

Principles concerning settings for bibliotherapy include the following:

1) The specific problems indigenous to the various types of settings must be realized. Those which could potentially threaten the bibliotherapy program (e.g., censorship, drug therapies, etc.) must be confronted by the therapist.

2) The objectives and techniques must reflect the problems and advantages inherent in the setting.

3) The milieu of the meeting room itself must be suitable for therapy. No matter what the context of the program, discussions must be held in comfortable, well lit, and cheerful rooms which allow for quiet, privacy, and relaxation. Refreshments, art displays, and music-playing can help to achieve the proper effect.

CLIENTS

Most bibliotherapy programs in the United States involve English-speaking children or literate adults with at least an average I.Q. and the ability to verbalize and to understand. No program with the Spanish-speaking or any other non-English-speaking people has been reported, nor have programs been attempted with the deaf. Yet, according to the 1970 U.S. Census, 35 million Americans do not speak English as a mother tongue. Over seven million are Spanish-speaking and approximately one-half million people use the American Sign Language (A.S.L.). The number of bibliotherapy projects with the blind, retarded, mute, and organically damaged elderly is miniscule. All of these populations need to be served by public and special libraries with both traditional and creative library services, including bibliotherapy. As Daniel Sweeney of St. Elizabeths Hospital in Washington, D.C. states it: "I do not think that many would debate the efficacy of bibliotherapy with the YAVIS group of institutionalized persons: the young, attractive, verbal, intelligent, and sophisticated. However, there may be a tendency to avoid using it with the elderly and other particularly difficult patient groups."[81] Dr. Sweeney, a psychologist, and Arleen Hynes, a librarian, lead bibliotherapy groups for elderly brain-damaged patients, aged 50 to 90-years-old, with diagnoses ranging from schizophrenia and senility to pre-senile dementia or chronic brain disorder. Rosalie Brown, a Certified Poetry Therapist, also at St. Elizabeths Hospital, leads a group of men in wheelchairs, some of whom cannot talk or move, yet she reports that the patients respond with memories, laughter, and appreciation communicated by signs.

Each client group, whether a bright active group or a listless unresponsive one, has its own problems which must affect the objectives and techniques of bibliotherapy with that group. For example, the retarded and brain-damaged will have obvious reading problems, and along with the speech impaired, will have trouble with verbalization. It is important that specialists such as speech therapists or clinicians be consulted and perhaps co-lead the bibliotherapy sessions. High interest/low vocabulary books and audiovisual materials are essential. Some objectives might be social interaction, increase in self-confidence, opportunity for speech practice, and understanding of the personal significance of the handicaps.

As another example, drug addicts tend to be introspective and are often avid readers. Alcoholics Anonymous and Synanon groups have taught many addicts to verbalize their feelings. More difficult materials can be used to achieve the goals of insight and behavior change. Delinquent adolescents, on the other hand, may be underachievers and school dropouts and therefore deficient in academic skills. Yet they, as the addicts, are often sophisticated and show interest in socially relevant themes. Self-esteem, insight, and attitude change are among the objectives for bibliotherapy with these groups.

Some basic principles governing bibliotherapy participants are:

1) Participation in bibliotherapy should be completely voluntary. In situations where the resident is court committed (mental hospitals, prisons) or non-voluntary (medical hospitals, sanitoriums) this principle may be difficult to implement but is nonetheless essential.

2) The clients' needs, abilities, and problems—besides diagnosis or criminal status—should determine both the techniques and the objectives. Also to be considered are chronological and emotional age, educational background, developmental and situational problems, reading preferences, etc.

3) The therapist must adapt the materials to the physical handicaps and reading abilities of the clients. Typography, format, size and illustrations are all important considerations for the use of print materials; auditory and visual quality, clarity, speed, and speech are relevant when using audiovisual materials.

4) The client must not be forced, rather the therapist must appreciate his "teachable moment." This is called by Zaccaria and Moses "bibliotherapy readiness."[90]

5) Unserved populations such as the Spanish speaking and the deaf and blind should be given access to bibliotherapy.

MATERIALS FOR BIBLIOTHERAPY

Selection of materials is a major part of the preparation for a program of bibliotherapy. It is well accepted that a good book collection reflects the community it is designed to serve. In bibliotherapy, the community is a limited, carefully delineated group of people and the book selection is tailored especially for the individual client, in compliance with the definition of "good librarianship" as the right book for the right person at the right time.

Dr. William C. Menninger stated in a 1937 article: "In considering the basis for the prescription of reading we have taken into account three factors: the present therapeutic needs, the background of the individual, and the symptomatic picture."[54] These three selection criteria can be further broken down. "Present therapeutic needs" include what Caroline Shrodes refers to as "the subject's characteristic modes of adaptation."[78] The crucial question in her research was whether the therapy was to be supportive or aimed at supplying insight.

> If the therapy indicated was supportive, the books selected were chosen to lend support to the subject's defenses, to encourage sublimation, to reduce his sense of difference from others and to increase his sense of belongingness, and to provide a sense of direction, values to live by, a radix, a philosophy for living. If the therapy indicated was to provide insight, the books selected might aim at establishing two different but related types of identification: identification with the self-figure or the nonself-figure. If the subject's sense of reality was distorted by stereotyped thinking, books were selected to provide correctives for stereotyped interpretations of reality. If the subject's life experiences allowed insufficient expression for emotions, books were chosen to arouse affect. If the subject gave evidence of intense rigidity and intolerance, the books recommended were focused on themes designed to being about recognition and acceptance of difference.[78]

Menninger's second criterion, the individual's background, includes ethnic affinity, reading level, sex, age, race, past experiences, and interpersonal relationships. The third criterion, the "symptomatic picture" or diagnosis, is even more complex. Numerous studies were done in the 1930's, 40's, and 50's to demonstrate what classification of patient likes, reads, or benefits from a particular type of literature. Unfortunately most of the results are vague and conflict with each other. Pomeroy (1931) and McFarland (1952) found that hospitalized psychiatric patients prefer fiction to nonfiction. Mayden (1952), and Lind (1927) found the opposite. Other studies are more specific. Frank Leslie's 1931 study at a Veterans Administration hospital showed that fiction readers included drug addicts, patients with encephalitis, mental deficiency, Raynaud's disease, hyperthyroidism, hysteria, psychoneuroses, and psychoses. Alcoholics and catatonics "preferred the useful arts" while hebephrenics and manic-depressives read in all categories and in the largest quantity.[40] In 1942, Salomon Gagnon reported a study comparing the reading interests of 529 patients with those of "normal individuals." He found that fiction was more popular, and nonfiction less popular, with patients than with the "normals." Patients devoted 58 percent of their reading time to fiction and 42 percent to nonfiction while "normals" devoted 52.3 percent to fiction and 47.7 percent to nonfiction. He then classified the types of fiction and nonfiction by male and female, and again by diagnosis. He found that paranoid schizophrenics were the only one of the 28 diagnostic categories he studied who read more nonfiction than fiction.[19] Unfortunately, Gagnon declined to interpret his data. Two years later, in a study of 147 patients, Mary D. Quint's findings contradicted Leslie's in that she found hebephrenics to be poor readers. Paranoid dementia praecox patients preferred nonfiction while syphilo-meningo-encephalitic psychotics and psychoneurotics preferred novels.

This type of classification of books by diagnostic category is no longer in vogue. The problems with such classification are many: the psychological labels are vague, they overlap, and reading interests rely on background and predispositions apart from the psychological problem and label.

Edwin Starbuck, and his colleagues, developed eight standards for selecting literature which they felt were good for "character training."[80] The criteria were unity, craftsmanship, emotional tone, effectiveness, artistry, truthfulness, refinement of fundamental human attitudes, and proper orientation. The first three criteria were literary, the next three educational, and the last two refer specifically to the use of literature to change children's attitudes. "The refinement of fundamental human attitudes" is explained as the redemption of man's basic tendencies and the transformation of his values toward " 'the eternally better . . .' Literature justifies its existence as it appeals either explicitly or implicitly to the fundamental attitudes in their refined forms." "Proper orientation" is defined as a true perspective on life which will help the individual to adjust to new experience. "In the last analysis (literature) helps in the adjustments of personality; it adds its share to the influences which create an individual who can move easily and familiarly in all spheres of valuable experience."[80]

A decade later, in 1940, Hazel Sample, an educator, wrote a book entitled *Pitfalls for Readers of Fiction*, in which she studied the novels of Zane Grey, Harold Belle Wright, Gene Stratton Porter, and Emilie Loring to determine each author's unstated assumptions.

Probably the most subtle influence which the author has on his reader is not through his expressed theme or thesis but through the values and ideas which he takes for granted, which are so much a part of the framework of thinking from which he writes that he himself is hardly conscious of the possibility or the needs of questioning them.[75]

Though she does not list criteria for book selection *per se,* she does list five sorts of evidence of an author's assumptions and encourages book selectors to examine them. They are: the structure of the story; the conflicts the author deals with and their outcome; the characters presented and the author's treatment of them; the goals of the characters; opinions and ideas expressed by the characters; and soliloquies of the author. Sample stresses that teachers, and other adults, should be aware of the author's biases and the reader's absorption of them. Most bibliotherapists seem to agree with her concern, and choose books accordingly. Materials that are moralistic, didactic, or prejudiced are avoided. For bibliotherapy, a piece of literature need not be the most current information or the most famous work of an author. Instead it must be an appropriate channel for the reader's ideas and emotions.

Jack Leedy's oft-quoted comment about therapeutic poetry applies to all literature:

> . . . some masterpieces of poetry may not be therapeutic whereas mediocre poems, never included in anthologies, may be extremely helpful or right for a patient, and may be his bridge to reality . . . a psychotherapist will choose verse that is useful in psychotherapy, however fine or poor it may appear to critics old or new. Some of it may be of the most inferior, some of the most superior order of poetry; for therapy, the standard is not whether it is great or good poetry, but whether it will help the ill.[39]

A number of authors have dealt with the problems of defining the qualities necessary for a book to be an effective instrument of therapy. Shrodes states that:

> The reality-unreality level of the book chosen is crucial in determining the potential impact upon the reader. The more illusion of reality the book conveys, the firmer it is embedded in the reader's mind and the more compelling it becomes in influencing future behavior. Obviously books appealing to the reader's interests, needs, and preoccupations will have a high level of reality and hence be more susceptible to intraception.[78]

Later in her dissertation, she presents another dimension of reality in literature.

> By realistic is meant that the author treats recognizably real people in real situations rather than stereotypes of people or situations contrived to demonstrate popular schematizations of experience. The characters will thus be governed by motives which are clearly recognizable as universally valid human motivations and the events will follow one another in an inevitable and logical sequence as the result of the interaction of the characters' psycho-biological natures with the world in which they have their being. Realistic literature presents not only the phenomena of experience but its genesis. The differing causes for the same behavioral manifestations are revealed in such a way that the reader is never left in doubt as to the internal consistency and the lawfulness of the personalities depicted.[78]

The concept that literature appears to be real if it applies to the reader, if it mirrors his/her emotional preoccupations and his/her values, is termed "emotional parallelism" by Louise Rosenblatt.[72] Selection of this type of materials, called the "isoprinciple" by Leedy,[39] is what leads to the identification of the reader with the material and leads to catharsis, understanding, insight, and change.

Who selects is a question which is still being debated. Although some practitioners allow the group members to choose materials to read, the author feels that selection should be done by the librarian or bibliotherapist unless the process of choice is in itself important for the client, for diagnosis, reality therapy, or responsibility training. In that case a few selections may be offered from which the client can choose. The rationale for this is twofold: The book must be well selected according to the criteria discussed above if bibliotherapy is to be effective; and most people choose material which is consistent with their beliefs and doesn't challenge their attitudes. Bernard Berelson's reading study demonstrated that "it is more often true that people select their reading to support their predisposition than that their reading changes their predisposition. This condition operates as a basic and powerful delimitation upon the psychological and social effects of reading. In this sense, what reading does to people is not nearly so important as what people do to reading."[4] Perhaps when readers discover the possibility of enriching their minds through reading, their book selection patterns will change. Until then, a librarian should help the reader to choose books which offer new insights. According to Wilbur Schramm's "fraction of selection," if librarians increase the reader's expectation of reward and decrease the effort required to read, people would read more.[76]

Imaginative vs. didactic literature and their relative value for bibliotherapy, is a current debate. Imaginative literature represents human behavior and emotions whereas didactic literature explains them. Caroline Shrodes states that:

> In general, didactic literature is more apt to contribute to man's intellectual awareness whereas imaginative literature is more likely to afford the reader an emotional experience without which effective therapy is impossible. So far as studying the dynamics of reading is concerned, and even as a basis for psychodiagnosis, one might well use an occasional piece of didactic literature, but for purposes of insight therapy it would seem that imaginative literature has greater power to effect changes in the reader. Unless direct or vicarious experience accompanies didactic and academic approaches to learning, there may be little carry-over into attitudes and behavior.[78]

A quotation from Freud's "Observations On Wild Psychoanalysis" corroborates Shrodes' opinion:

> The idea that a neurotic is suffering from some sort of ignorance, and that if one removes this ignorance by telling him facts (about the causal connection of his illness with his life, about his experiences in childhood, and so on) he must recover, is an idea that has long been superseded, and one derived from superficial ap-

pearances. The pathological factor is not his ignorance in itself, but the roots of this ignorance in his inner resistances; it was they that first called this ignorance into being, and they still maintain it now. In combating these resistances lies the task of therapy. Telling the patient what he does not know because he has repressed it, is only one of the preliminaries in [psycho] therapy. If knowledge about his unconscious were as important for the patient as the inexperienced in psychoanalysis imagine, it would be sufficient to cure him to go to lectures, or read [didactic] books. Such measures, however, have as little effect on the symptoms of nervous disease as distributing menu cards in time of famine has on people's hunger.[18]

Joseph Luft in his book *Group Process,* also uses a culinary metaphor: "Giving people information about food does not result in changes in food preferences, because personal attitudes remain unaffected by the mere presentation of facts."[45] Despite these strong statements in favor of the use of imaginative literature, it should be noted that some bibliotherapists do use didactic literature. The McClaskey study, discussed in Chapter Two, found no significant differences in behavior improvement between the bibliotherapy group using didactic literature and another using creative literature.

Literary genre. The relative advantages of one literary genre over another have not been studied with reference to bibliotherapy. A number of authors, however, have discussed the merits of specific genres, all of which have been used in bibliotherapy.

The novel is the most popular form of reading material in America. Studies of children's reading have found that fiction is much more popular than nonfiction, with biography in second place. By age twelve or so, sex differences in reading preferences begin to surface — girls continue to read mainly fiction while boys split their reading time between fiction and science materials. By fourteen, boys are reading as much nonfiction as fiction. Girls read adult fiction earlier than boys, although the reading of teenagers of both sexes is 90 percent fiction. In adulthood, fiction remains the most popular book choice for men and women. Publishing patterns both reflect and encourage the popularity of fiction. Of the 34 best-selling hardbacks of 1974 (17 fiction and 17 nonfiction) 2,140,759 novels were sold as compared to 3,116,824 total sales of all other types of books. Perhaps the mass-market paperback publication statistics are even more indicative than those of the hardbacks. In 1974, 1,695 new mass market paperback novels were published as compared to 1,107 new mass-market paperbacks in all other categories combined. Library use reflects the popularity of fiction also: 46 percent of all library materials borrowed are novels. Meckel maintains that the "novel has the virtue of possessing a greater range of stimuli for responses."[53] Whatever the reasons, novels continue to be extremely popular and have been used most often in bibliotherapy research.

Two studies deal with responses to fiction. The first, Henry C. Meckel's 1946 dissertation, examines and analyzes responses of adolescents to Walpole's novel, *Fortitude,* in order to determine what situations in the novel caused the most vivid responses, what aspects of the novel were liked and disliked, and what relationships appeared to exist between personality predispositions (defined in terms of personal and social adjustment) and reading response. Five groups of high school senior English classes (96 students) participated and answered structured questions; did a free writing exercise; and rated events, situations and ideas from the novel as to their interest. Meckel found that "close dynamic relationships exist between reading interests and individual meanings and interpretation. Interpretation appears to be a selective process. Psychological factors result in attention being given to certain aspects of reading content rather than others." Meckel concludes that:

> The findings of the investigation do not justify the conclusion that one may hand to a pupil with tensions and anxieties a novel which deals with the same tensions and anxieties and expect therapeutic results automatically. The data, on the contrary, suggest that such anxieties, if serious, may operate to repress and block desired response to the very situation and ideas which have potential therapeutic value. Wise discussion is a necessary technique which must supplement 'free reading.' Such discussion should be based on an understanding of the relationship between personality predispositions and reading response.[53]

A 1975 report by therapist Fred McKinney concentrated on studies of responses to the short story.[48] McKinney feels that short stories are important vehicles because they can be read at a single sitting and do not require a long commitment to reading. Because of their brevity, details of the story are often ambiguous, forcing the reader to bring his or her own experience and creativity to the story. Finally, he points out that many contemporary short stories deal with personality dynamics such as conflict and anxiety which are especially appropriate for bibliotherapeutic use. In McKinney's study, 114 psychology students selected stories which they rated in terms of their interest and involvement. A second group of 80 students also read stories, discussed them in groups, and filled out structured involvement forms. In both cases, the stories deemed bibliotherapeutic by the experimenter were the ones most likely to elicit positive responses. He had selected the stories according to readability, human/psychodynamics, and realism.

Biographies are the second most popular form of reading matter in the U.S. and are often used in bibliotherapy. The inspirational value of biography has long been accepted by educators and librarians. As Helen E. Haines asks:

> Is there anyone who has not responded to the ideal conveyed in some record of accomplishment, or to the revelation of what others have endured and suffered and overcome? . . . The reader of biography comes to realize that every difficulty or handicap may be overcome by the unconquerable mind of man—physical weaknesses or disabilities, lack of advantages, lack of the commonest necessities; that the spirit can dominate the material conditions of life . . . The inspiration of biography is that it is the mirror of man as he is. And in that mirror, more

and more readers seek to study themselves, to learn their own nature and observe the inner traits that make for self-conquest or self-defeat.[25]

This use of biography for identification and moral effect has been emphasized with children. Yet, Patrick Groff, an educator, has found that "quite to the reverse of what is believed about children and biography, a careful inquiry into the information about this relationship reveals that biography has little chance of exerting the extraordinary moral of psychological influences on children credited to it . . ."[23] He offers four fallacies in the theory that biography has bibliotherapeutic implications for children. One is that children under the age of seven or eight are not, according to Jean Piaget, able to vicariously accept the role of an adult, even when reading a biography. The other arguments against using biography for bibliotherapy apply equally to adults: the quality of biography is not always good, history is usually portrayed in a biased manner, and much biography is written in a dull fashion.

It seems that biography is not the best genre for bibliotherapy with children or with adults for still another reason. Biographies are written about people who were successful despite their difficulties or handicaps. By offering real success stories to readers with problems, unrealistic expectations can be raised. Not all blind people will be Helen Kellers and to even suggest that could be harmful to a reader. Biographies can, and have been, used successfully especially to raise a group consciousness, such as in the promotion of biographies of women during the Women's Liberation Movement. But caution and care must be used in selecting biographies for bibliotherapy.

Other practitioners have their own favorite genres. Bruno Bettelheim, the famed child psychologist, feels that fairy tales are the best vehicles for children.

> From them a child can learn more about the inner problems of man, and about solutions to his own—and our—predicaments in any society, than he can from any other type of story within his comprehension . . . Through the centuries (if not millenia) during which fairy tales, in their retelling, became even more refined, they came to convey overt and covert meanings at the same time; came to speak simultaneously to all levels of the human personality, communicating in a manner that reaches the child as well as the sophisticated mind of the adult. In terms of the psychoanalytic model of the human personality, fairy tales carry important messages to the conscious, the preconscious, and the unconscious mind, on whatever level these are functioning. By dealing with universal human problems, and especially those that preoccupy the child's mind, these stories speak to his budding ego and encourage its development, and at the same time relieve preconscious and unconscious pressures. As the stories unfold, they give conscious credence and body to id pressures and show how to satisfy these in line with ego and superego requirements.[6]

Bettelheim continues by saying that fairy tales are popular with children, because they are simple portrayals of their problems without belittling them and because fairy tales offer children a way to use their imaginations to deal with their concerns. Fairy tales encourage the child's use of daydreams, dreams, and imagination to structure his/her problems. Bettelheim warns that:

> Fairy tales may seem senseless, fantastic, scary, and totally unbelievable to the adult who was deprived of fairy tale fantasy in his own childhood or has repressed the memory of it. An adult who has not achieved a satisfactory integration of the two worlds of reality and imagination is put off by such tales. But an adult who in his own life is able to integrate rational order with the illogic of his unconscious will be responsive to the manner in which fairy tales help the child with this integration.[6]

Since ancient Greece, the fable has been a popular genre and a source of moral training and character education. However, when fables were used in primary schools in New York and other cities to teach values to children, Sadie Goldsmith's 1936 study showed that they had little or no influence on a child's values whether taught didactically or bibliotherapeutically.[21] Whether fables may have a delayed effect on the reader's values has not been determined. However, the fable is not a currently popular genre for bibliotherapy.

Science fiction and utopian literature have been considered by a few practitioners as therapeutic. Louis A. Rongione states:

> Science fiction is imaginative literature which deals with human response to the advances in science and technology. . . . Science fiction anticipates what science will realize and so it has much appeal as prophetic fiction. . . . Science fiction also offers some solace from the frustrations of modern man's greatest embarrassment, namely, his probing into age old problems has created so many more seemingly unsolvable problems.[71]

A more sophisticated rationale for the therapeutic use of science fiction is due to Robert Plank, a social worker. He distinguished science fiction from other fiction: "While most fiction invents individual characters, science fiction (and utopian literature) invents environments . . . science fiction presents an environment distinguished from our real one by some fictional technological or scientific innovations."[65] He feels that there is a similarity between the operations of science fiction and of the unconscious in that science fiction expresses human aggression, and—to a large extent—human anxiety. It typically presents an omnipotent hero similar to one in a child's fantasy. The hero is without a family, without much love or sexual outlet, isolated geographically and emotionally, yet possessing great powers. "The result is a warped and regressive picture of interpersonal relationships and of communications."[65] The therapeutic use of such literature may help an individual cope with technological changes, understand future possibilities, and gain insight into universal human problems. Unfortunately, no research experiments using science fiction in bibliotherapy have been reported.

Poetry therapy is a bibliotherapy technique which uses only poetry. Its practitioners call themselves poetry therapists rather than bibliotherapists and were organized in 1959 into a national organization called the Association for Poetry Therapy (APT) which boasts 500 members.

Since 1931 when R. H. Schauffler wrote *The Poetry Cure,* poetry has been seen as an especially effective medium for therapy. As poetry therapists Robinson and Mowbray explain it, "The etiology of poetry and psychotherapy both involve unconscious and preconscious materials, including dreams, daydreams, and fantasies. Both employ the defense mechanisms of condensation, sublimation, displacement, and symbolization."[70] The symbolic nature of poetry is especially significant because poetry is open to such wide, personal interpretations.

The condensation in poetry is also important, according to Jack Leedy, the founder of APT and editor of two books on poetry therapy: "A poem has been described as the shortest emotional distance between two points, the points representing the writer and the reader. This may explain why communication through poetry is established so readily, and why patients themselves are moved so frequently to attempt their own composition of poems."[39] The emotional density of poetry makes its impact powerful; often a short poem can elicit the feelings of a longer story or full length novel. Leedy states that rhythm is another important feature of poetry. "Poems with regular rhythms, those that most nearly approximate the beat of the human heart, affect many patients deeply."[39] Tedford and Symnott, two psychologists, tested the influence of a poem's rhythm on the meaning attributed to it. Some 129 college students were used to rate rhythmic patterns according to heaviness/lightness, sadness/happiness, and five other pairs of adjectives. Subjects judged fast speeds as light, slow speeds as heavy, and all rhythms happier as the speed increased. The differences in "feet" were investigated and the researchers concluded that poetry therapists should be aware of the importance of rhythm as well as the content of a poem.[82]

Although poetry therapy is based on theory very similar to that of bibliotherapy, it is considered a completely separate field because of three major differences between it and bibliotherapy. Poetry therapists use only poetry, and no other genres, in their therapy sessions; poetry therapy developed primarily through the work of poets and psychotherapists and not through library science; and poetry therapy stresses the writing of poetry as well as the reading and discussing of it. In addition to the APT, New York has a Poetry Therapy Center and classes in numerous locations. The Poetry Therapy Institute in Los Angeles, California, was founded by a psychologist, Arthur Lerner, in 1973. It is not a membership organization, but a consulting, educational group. Poetry therapy is an increasingly popular field. An estimated 500 to 2,000 poets, psychologists, psychiatrists, and others are currently involved in poetry therapy in private practices, hospitals, schools, prisons, and other settings.

Print and nonprint materials have never been tested for their comparative values for bibliotherapy. Although bibliotherapy practitioners use slides, films, records, realia, and other media besides books, the use of these other media have not received much attention. As Herman Axelrod, a special education professor, states:

> A paradox occurs when we speak of children who may be learning-disabled, emotionally disturbed, or diagnosed and judged with a myriad of other labels; we speak of children who very probably would benefit from bibliotherapy, but who may also, for various reasons, refuse or be unable to read . . . Thus, in many cases, due to the inability or unwillingness of large numbers of children with learning problems to engage in reading with any degree of consistency, the idea behind bibliotherapy has been eliminated as an operable alternative.[3]

He then suggests "audiovisiotherapy" as an alternate means of bibliotherapy. His concern with learning-disabled children must be extended to adults, also, and to blind and physically handicapped people who are unable to use conventional printed materials. It cannot be overemphasized that audiovisual and realia materials are essential to reach a larger audience. Even for readers, the use of nonprint can be a stimulating and welcome change.

Although there have been no studies comparing the bibliotherapeutic effects of print and audiovisual materials, advertising and broadcasting research has investigated the relative values of various media. Unfortunately, most of the research has dealt with the retention of information rather than the strength of emotional response. Joseph T. Klapper summarizes the laboratory experiments by stating that they indicate:

> a) that combined use of aural and visual presentations elicits better retention of simple, brief material than does the use of either method of appeal alone; b) that aural presentation of whatever sort elicits better retention of simple and brief material than does visual presentation; c) conflicting findings regarding the relative effectiveness of visual and aural presentation in eliciting retention of lengthy or complex material . . . the reading skill of the audience may be a major criterion; d) face-to-face discourse is a more effective persuasive agent than is a transmitted voice, which in turn is more effective than print. . . .[35]

Lee Loevinger postulates a "reflective-projective" theory of mass communication which is closely related to the theory of bibliotherapy.

> This theory postulates that mass communications are best understood as mirrors of society that reflect an ambiguous image in which each observer projects his own image of himself and society . . . while the mass media reflect various images of society, the audience is composed of individuals, each of whom views the media as an individual. The members of the audience project or see in the media their own visions or images in the same manner that an individual projects his own ideas into the inkblots of the Rorschach Test, commonly used by psychologists.[42]

He feels that broadcasting is increasingly popular and universal "because it is elemental, responsive to popular taste, and gives the audience a sense of contact with the world around it which is greater than that provided by any other medium . . . it is immediate, personal, and comprehensive. . . ."[42]

Each medium has its advantages and drawbacks. Print may be referred to numerous times and read as slowly or as quickly as the reader desires. It is also a portable medium. Aural media such as recordings and radio can be understood by nonreaders and can approach the personal level of face-to-face contact. Radio, especially, according to Klapper, is enjoyed most by the poorly cultured and suggestible. Along with television, it provides the individual with a sense of participation, and gives immediate gratification. The screen is a most persuasive medium in that it presents concrete visual images. Lee Loevinger explains that:

> The technologically most advanced media are the most elementary and primitive. Psychologically, man has advanced from simple sensation to perception, and then to abstraction . . . Speech conveyed by telephone or radio is understood more easily and is a psychological regression from the abstraction of printed language to the more elemental level of oral language. Finally, television is a medium which . . . conveys the most information in the most literal form by giving us oral language combined with visual perceptions and requiring the least effort to interpret the abstractions. Thus television is a multi-channel communication which is more elemental and therefore has greater immediacy and impact than other media.[42]

Because this author could find no research on the implications of these differences for bibliotherapy, she conducted an informal experiment with two groups each of eight incarcerated men who were already involved in a bibliotherapy program. One week, the first group read the short story version of Shirley Jackson's "The Lottery"; the second group viewed a film version which is remarkably faithful to the original both in concept and in dialogue. The group which watched the film reacted immediately and emotionally. Discussion of the film was so heated that word of it spread throughout the jail; the film had to be shown again for other men who had heard about it. The reading group, however, reacted slowly. Directly after reading the story, the men asked questions about specific details, debated the ending, and discussed the concept of a "scapegoat." It was not until a few days later that emotional reactions were evident. A month later, the readers were still talking about the story, while the film group had lost interest. It seemed that the film caused an immediate and intense, but temporary, reaction whereas the print version led to a delayed, longer-lasting impression. Of course, controlled research is necessary before any conclusions can be drawn.

Principles of selection of materials for bibliotherapy include the following:

1) The therapist should not use any materials with which he or she is not familiar.

2) The therapist should be conscious of length when selecting materials. Complex materials with extraneous details and situations are to be avoided until a group is able to deal with such material. Poems, short stories, one act plays, or single chapters of longer works are recommended. Short works are practical in that they are physically easier to read and recall, and less therapy time is spent on the reading itself.

3) The client's problems must be considered; the materials should be applicable to the problem but not necessarily identical with it.

4) The client's reading ability must be known and should influence the choice of materials. If reading problems exist, reading aloud or using audiovisual materials may be necessary.

5) Both chronological and emotional age must be considered and reflected in the sophistication of the material selected.

6) Reading preferences, both individual and general, are a guideline for selection; as Zaccaria and Moses note:

> "Reading preferences of children and adolescents go through a series of predictable stages. From the ages of two or three to about six or seven, children like to have stories read to them concerning familiar events. Then up to the age of ten or eleven years, there is an increasing interest in fantasy stories. Adolescents, too, go through several reading stages. The early adolescent (12 - 15 years) tends to be interested in . . . animal stories, adventure stories, mystery stories, tales of the supernatural, sports stories . . . Later on (15 - 18 years) reading preferences change to such topics as war stories, romance, and stories of adolescent life. Perhaps sparked by the realization that maturity is fast approaching, the reading interests in late adolescense (18 - 21) tend to focus on such types of stories as those that deal with personal values, social significance, strange and unusual human experiences, and the transition to adult life."[90]

Of course, these are just rough guidelines; the reading history of the client and his/her expressed interests are the best indication. For clients who do not read much, favorite TV programs and movies are good guides to possible reading interests.

7) Materials expressing the same feeling or mood as the client are often good choices. This is the "isoprinciple" which stems from the technique of music therapy and is commonly used in poetry therapy. The only exceptions to this principle, according to Leedy, are poems on suicide or ones which are hopeless or completely negative.

8) Audiovisual materials should be given as much attention and critical consideration as print materials.

PROCEDURES WITH ADULTS

Procedures with adults have not received much attention in the literature, which is mainly theoretical and anecdotal, yet an informal network of communication among bibliotherapy practitioners gives evidence of great diversity in technique. Individual reading guidance in the library, prescriptive reading on a one-to-one basis without follow-up, bookcart service in institutions, and the use of special bibliographies with patrons are often mentioned as bibliotherapeutic techniques. This book does not consider these activities to be bibliotherapy because they do not explicitly provide for subsequent discussion. This section will not deal with individual techniques used in medical bibliotherapy, such as bookcart service or individual conferences. Instead it will concentrate on group bibliotherapy because it is currently the most popular mode of bibliotherapy.

The procedures chosen for a bibliotherapy program depend on the evaluation of the setting, the study of the clients, and the selection of materials, as well as the talents and personality of the group leader who must choose a leadership style. Note that discussion of the material experienced by the clients is a fundamental aspect of all modes of bibliotherapy with adults.

For bibliotherapy with depressed, withdrawn or apathetic mental patients, Ruth Tews suggests "motivational group therapy":

> A short, simple story or factual material without dialogue is typed on single sheets with the sentences numbered; members of the group then take turns reading the sentences. The discussion leader should ask questions which require emotional or conceptual answers. The aim is only to elicit verbal responses. When the group advances to where the members respond easily, discussions which involve opinions and concepts may be gradually introduced. The sessions could also be recorded on tape. Playback of these tape recordings may be useful as the group progresses.[83]

The following method, which can apply equally well to adults, was used by Joseph Malkiewicz, in his work with twelve year-olds. Because of the school setting, the participants met daily and knew each other well. Malkiewicz read aloud a chapter of a book each day.

> A discussion followed in which the class identified the story's main problem, the character who was most involved, the secondary problems, and made an evaluation of the interactions between them. As the reading progressed, the discussion added a personal dimension. The class and the teacher related themselves to the characters and the action. In an atmosphere free from disapproval and ridicule, the children were encouraged to share their own similar experiences. At first this was possible only because the discussion was about a safe and remote person, the story character. When the children understood that others could discuss an individual's problems with compassion and empathy, acquired defenses were relaxed. Lively discussion revealing much insight followed.[49]

Arleen Hynes in her *Libri* article discusses a number of modes of conducting bibliotherapy sessions in the patients' library of a large mental hospital. She expresses them as a continuum from facilitator-directed to group run.

> Facilitator-directed reading and/or writing groups seem to be the most common mode used for bibliotherapy groups and is the one used most often in the Circulating Library. The facilitator chooses and reads the materials aloud or asks specific members to do so. The art of reading materials effectively is regarded as important since bibliotherapy is a form of communication. The goals of the group in relation to the significance of communication may vary and this should be kept in mind when deciding upon the importance of the interpretive reading . . . The group climate as a whole is sympathetic, cohesive, intuitional, and noncoercive. When literature is read, typed copies are usually provided for each member . . . Occasionally, in the drug unit and in others we read the words to a popular song, play the music on the cassette tapes that the library provides, and then discuss the ideas. The songs are effective because the youths are familiar with them and the message is written in the vernacular; the music adds to the emotional impact . . .
>
> Directed readings and discussion is an early form of bibliotherapy. A number of popular mental health books, as well as fiction and drama, are considered by some to be helpful in improving self-understanding and in recognizing and learning to solve difficult problems . . . With both the young drug addicts and the middle-aged men in the Alcoholics Anonymous unit, we excerpted Erich Fromm's *The Art of Loving* into twenty-three sections and gave typed copies to the group members . . .
>
> Team leadership consisting of a bibliotherapist and a mental health worker proved to be a mutually supportive mode of cooperative bibliotherapy. In the last year the bibliotherapist has had the privilege of working with two psychologists and a clinical nurse specialist in three ongoing weekly groups. The librarian chooses the material and reads aloud to the group which is often furnished with copies of the selections. The co-leaders work together to ask appropriate questions or to make group statements which enable the members to delve as deeply as possible into their reactions. The goals, the mode of procedure, the balance between aesthetic enrichment and the depth of psychological insight are the product of mutual cooperation of the co-leaders as well as the mental states of the patients in the group . . .
>
> A final step in the continuum of bibliotherapy demands more of the participants than any mentioned previously. The group members all read the selected material before they arrive at the discussion meetings. In this mode of bibliotherapy, the group and its leader decide on the goals, what will be read, and how the discussion will be structured . . . The group meets regularly and discusses what they have read. . . .[30]

This last method—in which the participants read the material ahead of the discussion meeting—was used by both Harris McClaskey and Lesta Burt in their research studies. Prior to her study, Burt held a workshop with the discussion group leaders to standardize their approach. Each group was to be led by two librarians working as co-therapists. She instructed them to:

> a) keep the discussion operating at an objective, fact-documented level, b) hold identification with the leader at a minimum through focusing members of the group continuously on the book and the author's ideas, c) ask a question to

stimulate discussion but not inject their own views, d) allow no one to monopolize the discussion or violate the rules of common courtesy, e) gently encourage critical, evaluative, and increasingly more discriminating comments.[10]

These instructions are similar to those used by other practitioners with the exception of "a"—most bibliotherapists allow the discussion to flow in whatever direction it chooses, and encourage personal emotional statements.

The method used by Bruce Bettencourt and Clara Lack of the Santa Clara County bibliotherapy project in the Agnews State Hospital emphasizes a friendly, informal milieu. The bibliotherapy room has been specially furnished for comfort and beverages are served. They ask the group participants to introduce themselves by first name only so that the interactions remain informal. One of the leaders then explains the format of the session. Bruce Bettencourt's description follows:

> I am going to read a short story out loud to the group. Usually it is 10-15 minutes in length. Then we spend the rest of the time talking about the story, the characters, the situations they have gotten themselves into, and their problems. We might discuss what the people in the story did to extricate themselves from their situation or problem. Or we might speculate as to why the characters acted or felt as they did. We try and get below the surface of the plot and discover what the characters' motivations are, what makes them tick. Sometimes, we talk about experiences or feelings that we have had that are similar to those of the people in the story. Or we might talk about ways in which our experiences have been different or opposite. We often discuss whether or not we agree with the course of action taken by the character in the story. But I do want to emphasize that this is not like an English or literature class in school. We are not interested in analyzing symbolism, or discussing the author's life, or his reason for writing the story. We can speculate as to what we think happened next after the story ended. We can try to fill in the details that the author leaves to our imagination. In general, our discussions are at a feeling level, rather than at an intellectual level.[7]

Bettencourt then reads the story and waits for discussion to begin, encouraging but not directing comments as he feels that the leader's participation should be minimal. Any constructive discussion is allowed to continue uninterrupted; he intervenes only when someone digresses or when the discussion lulls. Clara Lack uses a similar procedure but also uses plays which the participants read aloud and then discuss.

This author used a procedure similar to that described by Bettencourt. When running bibliotherapy groups in a jail, she divided the twenty volunteer participants into two sections based on reading skills. Group A (composed of 11 men who read at a grade level of 6.7 or above) met once a week for an hour as did Group B (nine men with an average reading level of 4.4). Both groups dealt with the following topics: joy and sorrow, loneliness, self-concept, anger and revenge, scapegoats, imprisonment, addiction, and fantasy. However, the materials selected and the method varied between the groups.

Group A used primarily written materials which were read aloud at the beginning of each session. Poems were read by members of the group who volunteered, with often more than one man offering his rendition; longer works were read by the entire group with each member, including the leader, reading in turn. Discussion followed with minimal direction from the leader. Invariably the discussion followed a pattern of intellectualization about the material, discussion of it from a literary point of view, and finally personal reactions to the material. At the end of the session, each participant was allowed to keep his mimeographed copy of the material; this proved to be very popular. The men were urged to write down any comments or further reactions to the material and to bring them the following week.

Group B saw films and listened to records; the participants were never expected to read. Before and after playing records, the leader read aloud the verse which often was hard to understand because of the quality of the recordings. The subsequent discussion usually required some participation and direction from the leader as the group members tended away from verbalization. Often the discussions did not progress as far with this group as with the first during the hour session, but discussion continued informally in the cells during the week and was resumed at the following session. No mention of writing between sessions was made.

The above examples demonstrate a number of differences in the adult group bibliotherapy procedure. Some therapists stress the use of a team while others work alone; some have the participants read material ahead of the meeting or aloud before the group while others have the participants only listen; and some combine bibliotherapy with other therapies such as therapeutic writing.

Ruth Tews has long been a proponent of the interdisciplinary team approach: "Each of the members [of the team] must have three necessary features—1) the ability to contribute some knowledge the others do not have; 2) a willingness to receive and absorb what the other members offer; and 3) the ability to make decisions and carry out plans in his area."[84] In "The Role of the Librarian on the Interdisciplinary Team" she continues by stating that if the librarian's expertise is to contribute to the team, it is necessary,

> . . . that we organize a library service that is meaningful and structured on the principles of theory; that we not only have the qualities and qualifications of a specialist but that we can relate them as a contribution; that we show the interrelatedness of the book to life and of book content to overt behavior as it can be related to therapy; that we can evalute the role of the librarian in the planning of the goals for the patient; that we are able to analyze literature or its emotional content to fit the patients' need . . .; that we can be flexible and able to re-evaluate our program to fit the emotional situation.[84]

Tews, herself, was not a member of a structured interdisciplinary team but only had informal contacts with other members of the total rehabilitation team. That situation is common, so it is important that librarians establish at least informal contacts that can provide some support and knowledge of a team.

A common technique in poetry therapy, also used by some bibliotherapists, is the combination of therapeutic reading and writing. Hynes reports two ways that creative writing is used in her bibliotherapy program.

> For almost four years bibliotherapy programs have been held in the drug addiction unit . . . We have used a great deal of poetry, some plays, and creative writing. Each selection was discussed with great insight although the educational level of most members was low and they were generally unfamiliar with poetry. For instance, we read some examples of Japanese haiku, an art form with which they were unacquainted, and then each group member wrote his own haiku, a description of an emotion that he wanted to communicate . . . With very old and disturbed patients or young and unlettered children, we may read a story or poem aloud and ask each person for a one word response or a one line response. A blackboard may be used to record these reactions and the total group response is considered a poem.[30]

Robinson and Mowbray, two poetry therapists, feel that "the production of a poem may be considered a problem-solving activity. To translate feelings into a verbal unit suggests an awareness of self. To probe for insights requires experimentation with language and economy of words. To give form to thought represents a maturity of effort, a growth producing experience compatible with therapeutic aims."[70] On the other hand, some authors warn against the patients writing and discussing their poetry. If technique is overly important to the person, if he or she is concerned primarily with the look and sound of writing, using writing for therapy may not be a possibility. Similarly, for a person whose own ego won't allow dissection of his/her poetry, therapeutic writing may not be effective.

Another type of therapeutic writing which can be used in conjunction with bibliotherapy is the diary or autobiography. The writing creates an emotional and psychological distance between the client and therapist and thereby allows the client to express himself freely. In relation to bibliotherapy, the diary could be used to record thoughts connected with the bibliotherapy readings and any resultant actions. In a similar vein, one psychologist has students in his class on bibliotherapy keep a diary in order to record long-term effects and to have a cumulative record of the class experience. Others stress the writing of life histories.

Franklin Berry, a psychologist interested in bibliotherapy, has suggested a systematization of literature-based therapies to delineate four different modes of bibliotherapy or poetry therapy. In his view, the four methods can be analyzed by the participant's response to the therapy. Such responses can be written or oral, receptive or expressive. If a piece of literature is read by a patron, his/her response would be considered receptive/written. If he or she writes a poem, for example, the response would be expressive/written. Oral/receptive

methods are those used by Shiryon and others who tell stories or anec-
dotes to patients for their response. Oral/expressive is a potential form
of bibliotherapy in which creative material is produced by the patron
but spoken rather than written. Perhaps the combined use of psychodrama with bibliotherapy would also fit into the category of oral/
expressive. (See figure 7).

Therapists may use psychodrama and bibliotherapy jointly,
employing techniques of psychodrama to re-enact memories evoked by
literature. Three types of psychodrama have been delineated: The first
is role playing, *per se,* in which a person portrays another. The second
is psychodrama in which a personally meaningful life experience or
situation is re-enacted. Sociodrama is the last type; it is an enactment
of a significant life situation applicable to a number of people and can
often demonstrate different approaches and solutions to a common
situation or problem. It is important that role-playing be used by an
experienced therapist, and only after the group members are comfortable with each other.

Some poetry therapists and bibliotherapists use group sensitivity
techniques in order to relax the participants and to establish the group
rapport which is a prerequisite to role playing and similar activities.
Among these techniques are emotion sharing exercises such as sharing
an important experience with the group, telling of a happy moment,
or describing oneself as an animal. Others are sensory awareness techniques such as stretching, experiencing music with the eyes closed,
taking a blind walk, etc.

Music and art may also be used conjunctively with bibliotherapy.
Music therapists believe that music can be used in therapy to help establish a counseling relationship, to provide an opportunity for the
person to participate in a pleasurable activity, and to condition
changes in the person's mood. This last is effected by matching the
music to the client's mood and then changing the type of music to influence his or her mood.

The techniques of art therapy, especially the variation in which
one creates a piece of art which will be analyzed, can be another
adjunct to bibliotherapy. The art work provides an emotional release
and an expression of affect similar to that of the writing of poetry.
Special expertise in music and art are of course necessary to implement these therapies and perhaps can best be done in cooperation with
an expert.

In institutions, especially those subscribing to the milieu or total
therapy concept, bibliotherapy may be used in relation to all of the
above and to recreational, occupational, physical, and/or educational
therapies.

Principles of procedures with adults include:

1) The setting, the clients, and the program objectives determine
   the procedures to be used.

A Systematization of Literature-Based Therapies

Cells A, B, C, and D are all variants of literature-based therapies. The type of literature presented to the patient, whether in writing or orally, or the type of literature created by the patient further delimits the type of therapy.

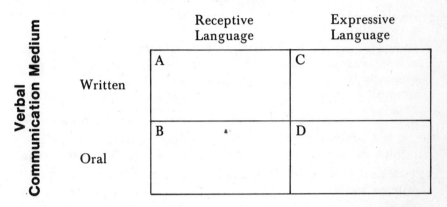

Nature of Patient's Linguistic Response

A—Traditional Bibliotherapy. Written material read by the patient.

A and B—Literatherapy (as defined by Shiryon). Literature read by, or spoken to, the patient.

C—Creative Writing Therapy. Writing emphasis.

D—Creative Orating Therapy (A potentially useful version of poetry therapy for illiterate persons)

D'—Oral Linguistic Response in which the response is the reading of a pre-existing work that he/she has selected to present to the therapist.

Models of therapy:
- Therapist presents selected material to individual patient—A
- Therapist-Selected or Patient-Selected Materials Shared in Group Therapy—A, B, and D'
- Therapist Urges Patient(s) to Write—C
- Mixed Modality: Therapist presents selections to patient(s) and patient(s) is urged to write—A, B, C, and D'
- Nontraditional creative writing instruction (poetry therapy without patient and therapist roles)—B, C, and D'
- Non-patient reads/writes, uses literature as a coping resource—A and/or C

FIGURE 7

2) The bibliotherapist must do an honest self-appraisal to determine what methods and styles of leadership are consistent with his talents and personality.

3) Techniques from other therapies may be borrowed for bibliotherapy but the distinct contributions of the library and its materials should not be overlooked.

4) The therapist decides whether the material is to be read ahead of, or at, the meeting; whether it is read aloud by all or by one reader; and whether every participant is given a copy of the literature.

5) The procedure chosen must be a comfortable one for the clients; informality and freedom are necessary for bibliotherapy.

6) Writing during or after the sessions may be encouraged.

7) The clients should be steered away from intellectualization and toward personalization.

8) A formal or informal interdisciplinary team may prove useful.

9) Sensitivity techniques may be used in the bibliotherapy group.

10) The optimum size of the group seems to be 6-12 and the ideal length of time, 1-1½ hours.

BIBLIOTHERAPY WITH CHILDREN

Bibliotherapy with children is necessarily different from that with adults. The small vocabulary, limited range of experiences, problems with verbalization, and short attention span of children all affect the method to be used. Both material selection and procedure must be adapted to children who cannot be confronted as directly as can adults.

With very young children, reading an assigned piece of literature is out of the question. Instead, audiovisual presentations must be used, or stories must be read or told to the children. May Hill Arbuthnot, whose classic *Children and Books* discusses the values of reading aloud, notes that:

> As a teacher reveals her understanding and sympathy with the plights of fictional characters, she also reveals her potential of understanding and sympathy for the plights of the children in her class. As she reveals her delights in a vivid phrase or a fresh bit of imagery, she is also revealing something very personal about herself. It is an act of trust to which children are very responsive. Once that mutual trust is established, the child finds it easier to cope with threatening moments of tension.[1]

This bond of trust is especially important in order for therapy to be successful. Both storytelling and reading aloud provide the opportunity for a relationship to develop. Storytelling is a more difficult technique and needs more preparation and skill than does reading aloud, but is worthwhile because it allows a more direct relationship between the teacher or librarian and the child. Arbuthnot warns the librarian that there are some stories which should be read and not told; she discusses these and the related techniques. One piece of advice is especially pertinent for bibliotherapy: "When you read stories that portray real situations and concerns in fictional form, the reading should be straight and unforced. If there is a message there for children, they will receive it. This is especially true when reading books with such delicate themes as size, loss of pet, and death."[1]

When selecting books for storytelling and reading aloud to children who do not yet read, the illustrations assume a great deal of importance. Gertrude Whipple has compiled the following facts about illustrations:

> Illustrations may exert a negative as well as a positive appeal. The larger the total number of illustrations in the book, the higher the interest level. This point holds true up to an undefined point of saturation . . . The larger the average size of the illustrations, the higher the interest level, other things being equal. An illustration in several colors has greater merit than one that is black and white . . . An illustration with a center of interest that draws the eye to a particular point offers great appeal to children than a picture with no recognizable center of interest or one subordinated by too many details. The more action and the more interesting the action, the more appealing is the illustration. The subject matter of the illustration has marked effect upon its interest to children. Eventful topics depicted in the illustration have greater merit than still life topics.[88]

Whipple also points out that racial discrimination—even indirect or subtle—in illustrations must be avoided because the biased message will get through to the child.

According to Patricia Jean Cianciolo, illustrations facilitate identification and help to develop self-concept in children.

> The visual message transmitted by a book's illustration may determine in large measure the concept of self that the viewer constructs. Illustrated books may be used to help the reader view himself in an adequate and positive manner; they may help him to consciously accept himself in the social setting in which he must function and grow up . . . Illustrated books can be used to help children of all ages realize that their wishes, feelings, and actions are a normal part of the process of growing up . . . We become as we imagine ourselves to be. Illustrated books might help the readers become beautiful, functioning human beings.[13]

Illustrations can also extend the child's world:

> A picture is a window and it is through this window that the reader may learn about individuals who live in an environment which differs from his own. Illustrations constitute a powerful and pervasive means of communicating a respect for the concept that minorities should not be permitted to lose their identities in anonymity. One should appreciate the challenge of being different . . . Each illustration should emphasize the richness and diversity of the human experience, for it is especially in the affective domain of the educative process that art leads the reader to a better understanding of himself and others.[13]

The findings of two recent studies of children's reactions to picture books necessitate a word of caution, however. In one of these, Gail Marshall based her studies on Jean Piaget's work on the development of the child's thinking processes and his conclusion that the child views the world differently from the adult. She read five books which had won the Caldecott Award for meritorious picture books to two groups of ten kindergartners, and then interviewed the children individually about the books. The children were asked to retell the story, using the book's illustrations as a guide. Although the groups varied in socioeconomic status, and in auditory and visual association tests scores, they both demonstrated the same fact—the children distorted the stories and misunderstood the pictures. A lack of understanding of time and causality led them to misinterpret the text and the illustrations to fit their misunderstanding. In a follow-up study, Marshall did not allow the children to see the pictures when retelling the story. Twelve children, who ranged from five to nearly eleven years of age, were read *Make Way for Ducklings,* which was familiar to all of them. But when they retold the story, without the aid of the illustrations, they altered the story by shortening it and paying no attention to chronological order. In "Stories for Children and Children's Stories" she reports: "When children are given a long and complex story, with ambiguous sections, distortions occur if the children try to tell the story while looking at the pictures. When they tell the story without the pictures, ambiguous elements are omitted, and at least with older children, the sequence of the story is changed."[51]

Picture books, even sophisticated ones, should not be avoided because of these problems, but librarians and teachers must be aware of them and of the child's thought processes. "To transform, to think out a story or a poem, the child needs time. It may not always be in the best interest of the child to move rapidly through material teachers deem important. To allow the child time to dig more deeply, to learn and explore may serve him well."[51]

Young children are especially affected by stories and picture books, according to Lili E. Peller, because such materials nurture their daydreams. Animal characters are especially good for this purpose because the considerations of sex, age, and race are not involved; the child can concentrate on the content of the story and of his daydreams.[63] Jacob Panken, a Juvenile Court Judge who is a proponent of bibliotherapy, also stresses the importance of the child's daydreams.

As a result of daydreams, various needs develop in the child, tendencies indicating what the child would like to be, what he would like to accomplish. Many children who are delinquent and brought to court repeat their conduct. They are prone to be recidivistic. Those helped by the reading of books show a very low percentage of recidivism. We find in these cases some who have actually identified themselves with personalities they had met in books, history or even romance. Children because of imagination, or by a process of reasoning, have lifted themselves out of the noxious environment that was responsible for their antisocial life.[62]

The problems of selecting materials for therapeutic use with children are many. In addition to being aware of the child's limitations and abilities, needs and fantasies, the book selector must be aware of his or her own prejudices and attitudes. Some materials which adults scorn are popular with children, and have potentially great effects on them. Sister Lorang did two studies, one in 1945 and one in 1968, of large groups of high school students to ascertain what books and magazines had affected them. The publications which the students listed as having had good or bad effects on them were then sent to a panel of adult judges who rated them and declared that 31 percent of them were unfit for juveniles. Yet, according to the students' reports, 86 percent said that the publications aroused emotions, 53 percent said that they had tried to imitate a character, and 42 percent had been motivated to act after reading.[43]

Once the children reach puberty, the direct use of literature and group discussion of it is applicable, as demonstrated in Malkiewicz's work.[49] However, the procedures must be adapted for use with younger children. Practitioners agree that it is preferable to present the stories to young children without any preliminary explanation of the therapy or discussion of goals. Yet books should not be used until a good rapport is established between the child and the therapist. To this end, play therapy is an increasingly popular technique which is similar to art therapy. In a typical situation a child is brought to a room of toys and play materials, and is allowed to do whatever s/he likes with the toys without any suggestions or comments from an observing therapist. Through the child's own choice of activity, s/he and the therapist become acquainted and the child's problems are brought to the surface. Here is an example from an actual play therapy session, described by Virginia M. Axeline.

> He dabbed blotches of color on a piece of drawing paper in the same deliberate, rigid sequence. I attempted to keep my comments in line with his activity, trying not to say anthing that would indicate any desire on my part that he do any particular thing . . . I wanted him to lead the way. I would follow. I wanted to let him know from the beginning that he would set the pace in that [the play therapy] room and that I would recognize his efforts at two way communication with some concrete reality basis of a shared experience between the two of us . . . All people proceed with a caution that will protect the integrity of their personality. We were getting acquainted. These things Dibs mentioned, objects in the room that were not involved in any serious affect, were the only shared ingredients at this point for communication between us. To Dibs, these were safe concepts.[2]

The play activity can then be used as a "jumping off" place for discussion.

Another technique which can be used singly or in conjunction with bibliotherapy is mutual storytelling. In the technique used by Richard Gardner (there are a number of variations), the child tells a story and the therapist then tells one back. The therapist's story is based on the child's and should be recognizable to him/her, yet the new story provides significant new aspects which can impart resolutions, insights, and alternatives. The child's story is similar to free association or dream analysis with adults but is less complex. Similarly, the therapist's response is not a psychoanalytic explanation but a story told in the child's own language. Gardner explains:

> One could almost say that in this method, the therapist attempts to bypass the child's conscious with his interpretations, and instead to address the unconscious in the hopes that the interpretations will be received by it . . . Such characteristic measures of parents and teachers as direct verbalization, confrontation, and interpretation, are avoided entirely; and there is no need to burden the analytic situation with interpretations of a sort that the child would very likely be unable to comprehend if he did receive them . . . There are some children, of course, who are able to profit from conscious awareness of their unconscious process . . . But there are others who do not seem able to utilize that mode of treatment. Such children, however, may enjoy telling stories. It is for children in this latter group that the mutual storytelling technique may prove to be a valuable therapeutic tool.[2]

Principles of bibliotherapy with children include:
1) Story telling or reading aloud may be used with children who are unable to read; audiovisual presentations are another alternative.
2) Because of the child's attention span, short stories should be used; sessions should last no longer than 30 minutes to an hour with older children.
3) The illustrations in picture books play an important role.
4) Books may be reread numerous times so that children are able to absorb and understand them.
5) Animal stories and fantasies allow the children to daydream.
6) Realistic stories about real situations must be presented directly and carefully.
7) Play therapy or the mutual story telling technique may be used before introducing bibliotherapy. Of course, special expertise or a team of experts is necessary.
8) With younger children, the theory of bibliotherapy and the objectives are not discussed; with older children a more direct approach is possible. By the time children reach puberty, adult procedures may be used successfully.

RECORD-KEEPING AND REPORTS

There are three types of records which can be kept in conjunction with bibliotherapy. The first are internal records for the future use of the bibliotherapist; the second are reports to other people involved with the client; the third are records kept for research purposes. Hynes, among others, keeps a record which is essentially an inversion of the traditional reader guidance files (lists of topics of interest and books read, organized by individual patrons). Instead, her files are organized by bibliotherapy materials; one file of each author and title, listing all materials used with a brief notation of when, where, and how the piece was received.

This author keeps an author-title file and an additional file of index cards organized by topic or emotional theme. The cards include author, title, and full bibliographic detail as well as remarks on the group's reactions to it, the date and place or use, and any other comments. The use of the above types of records, for internal use, do not appear to have any ethical overtones.

Reports to others, however, are highly controversial. Margaret Kinney in "The Patients Library in a Psychiatric Hospital" states that a bibliotherapy program with psychiatric patients necessitates such reporting. "An important aspect of such a program is the regular reporting to the physician concerning the patient's participation."[33] This idea may stem from the practice of early mental hospital librarians to report all reading behavior to the medical team for inclusion in the patient's files. Mary Graham, in a 1930 article, refers specifically to a "fifteen-day behavior report" of all materials the patient read during the first fifteen days of his hospitalization.[22] Dr. Menninger similarly demands that the hospital librarian make "written report of the patients' comments and reactions to their reading for the physician's information."[54] It should be noted that for Menninger, and others, only a physician can direct and choose the materials for bibliotherapy. The librarian, he states, "is the tool which carries out the mechanics and reports the observations."[54] Dr. G. O. Ireland goes so far as to present a "prescription form" for the doctor to fill out on a patient suggesting to the librarian types of books to use and types to avoid. The librarian would then keep a file of these forms and, in addition, keep a "worksheet" on each patient listing his or her name, family history, home environment, education, tastes and dislikes, review of events prior to hospitalization, present condition, and books read.[31]

The librarian's subservient role to the physician is not as prevalent today as it was in the 1930's; the concept of the therapeutic team is now a popular one. The librarian, whether formally or informally involved in the team, may be asked to add comments on the patient's chart, to attend staff meetings, or to report in other ways.

In spite of the latitude allowed in almost all aspects of group bibliotherapy, the librarian, whether he is group bibliotherapist, a co-leader of the group, or a resource person, has a definite role as a member of the interdisciplinary team in planning, reporting, and evaluating the progress of the group. He has the major responsibility for selecting materials for use in the group sessions, for discussing books, interests, and ideas with the readers, and for keeping records of the meetings.[57]

Margaret Hannigan in her *Library Trends* article suggests: "The bibliotherapist will be wise to establish a system of reports to be routed to
other team members and to be included in his own files . . . they are
essential because they establish a written record for future reference
and comparisons. They also give other staff members an understanding of the potential of bibliotherapy."[26]

In the hospital settings to which all of these authors refer, bibliotherapy reports may be an excellent idea. In other settings—correctional ones for example—such reports can be used as a source of
reward or punishment by an authority (i.e. the parole board) which
has access to all records. The knowledge of such reports can under-
mine the participant's honesty and sincerity in the group and can
destroy his or her trust in the bibliotherapist. Therefore, the question
of record-keeping and external reports can have significant ethical implications. Bibliotherapy practitioners should weigh the alternatives,
consider the setting, and reach a decision based on the interests of the
participants.

The third type of record-keeping is for research purposes. An early
example is Kathleen Jones' records at the Metropolitan State Hospital
in the 1930's which were used by Gagnon in his study of the therapeutic effects of literature on specific types of mental patients. In this
study, the information recorded included the age, sex, marital status,
education, and socioeconomic status of the reader plus a psychiatric
and medical diagnosis. The librarian then noted all types of materials
borrowed by the patient.[19] More than a decade later, Melvin C.
Oathout called for a similar type of system using punched cards with
notations of reactions to the materials; he suggested that "a series of
reactions must be defined—ranging from those indicating severe
maladjustment to those demonstrating marked psychological improvement—and codified for use on the reading cards."[60] Although this is
not a currently popular form of research, as it is empirical rather than
experimental, some institutional librarians do keep similar records to
aid in future book selection and to analyze readers' interests. Such records can also be useful in evaluating a program.

EVALUATION OF BIBLIOTHERAPY PROGRAMS

That evaluation of the social sciences is difficult is a truism. Studies
to evaluate the effectiveness and value of various therapies have
resulted in inconsistencies, contradictions, and rather negative results,
although the common assumption remains that therapies "work." A
recent book about Jung, *Jung and the Story of Our Time* states that:

> Asked once how many of all the people who came to him had been healed, he re-
> plied that he made a rough assessment once. He thought that one third of the
> vast number had not been healed, one third partially, and one third entirely. He
> added that the middle category was most significant and most conclusive because
> he was constantly amazed how persons included in it saw the meaning of what
> they had learned in their work with him only years later and so indicated thereby

that the number healed could be far greater than he in his most conservative estimates had calculated.[86]

According to a 1975 study by Allen E. Bergin, Jung's estimates
were too conservative. Assessment of nearly 1,000 cases reported in a
dozen or so controlled studies, demonstrated that of the untreated
(control) groups, 40 percent improved, 55 percent were unchanged,
and 5 percent deteriorated. In contrast, the therapy groups showed
that 65 percent improved, 25 percent were unchanged and 10 percent
deteriorated. In other words,

> . . . that leaves us with 25 percent whose improvement can fairly be attributed to
> the benefits of therapy. The fact that less than half as many of the therapy groups
> show no change in their condition, compared to the untreated controls, gives
> clear proof of the effectiveness of therapy. But change was not always beneficial.
> Ten percent of therapy cases deteriorated significantly after treatment, twice as
> many as in the untreated groups . . . In half of these cases the deterioration can
> fairly be blamed on the therapy itself.[5]

The study concluded that the critical factor may be the therapist's personality rather than the type of therapy. Because of the personality factor, which is very difficult to control, evaluation of therapy is difficult.

Most so-called "evaluations" of bibliotherapy programs which
have been reported have been unstructured subjective value statements by the therapist and/or the clients. Statements as to the merit of
bibliotherapy are often based on an individual's experience with bibliotherapy. But for an evaluation to be useful in terms of future decision making, for use with reluctant administrators seeking to choose
between alternative techniques, or to improve the field of bibliotherapy, specific objective effects and criteria must be used. Carol Weiss, in
a book on evaluation research, states that:

> The purpose of evaluation is to measure the effects of a program against the goals
> it set out to accomplish . . . 'The effects' emphasizes the outcome of the program
> rather than its efficiency, honesty, morale, or adherence to rules or standards.
> 'The comparison of effects with goals' stresses the use of explicit criteria for judg-
> ing how well the program is doing. The contribution to subsequent decision mak-
> ing and the improvement of future programming denote the social purpose of
> evaluation.[87]

Evaluation, then, is dependent on enunciating goals, objectives (or
desired outcomes), purposes (often the same as the goal) and criteria.
Unfortunately, most of the bibliotherapy literature does not reflect
these thought processes. The goals are often vague, the measure of ac-
complishment has usually been participants' reactions, and the criteria
of evaluation are usually unstated.

If a program is unsuccessful it may be due to a program failure or
a theory failure. Program failure occurs if the causal process assumed
to be operative (e.g., identification with a fictional character) is not set
into motion by the program (e.g., bibliotherapy). On the other hand,
theory failure occurs when the program does motivate the causal pro-

cess, but this process does not result in the desired effect. As Edward Schumann has said: "program failure is a failure to reach proximate goals; theory failure occurs when the achievement of proximate goals does not lead to final desired outcomes."[77] Another obvious weakness of the bibliotherapy literature is that it does not distinguish between these two types of failure. Rather, it assumes the theory is correct and only examines the process.

A number of methods are available to evaluate processes—they run the spectrum from subjective remarks by participants to evaluations utilizing the experimental method. The latter was used by Alexander, McClaskey, Burt, and a few other doctoral researchers. The classic experimental design uses at least one experimental group which participates in the program and one or more control groups which do not. Measure of the criteria (e.g. personality assessment) are taken before the program begins and after it is over. If the difference between the experimental group's scores before and after the program is greater than the difference between the control group's scores before and after, the program is considered a success. The experimental method of evaluation is considered one of the most reliable.

Besides the technical difficulty involved in an intricate evaluation, another explanation for the reliance on more subjective measures to evaluate bibliotherapy is offered by Shrodes. "Since the reading of literature provides an emotional context, the expression of attitude is likely to be a more reliable index of the subject's actual behavior than the ordinary questionnaire which is unlikely to evoke an affective response and which is commonly filled out with an awareness of the response that is wanted by the experimenter."[78] Because of this philosophy, Shrodes asked her subjects for subjective responses to twenty carefully structured questions. For example, she asked "What is the author's attitude toward life? Toward main characters? What character do you like best or study with greatest interest? Why? Whom did he remind you of? . . ."[78] A structured questionnaire was also used for evaluation by Robert Tyson to evaluate his study of psychiatrists' opinions of bibliotherapy.

The rating scale is another popular evaluation technique. Gratton C. Kemp suggests that all group therapies use a "members' self-evaluation scale" to evaluate the individual's role in the group. The participant rates him or herself on eight different aspects of group membership. For example, on listening from "1" "(I only partially hear the idea and not the persona and what it means to him") to "8" "(I hear the idea and to some degree understand.") The participant similarly evaluates sense of belonging, acceptance of others, concentration, participation, silence, and sense of responsibility.[32] The therapist may also rate the group members with a "behavior analysis form" such as that used by Helen I. Driver. She uses it in conjunction with self-appraisal techniques such as value statements and autobiographies, and with sociograms in which the participant rates the fellow members and him or herself.[16] These techniques appear to be applicable to group bibliotherapy but have not yet been used.

It is essential that bibliotherapy be better documented, better researched, and better evaluated. Some of the techniques discussed here should be utilized in bibliotherapy research so that scientific results can be recorded. In 1939, Alice I. Bryan discussed the need for a scientific approach. Although some progress has been made during the last four decades, the need for the application of scientific principles remains.

REFERENCES

1. May Hill Arbuthnot and Zena Sutherland, *Children and Books* (4th ed; Glenview, Illinois: Scott, Foresman and Co., 1972).

2. Virginia M. Axeline, *Dibs: In Search of Self* (Boston: Houghton Mifflin, 1964).

3. Herman Axelrod and Thomas R. Teti, "An Alternative to Bibliotherapy: Audiovisiotherapy" *Educational Technology* 16:36-38 (1976).

4. Bernard Berelson, "The Public Library, Book Reading, and Political Behavior" *Library Quarterly* 15:299 (1945).

5. Allen E. Bergin, "When Shrinks Hurt," *Psychology Today,* November 1975.

6. Bruno Bettelheim, "The Uses of Enchantment" *The New Yorker* December 8, 1975.

7. Bruce Bettencourt and others, "Agnews State Hospital Patients Library Bibliotherapy Project Final Report" March 1972, Part IIA.

8. L. M. Brammer and E. L. Shostrum, *Therapeutic Psychology* (Englewood Cliffs, New Jersey: Prentice-Hall, Inc., 1963).

9. Rosalie M. Brown, "Let's All Pull Together: The Birth and Blossoming of a Bibliotherapy Group" speech presented at the Bibliotherapy Round Table, January 1976.

10. Lesta Norris Burt, "Bibliotherapy: Effect of Group Reading and Discussion on Attitudes of Adult Inmates in Two Correctional Institutions" (unpublished Ph.D. dissertation, University of Wisconsin, 1972).

11. Genevieve Casey, *Libraries in the Therapeutic Society* (Chicago, Illinois: Association of Hospital and Institution Libraries, 1971).

12. P. J. Cianciolo, "Children's Literature Can Affect Coping Behavior," *Personnel and Guidance Journal* 43:897-903 (1965).

13. Patricia Jean Cianciolo, "What Can the Illustrations Offer?" in Virginia M. Read, ed. *Reading Ladders for Human Relations* 5th ed. (Washington D.C.: American Council on Education, 1972).

14. Sadie Petersen-Delaney, "Bibliotherapy for Patients in a Drug Antabuse Clinic" *Hospital Books Guide* 16:140-141 (October 1955).

15. Sadie Petersen-Delaney, "The Place of Bibliotherapy in a Hospital," *Library Journal* 63:307-308 (April 1933).

16. Helen I. Driver, *Counseling and Learning Through Small Group Discussions* (Madison, Wisconsin: Monona Pub., 1958).

17. Maurice Floch and Genevieve Casey, "The Library Goes to Prison," *American Library Assn Bulletin* 49:126-218 (March 1955).

18. Sigmund Freud, "Observations on Wild Psychoanalysis" in Ernest Jones, ed., *The Collected Papers of Sigmund Freud.* (vol. 2; New York: Basic Books 1959).

19. Salomon Gagnon, "Is Reading Therapy?" *Diseases of the Nervous System* 3:206-212 (1942).

20. Richard A. Gardner, M.D., "Mutual Storytelling as a Technique in Child Psychotherapy and Psychoanalysis," in J. Masserman, ed., *Science and Psychoanalysis* (vol. 14, New York: Grune and Stratton Pub., 1969).

21. Sadie Goldsmith, "The Fable as a Medium for Character Education" *Elementary English* 16:223-225 (1939).

22. Mary B. Graham, "Motivation of Reading Among Neuropsychiatric Patients," *U.S. Veterans Bureau Medical Bulletin* 6:1088, 1090, (1930).

23. Patrick Groff, "Biography: The Bad or the Bountiful?," *Top of the News* 29:211 (April 1973).

24. Leah Ann Griffith, "The Agnews State Hospital Bibliotherapy Program," *News Notes of California Libraries* 66:400-404 (Summer 1971).

25. Helen E. Haines, *Living with Books: The Art of Book Selection* 2nd ed. (New York: Columbia University Press, 1950).

26. Margaret C. Hannigan, "The Librarian In Bibliotherapy," *Library Trends* 11:194 (October 1962).

27. Margaret Hannigan and William Henderson, "Narcotic Addicts Take Up Reading" *Bookmark* (New York State Library) 22:140-141 (October 1955).

28. Lore Hirsch, "Book Service to Patients," *Wilson Library Bulletin* 27:634-635 (April 1953).

29. Arleen Hynes, "Bibliotherapy at St. Elizabeths Hospital" *HRLS Quarterly* 1:18-19 (October 1975).

30. Arleen Hynes, "Bibliotherapy in the Circulating Library at St. Elizabeths Hospital," *Libri* 25 (December 1975).

31. G. O. Ireland, "Bibliotherapy: The Use of Books as a Form of Treatment In a Neuropsychiatric Hospital," *U.S. Veterans Bureau.*

32. Gratton C. Kemp, *Small Groups and Self Renewal* (New York: Seabury Press, 1971).

33. Margaret Kinney, "The Patient's Library in a Psychiatric Setting," *AHIL Quarterly* 6:15 (Winter 1966).

34. Clara J. Kircher, "Bibliotherapy and the Catholic School Library" in Brother David Martin, ed., *Catholic Library Practice* 2nd ed. (Portland, Oregon: University of Portland Press, 1950). *Character Formation Through Books* (Washington, D.C.: Catholic University of America Press, 1945).

35. Joseph T. Klapper, "The Comparative Effects of the Various Media" in Wilbur Schramm, ed., *The Process and Effects of Mass Communication* (Urbana, Illinois: University of Illinois Press, 1954).

36. Kenneth Koch, *Wishes, Lies and Dreams: Teaching Children to Write Poetry* (New York: Chelsea House Publishers, 1970).

37. Clara Lack and Bruce Bettencourt, "Bibliotherapy in the Community" *News Notes of California Libraries* 67:372 (Fall 1973).

38. Clara Lack, "Group Bibliotherapy," *HRLS Quarterly* 1:19-20 (October 1975).

39. Jack Leedy, *Poetry Therapy* (Philadelphia, Pennsylvania: Lippincott and Co., 1969).

40. Frank Leslie, "Choice of Reading Matter by Neuropsychiatric Patients" *U.S. Veterans Bureau Medical Bulletin* 7:779-780 (1931) as discussed in Jerome M. Schneck, "Bibliotherapy and Hospital Library Activities for Neuropsychiatric Patients" *Psychiatry* 8:207-228 (May 1945).

41. H. M. Lindahl and K. Koch, "Bibliotherapy in the Middle Grades," *Elementary English* 29:390-396 (1952).

42. Lee Loevinger, "The Ambiguous Mirror: The Reflective-Projective Theory of Broadcasting and Mass Communication" in *Mass Media: Forces in Our Society* (New York: Harcourt Brace, 1972).

43. Sister Mary C. Lorang, *Burning Ice: The Moral and Emotional Effects of Reading* (New York: Scribner's, 1968).

44. Clara C. Lucioli, "Bibliotherapeutic Aspects of Public Library Services to Patients in Hospitals and Institutions," in Margaret Monroe, *Reading Guidance and Bibliotherapy in Public, Hospital, and Institutional Libraries* (Madison, Wisconsin: University of Wisconsin Library School, 1971).

45. Joseph Luft, *Group Process: An Introduction to Group Dynamics* (Palo Alto, California: Mayfield Publishing Co., 1970).

46. David J. McDowell, "Bibliotherapy in a Patient's Hospital" *Bulletin of the Medical Library Assn* 59:450-457 (July 1971).

47. John H. McFarland, "A Methodology of Bibliotherapy," *American Journal of Occupational Therapy*, 6:66-73 (1952).

48. Fred McKinney, "Explorations in Bibliotherapy: Personal Involvement in Short Stories and Cases" *Psychotherapy: Theory, Research, and Practice* 12:112 (Spring 1975).

49. Joseph E. Malkiewicz, "Stories Can Be Springboards" *The Instructor* 79:113+ (April 1970).

50. Gail Marshall, "Make Way for Children" *Elementary School Journal* 76:159 (December 1975).

51. Gail Marshall "Stories for Children and Children's Stories" *Elementary School Journal* 76:159 (December 1975).

52. P. M. Mayden, "What Shall the Psychiatric Patient Read?" *American Journal of Nursing* 52:192 (1952) and Lind, J. E. "The Mental Patient and the Library" *Bookman* 65:138-141 (1927).

53. Henry C. Meckel, "An Exploratory Study of Responses of Adolescent Pupils to Situations in a Novel" (unpub. Ph.D. dissertation, University of Chicago, 1946).

54. William C. Menninger, M.D., "Bibliotherapy," *Bulletin of the Menninger Clinic* 1:263-273 (November 1937).

55. Margaret E. Monroe, "Services in Hospital and Institution Libraries", in Genevieve M. Casey, *Op. Cit.*

56. Mildred T. Moody, "Bibliotherapy for Chronic Illnesses," *Hospital Progress* 45:62-63 (January 1964).

57. Mildred T. Moody and Hilda Limper, *"Bibliotherapy: Methods and Materials* (Chicago: American Library Assoc., 1971).

58. Mildred T. Moody, "Bibliotherapy: Modern Concepts in General Hospitals, and Other Institutions," *Library Trends* 11:147-158 (October 1962).

59. Harold A. Moses, "Counseling with Physically Handicapped High School Students," (unpublished Ph.D. dissertation, University of Missouri, 1965).

60. Melvin C. Oathout, "Books and Mental Patients" *Library Journal* 79:405-410 (March 1954).

61. M. Ohlsen, *Guidance Services in the Modern School* (New York: Harcourt, 1964).

62. Judge Jacob Panken, "Psychotherapeutic Value of Books in the Treatment and Prevention of Juvenile Delinquency" *Journal of Psychotherapy*, January 1947.

63. Lili E. Peller, "Daydreams and Children's Favorite Books" in Judy Rosenblith and Wesley Allensmith, eds., *The Causes of Behavior* (Boston: Allyn and Bacon, 1962).

64. Charles J. Perrine, "A Correctional Institution's Library Service," *Wilson Library Bulletin* 30:249-252 (November 1955).

65. Robert Plank, "Science Fiction" *American Journal of Ortho-Psychiatry* 30:801 (1960).

66. Esther B. Pomeroy, "Aims of Bibliotherapy in Tuberculosis Sanitoria" *Library Journal* 65:687-689 (September 1940).

67. Elizabeth Pomeroy, "Hospital Libraries," *Medical Bulletin of the Veterans Administration* 7:986-991 (1931).

68. Mary D. Quint, "The Mental Hospital Library" *Mental Hygiene* 28:263-272 (1944).

69. Virginia M. Reid and others, *Reading Ladders for Human Development* 5th ed. (Washington, D.C.: American Council on Education, 1972).

70. S. Sue Robinson and Jean K. Mowbray, "Why Poetry?" in Jack Leedy, ed., *Poetry Therapy. Op. Cit.*

71. Louis A. Rongione, "Science Fiction: The Psychological Aspects of Science Fiction Can Contribute Much to Bibliotherapy" *Catholic Library World,* October 1964.

72. Louise M. Rosenblatt, *Literature as Exploration* (New York: Appleton-Century-Crofts, 1933).

73. R. Rovin, "Identification Patterns of High School Students with Literary Characters: A Study in Bibliotherapy," *The School Counselor* 14:144-148 (1967).

74. David H. Russell and Caroline Shrodes, "Contributions of Research in Bibliotherapy to the Liberal Arts Program," Part I *School Review* 58:335-342 (September 1950). Part II *School Review* 58:411-420 (October 1950).

75. Hazel Sample, *Pitfalls for Readers of Fiction* (Chicago, Illinois: National Council of Teachers of English, 1940).

76. Wilbur Schramm, "Why Adults Read" in National Society for the Study of Education. *Adult Reading* (Chicago, Illinois: University of Chicago Press, 1956).

77. Edward A. Schuman, "Evaluating Educational Programs," *Urban Review* 3:16 (1969).

78. Caroline Shrodes, "Bibliotherapy: A Theoretical and Clinical Experimental Study." (unpublished Ph.D. dissertation, University of California, 1950).

79. N. B. Smith, "Some Effects of Reading on Children," *Elementary English* 25:271-278 (1948); "The Personal and Social Values of Reading" *Elementary English* 25:490-500 (1948).

80. Edwin Starbuck, *A Guide to Literature for Character Training* vol. 1. (New York: Macmillan, 1928).

81. Daniel Sweeney, "Bibliotherapy and the Elderly" Speech given at the East Coast Bibliotherapy Round Table meeting, Washington, D.C., January 11, 1976.

82. W. H. Tedford and Carolyn Symnott, as reported in *Psychology Today* (January 1973).

83. Ruth Tews and Mildred Moody, "The Practice of Bibliotherapy," in *Institutional Library Service: A Plan for the State of Illinois* (Chicago, Illinois; American Library Assn., 1970).

84. Ruth M. Tews, "Role of the Librarian on the Interdisciplinary Team" in Margaret E. Monroe *Reading Guidance in Bibliotherapy.*

85. Robert Tyson, "The Validation of Mental Hygiene Literature," *Journal of Clinical Psychology* 4:304-306 (July 1948).

86. Laurens Van der Post, *Jung and the Story of Our Time* (New York: Pantheon Books, 1975).

87. Carol H. Weiss, *Evaluation Research: Methods of Assessing Program Effectiveness* (Englewood Cliffs, New Jersey: Prentice-Hall Inc., 1972).

88. Gertrude Whipple, "Practical Problems of School Book Selection for Disadvantaged Pupils" in J. Allen Figurel, ed., *Reading and Realism,* Proceedings of the 13th Annual Convention of the International Reading Assn., Newark, Delaware, 1969, 13:195+.

89. Paul A. Witty, "Promoting Growth and Development Through Reading," *Elementary English* 27:493-500 (1950); "Reading to Meet Emotional Needs," *Elementary English* 29:75-84 (1952); "Meeting Developmental Needs Through Reading," *Education* 84:451-458 (1964).

90. Joseph S. Zaccaria and Harold A. Moses, *Facilitating Human Development Through Reading: The Use of Bibliotherapy in Teaching and Counseling* (Champaign, Illinois: Stipes Pub. Co., 1968).

Chapter Four
Education and Training for Bibliotherapy

Although bibliotherapy is an outgrowth of many professions, each of which has contributed to the techniques now used in bibliotherapy, none of these disciplines has trained bibliotherapists. The need for a specially tailored training program which would include aspects of librarianship, psychology, literature, and counseling is strongly felt by practitioners.

In 1962, Margaret Kinney, long active in institutional librarianship, called for special education for bibliotherapy. Her article, "The Bibliotherapy Program: Requirements for Training" remains one of the strongest statements on the subject. In enumerating the ideal qualities for a bibliotherapist, she notes that he or she "needs the personal qualities, the emotional stability, the physical well-being, the character, and the personality necessary for him to work successfully with people. . . . The demands of his work require a willingness to recognize the misfortunes of others and to react with sufficient facility to be of help. In addition, such a specialist has to understand the goal desired in each instance, be willing to accept responsibility for action taken, and be able to assume authority whenever necessary." She emphasizes that it is imperative:

> . . . to recognize and control personal prejudices, to be receptive to new learning, and to direct and channel personal feelings in a manner that will not impair his helpfulness to others. As a bibliotherapist, such a person needs to assume responsibility for the selection of reading materials; his selections would be based upon the understanding of cause and effect as they relate to the physical, emotional, and cultural factors related to the reader. An understanding of and a feeling for what goes on when one person talks and another listens are of primary importance to anyone undertaking this aspect of librarianship.[9]

Kinney's list of criteria for a good bibliotherapist includes at least a dozen other skills and characteristics which she deems important. A decade later, Father Louis Rongione presented another formidable list of qualifications in his *Catholic Library World* article "Bibliotherapy: Its Nature and Uses." He includes the following: emotional stability; a willingness to recognize the misfortunes of others and the ability to provide help; a good psychological adjustment; ability to cooperate with others in a therapeutic team; respect for the reader's own wishes and rights; willingness to accept responsibility; tolerance; ability to be objective and not to be influenced by personal prejudices; ability to direct others; willingness to learn; relative freedom from personal problems of one's own; cheerfulness; a high degree of perceptiveness and sensitivity; patience; mature judgment; ability to communicate clearly, ability to be a good listener; powers of intelligent observation; flexibility; the type of mind that organizes facts well; competence to instruct; ability to channel personal feelings; the discernment to discard the erroneous and irrelevant and draw only warranted and valid conclusions; a deep and abiding interest in other people as individuals.[16]

Both Kinney and Rongione describe a person "too good to be true," the perfect librarian and mental health worker. A more reasonable set of expectations is offered by Lucy Fairbanks, an activity therapist writing about bibliotherapy. She states simply that the bibliotherapist works much like the activity therapist who uses art, music, cooking, crafts, dance, etc. for therapeutic purposes. "Above all, he must be sensitive to what is going on, so that he reacts not just to the spoken word, but to the nonverbal message the patient is trying to convey."[4] She points out that this ability is partially learned and partially a matter of personality.

In their research on "helping professionals," Arthur Coombs et al. discovered that effective helpers and ineffective ones could be distinguished from each other by personality factors. Their beliefs about others, themselves, their goals, and their methods affected their ability to be helpful more than did their formal training. Good practitioners believe that others are capable, friendly, worthy of respect, internally motivated, dependable to behave in certain patterns, and potentially fulfilling to the helper. These effective professionals see themselves as identified with others, basically adequate, trustworthy, wanted, and worthy of respect. Their purposes are identified as freeing, concerned with large issues, self-revealing, personally involving, process-oriented, and altruistic. The approaches of a good helper are oriented toward people rather than objects, and toward perceptual experiences rather than objective facts.[2] These findings suggest that it is the personality and maturity of the practitioner, more than the educational background, that determines a good bibliotherapist.

The eminent psychologist, Carl Rogers has also discussed "the necessary and sufficient conditions of therapeutic personality change." In his 1957 article of the same title, he discusses several which have great relevance to an understanding of the essential qualities for a bibliotherapist.

> Two persons are in psychological contact. The first, whom we shall term the client, is in a state of incongruence, being vulnerable or anxious. The second, whom we shall term the therapist, is congruent or integrated in the relationship. The therapist experiences unconditional positive regard for the client. The thera-

pist experiences an empathic understanding of the client's internal frame of reference and endeavors to communicate this experience to the client. The communication to the client of the therapist's empathic understanding and unconditional positive regard is to a minimal degree achieved.[14]

Roger's portrayal of the ideal therapist is perhaps the best and clearest list of personality requirements for bibliotherapists. The therapist should be "a congruent, genuine, integrated person. It means that within the relationship he is freely and deeply himself, with his actual experience accurately represented by his awareness of himself. It is the opposite of presenting a facade, either knowingly or unknowingly." In addition, the therapist should experience "unconditional positive regard" which Rogers defines as "experiencing a warm acceptance of each aspect of the client's experience as being part of that client . . . It means a caring for the client as a separate person with permission to have his own feelings, his own experience . . . ." The other characteristic which Rogers considers essential is that the therapist be capable of "experiencing an accurate, empathic understanding of the client's awareness of his own experience. To sense the client's private world as if it were your own, but without ever losing the 'as if' quality—this is empathy, and this seems essential to therapy." The "as if"—the recognized boundary between the client and the therapist's identities—is essential in the relationship.[14]

Arthur Lerner, a poetry therapist, echoes Rogers, in describing a capable poetry therapist. In personal correspondence he states:

> I believe that it is most important that the poetry therapist be authentic in his use of poetry with others. He must know his limitations as well as his potentials and be able to admit when he does not know something or when he feels uncomfortable. Honesty has a way of becoming evident in therapy. Being authentic also means recognizing one's blind spots so that the other person's authenticity and growth are not affected.[10]

The bibliotherapy literature dwells more on the personal characteristics necessary for bibliotherapy than on professional qualifications. Bibliotherapy is currently practiced by librarians, physicians, psychologists, social workers and educators; each of these professions seems to assume that the use of literature as therapy is its exclusive province. Librarians have futilely debated whether the bibliotherapist should be a librarian with special training in psychology, or a psychologist with extra education in librarianship. It seems that either approach is viable if the therapist has the necessary personality qualifications and knowledge of both the patron and the necessary materials. Opler's 1967 survey (see Chapter One) asked librarians: "Who should be a bibliotherapist?" The majority responded with "any sensitive person with some experimental wisdom and basic understanding of the group process" or with "any professional person." An important 1964 workshop on bibliotherapy and mental health sponsored by the Association of Hospital and Institution Libraries of the American Library Association and funded by the National Institutes of Mental Health favored an interdisciplinary approach. Psychologists, psychiatrists, librarians, an occupational therapist, an activity therapist, a social worker, and a nursing educator were represented on the program. This conference, together with the dissemination of articles on bibliotherapy in the journals of these and other fields, demonstrates that bibliotherapy does not belong to only one profession and that motivated, trained professionals in numerous fields can be good bibliotherapists.

In her 1939 article "The Psychology of the Reader," Alice I. Bryan recommended that in order to provide bibliotherapy, a professional librarian should be appointed as a staff member or consultant to every psychiatric clinic and psychiatrists be appointed to all libraries, but her idea was never implemented.[1] The concept of bibliotherapy as a team effort of a physician or psychologist and librarian has long been a popular one. Besides the advantages of the pooling of expertise, the team provides a more efficient use of its members' time. Margaret Hannigan warns that if a librarian is going to do bibliotherapy alone s/he may have to streamline or abandon some of his or her other library tasks in order to be effective in therapy.

For the past ten years, even the title "bibliotherapist" has been contested by librarians because its professional basis and training requirements were unclear. An alternative term, "clinical librarian," which was first discussed at the 1964 bibliotherapy workshop, was also considered unacceptable because "the term 'clinical librarian' implies that the librarian, by aptitude, training, and experience, is qualified to participate in the remedial, therapeutic, and rehabilitative care of the individual in hospitals and institutions," although no professional training programs existed. At this time, "clinical librarian" (or "clinical medical librarian") is being used to designate a hospital librarian who attends medical rounds in order to provide appropriate information to the medical team members.

Because of the great shortage of workers in the mental health field, many people without certification are providing needed services. Indeed, the federal government has urged the mental health profession to recruit personnel from other public service fields. Mental health professionals seem less concerned with labels and certification than with the provision of services. Librarians must also follow this trend. Bibliotherapists are needed; their professional background should be less important than their current capabilities. Yet, there have been few opportunities for education and training in bibliotherapy.

EDUCATION FOR BIBLIOTHERAPY AND POETRY THERAPY

"Psychotherapy is an undefined technique applied to unspecific problems with unpredictable outcome. For this technique, we recommend rigorous training." So states a psychology training manual. Unfortunately, most of the pleas for the teaching of bibliotherapy follow this line of reasoning. Because no specific needs are outlined and no exact techniques endorsed, the number of educational opportunities in bibliotherapy have been few.

In her classic article on bibliotherapy education, Kinney states that "the bibliotherapist is primarily a librarian who goes further in the field of reading guidance and becomes a professional specialist."[9] She describes a model training program for bibliotherapy starting at the graduate level. The student would need basic library science courses, experience working in a library, and a broad knowledge of literature. She also stresses the need to study the principles and techniques of psychology because the therapist must evaluate the emotional significance of the client's responses, relate the reading selections to his or her needs, and make valid interpretations of his or her reactions.

Kinney, and many others, emphasize the need for field service training in bibliotherapy. On-the-job training has been successful in medicine, psychology, and social work, and could be equally so in bibliotherapy. No amount of book study can substitute for the experience of seeing another professional at work, observing the patron's responses, and trying out the newly learned skills. As Ruth Tews has said at a speech at the University of Wisconsin Library School: "The art of bibliotherapy cannot be taught; skill within an art depends on practice, not precept. We gain our professional knowledge, which is based on scientific principles, through study, but bibliotherapy, which is an art, must be learned by experience."[18] In her description of an ideal bibliotherapy training course, she makes the valid point that field service, in addition to courses in psychology, group dynamics, speech, and others, will serve the librarian in many ways. It will provide the needed professional expertise and the self-confidence which stems from experience. In addition, it will establish the bibliotherapist's role as an expert in relationships to other therapists.

While these ideal programs and future possibilities were being discussed in the United States, one republic in Russia established a central office for bibliotherapy research and training. The *International Library Review* reports that in 1962, the Ukranian Institute for Medical Education established a "Chair of Psychotherapy, Psychohygiene, and Psychoprophylax."

> The terms of reference of the chair consist also of the working out of scientific methodology and the naturalization of bibliotherapy into the practice of sanitoria. Many plans were made to use the libraries in the sanitoria of the Ukraine for therapeutic purposes. The experience so gained was then to be published and distributed to other sanitoria . . . [In one hospital] there has been created a consultative advice center for bibliotherapy. It consists of eight persons — four doctors and four librarians. To this advisory center, there also belong scientists as well as practicing members of both professions. The center intends from

1970 onwards to instruct the librarians of the sanitoria of the Ukranian S.S.R. on the basis of medical psychology and on the reading of the sick in the sanitoria; a permanent seminar will be held in the autumn of each year. Each group of librarians, consisting of 10-12 persons, will receive instruction for a whole week.[11]

Although the United States does not have any such body coordinating the work and training of bibliotherapists, courses in bibliotherapy and poetry therapy have been offered irregularly in various parts of the country. Most common have been guest speakers on the theory of bibliotherapy at colleges, professional associations, and experiential workshops. The latter, usually part of a longer conference, have been given by a number of current bibliotherapy practitioners. For example, the American Psychiatric Association (APA) has had poetry therapy pre-conferences; the Mental Health Librarians of the APA have had ones dealing with bibliotherapy in their agendas; and the International Federation of Library Associations has included a bibliotherapy panel discussion in its programs. Since 1972, the Association for Poetry Therapy has sponsored an annual poetry therapy conference which combined speeches by practitioners, demonstrations, and small group poetry therapy experiences. Courses offered at universities for regular academic credit are less common.

Since bibliotherapy has been considered a segment of institutional librarianship, it seems appropriate to mention the educational opportunities for hospital and institutional librarianship. In 1937, the University of Minnesota's Division of Library Instruction began offering annually a quarter course in hospital librarianship. It was both theoretical and practical and included six weeks of internship. Bibliotherapy *per se*, was not taught, although book selection and the use of materials with mental patients were included in the course content. Other courses in hospital librarianship have been offered from time to time at various library schools but as of now, only four library schools have ever offered a course devoted solely to bibliotherapy.

There have been references in the literature to a 1962 group bibliotherapy with long-term patients' training in a VA Hospital; a 1969 course on "poetry and interpersonal communication" offered cooperatively by the English and Psychology departments at Dowling College; a 1971 course in poetry therapy given by the guidance and counseling department of Long Island University; a 1971 summer course in poetry therapy at the Institute for Sociotherapy in New York; and a course on psychotherapy and poetry in the psychology department of Northeastern Illinois University in 1974. There is no way to determine how many other courses have been attempted.

A discussion of a few of the longer-lasting training programs in poetry therapy and bibliotherapy should help to give a perspective on what is currently available. The first college course in bibliotherapy for academic credit was offered in the fall of 1970 at Villanova University in Pennsylvania and has since been taught annually by Father Louis Rongione in the graduate library science program. The course description reads "Selection, evaluation, and acquisition of books and non-book materials as therapeutic adjuvants in medicine and psychiatry; and guidance in the solution of personal problems through directed reading." The course includes a definition of the field and its objectives: bibliotherapy in librarianship; bibliotherapy as a guidance technique, and the use of other media (music and poetry) for therapy. In personal correspondence, Father Rongione describes his course as "basic and strictly theoretic" with "no practicum or field experience required of the students . . . The course limits itself simply to what a librarian ought to know *about* bibliotherapy, not what he ought to know to *practice* it."[16]

In the same year, 1970, Morris R. Morrison taught the first course in poetry therapy in a school of higher education. At the New School for Social Research in New York, he taught a non-credit course entitled "Poetry and the Therapeutic Process." From 1973 on, Morrison, through the psychology department of the New School, taught a revised course entitled, "The Use of Poetry in the Treatment of Emotional Dysfunction," for three undergraduate credits. Prof. Morrison, who is also the President of the Association for Poetry Therapy and a co-director of the Poetry Therapy Center in New York, describes his course as dealing "with the theoretical basis of poetry as a healing modality, as a vehicle for self-discovery and interpersonal exploration . . . The last six sessions of the course will consist of workshops, intended to demonstrate the dynamics of poetry as a focal activator in the group setting." In 1973, he also began teaching an in-service poetry therapy course entitled, "Poetry Therapy in the Classroom," which is sponsored by the Professional Development Program of the New York City Board of Education; it serves as a human relations course for incremental credit for teachers and counselors.

Meanwhile, during the summers of 1972-1974, Indiana University of Pennsylvania offered a three-week interdisciplinary (English and Psychology) course in poetry therapy, which was also offered in 1976. The class, which results in graduate credit for the participants, is theoretical and experiential, with the emphasis on the latter. Kenneth Edgar and Richard Hazley, who teach the course, are well known among poetry therapists for their experimental work and their 1969 curriculum proposal for poetry therapists.

In it, they propose an interdisciplinary program including conventional clinical psychology classes and specially designed literature courses. They recommend a traditional undergraduate program with a major in either English or psychology and a minor in the other. In order to offer an M.A. in Poetry Therapy, the master's level curriculum would have to be specifically designed and taught by an interdisciplinary team. They recommend the following psychology courses: developmental psychology, abnormal psychology, psychology of personality, social psychology, projective tests, plus surveys of the techniques of psychotherapy and group psychotherapy. In the area of literature they recommend language as behavior, psychology and literature, psychological themes in poetry, and a seminar involving individual research and practice in poetry therapy. Further, they suggest that nine credits of internship be offered in conjunction with a local hospital where observation, assistance, and finally supervised leadership of group poetry therapy would be required. The proposed curriculum is still merely a proposal; it has never been officially adopted as a course of study and is not currently being used at any university. Even so, it is relevant for future planning in bibliotherapy education.[3]

Dr. Michael Shiryon, a proponent of literatherapy, taught a University of California Extension course in June 1972 which was repeated in 1973. Although he introduced some theory, Shiryon's course was primarily experiential. The students brought in favorite poems to discuss and were encouraged to keep a diary to help them become aware of subtle changes and new ideas that might occur between sessions. Each class was organized as a poetry therapy group with the students as participants and two as recorders who noted the interactions and the high points of the discussion. Their reports, which were read at the beginning of the next session, gave the participants two perspectives besides their own in viewing the poetry therapy experience.

The Poetry Therapy Institute in California is a training institute rather than a membership organization, and offers seminars and workshops through university extensions and professional and lay interest groups. Many courses are taught by Arthur Lerner, the founder, and are both theoretical and experiential and include the theory and practice of poetry therapy, poetry workshops and readings, psychodrama, and a poetry therapy marathon.

Arleen Hynes, the librarian in the Patient's Library at St. Elizabeths Hospital, is currently teaching bibliotherapy classes at the University of Denver and at The Catholic University (Washington D.C.) Graduate Library School. The first is a "mini-course" for one or two undergraduate credits; the second is a three-credit graduate library science class. Both are introductory in nature and deal with definitions, goals, processes, techniques, and psychological concepts in addition to providing bibliotherapy experience. More important is a two-year training program which she implemented in 1973, the most significant bibliotherapy education program that has been attempted. Her nonstipended trainees and interns come from library and other fields to participate in a two-year training program which includes a minimum of four hundred and forty-eight training hours. The first year is a trainee year and the second is an internship. As of mid-1976, one intern had completed the nonstipended program and thereby met the requirements of the Association for Poetry Therapy for certified poetry therapist (CPT). Four others were registered for future certification. Hynes explains that "There is no national organization of bibliotherapists to grant certification. Since poetry is the main tool used in the St. Elizabeths program, we sought certification from the

Association for Poetry." Future planning envisions stipended biblio-therapy trainees in the nine-month core curriculum program of St. Elizabeths. For more details on this vigorous training program at St. Elizabeths, see Appendix III A.

Although the handful of bibliotherapy classes and programs dis-cussed here are excellent, the need for bibliotherapy education far exceeds what is available. Unfortunately, many practitioners do not want to offer courses until they know what the certification require-ments would be. And most librarians balk at discussion of certification because classes are not available. It appears that people interested in bibliotherapy must work on both simultaneously—offering classes and developing certification standards. At this time, the poetry therapy certification is the most appropriate model.

POETRY THERAPY CERTIFICATION

Proposed standards for the certification of poetry therapists were published in 1973 in the *AHIL Quarterly*. Written by Morris Morrison with the Association for Poetry Therapy (APT) named as accrediting body, the full text appears in Appendix III B.

To qualify for certification under these standards, a person must have a bachelor's degree (or its equivalent) in humanities or the behavioral sciences. The trainee must then work, either as a volunteer or as a salaried employee, for two years under the supervision of a cer-tified poetry therapist.

Although some English teachers and psychological workers intern with Leedy and Morrison at their Poetry Therapy Center in New York in preparation for the APT certification, most poetry therapy trainees have devised their own training situations in appropriate in-stitutions under qualified supervisors and have approached APT indi-vidually. As of Spring 1976, APT had certified 40-50 people who were thereafter allowed to used the "CPT" designation after their names. Most of the CPTs were psychiatrists, psychologists, educators, and counselors. The minority have been poets and librarians; only a few li-brarians have been certified. The Poetry Therapy Institute in Califor-nia is also considering certification of poetry therapists but has not yet begun such a program.

BIBLIOTHERAPY CERTIFICATION

Currently, there is no bibliotherapy certification and many basic questions remain unanswered. What should be taught, to whom, and by whom still needs to be decided. The efforts in this direction thus far have been by individuals. The universities and the library schools should take a more active role both in supplying bibliotherapy courses and in lending legitimacy to this concern. As of now, there is no accrediting agency for bibliotherapy and few guidelines for certifica-tion.

Since there are librarians and other professionals currently calling themselves bibliotherapists, or providing a service they call bibliotherapy, it is necessary to examine their job descriptions before discussing certification.

Job descriptions. Many hospital librarians define themselves as bibliotherapists but correspondence with some of these practitioners discloses that their job classifications are generally "Librarian" or "Supervisor Librarian" and bibliotherapy is just an activity they have taken upon themselves. At the Central Louisiana State Hospital in Pineville, Louisiana, the 1972 Librarian II position description includes the statement "conducts bibliotherapy groups for adolescents and adults" and "the most important duty of this position" is listed as "complete responsibility for the bibliotherapy program at the Forest Glen Library." The 1972 U.S. Civil Service Commission GS-1410-9 librarian job description includes this statement under "duties": "The major portion of my patient work is specialized group work. Delegated authority by the Chief Librarian for making all contacts necessary for library therapy projects, I organize all groups with the approval and cooperation of ward personnel involved . . . Delegated authority and responsibility for the bibliotherapy programs, I conduct projects on a regularly scheduled weekly basis . . ." This description is used in a Tennessee Veterans Administration Hospital. At St. Elizabeths Hospital in Washington, D.C., the description stresses bibliotherapy as a library service and training of future bibliotherapists. (See full text in Appendix III A).

Both of these job descriptions are for librarians. The first position classification for a bibliotherapist *per se* is in the County of Santa Clara (California) where both a Bibliotherapist I and a Bibliotherapist II classification exist. In the original position description, a Bibliotherapist I needed a B.A. with a major in psychology or the humanities and six months experience in mental health work; the Bibliotherapist II needed, in addition, an M.L.S. and two years' experience in bibliotherapy. The 1974 descriptions are less oriented to library science and do not require a clinical training period, although Clara Lack, the present Bibliotherapist II, wanted this included. The employment requirements for the Bibliotherapist I include a B.A. (or its equivalent) in psychology or counseling, and experience working with emotionally disturbed people. Additionally required are a knowledge of library reference materials, literature, and group-leadership techniques, and the ability to "relate literature to individual and group needs, research and select literary materials suitable for emotionally disturbed patients, lead groups in discussion of literary materials and relate such materials to personal experiences, evaluate patients' participation in a bibliotherapy program for use by mental health personnel, speak and write effectively, maintain effective relationship with patients and professional personnel." The Bibliotherapist II requirements are similar but include supervisory skills and the ability to train the Bibliotherapist I. At present, the Bibliotherapist I is a college graduate in psychology and the Bibliotherapist II has a B.A. in English and psychology and a Master's in Library Science. (See both job descriptions in Appendix III C.)

Other helping professions. Another approach to the problem of bibliotherapy certification is provided by an examination of the certification programs of other "helping professions." Three modes of certification, or registration as it is sometimes called, are common. These include: certification by completion of a formal educational curriculum at an accredited college; by experience under a trained therapist after minimal normal education; by a combination of formal education and clinical training. Examples of the first type are library science, occupational therapy, and social work. Professional librarianship now requires a Master's degree in Library Science granted by a university which has been accredited by the American Library Association. Occupational Therapists are registered by the American Occupational Therapy Association after completing an accredited baccalaureate curriculum available at fifty colleges, or a Master's degree, offered at six. Six to nine months of field work is an optional requirement. Similarly, social workers are registered after the completion of a university curriculum accredited by the Council of Social Work Education.

Certification through clinical experience is common with the "creative therapies." It usually requires an internship and minimal formal education, and is exemplified by the APT, discussed before, and the American Dance Therapy Association. In order to be registered, dance therapists are required to have paid experience as a dance therapist for at least 2 years full time or 3,640 hours during five years, or 2,548 hours as a dance therapist and 1,092 hours as a dance therapy instructor; thorough dance training including three years with three to ten classes per week; experience teaching dance to normal students; a B.A. or its equivalent; dance therapy training under a registered dance therapist; and three references including one from another dance therapist.

Examples of certification through a combination of formal education and clinical experience are found in music therapy and recreation therapy. The National Association for Music Therapy began registering therapists in 1950; now thirty-two colleges in the U.S. offer baccalaureate, and a few offer Master's degrees, in music therapy. One of the additional requirements for the degree is a six-month practicum in an approved clinical facility under the direction of a registered music therapist. The National Therapeutic Recreation Society of the National Recreation and Park Association registers therapeutic recreation specialists with an M.A. in therapeutic recreation; or an M.A. in recreation plus one year's experience; or a B.A. in recreation plus three years' experience; or a B.A. in another field plus five years' experience. They also recognize Master Therapeutic Recreation Specialists with an M.A. in therapeutic recreation plus two years' experience; or an M.A. in recreation plus three years' experience; or an M.A. in another field plus four years' experience; or a B.A. in Therapeutic Recreation plus five years' experience and some graduate work; or a B.A. in another field plus seven years' experience and some graduate work. The National Therapeutic Recreation Society also recognizes Therapeutic Recreation Assistants, Therapeutic Recreation Technicians, and Therapeutic Recreation Leaders, all of which are paraprofessional positions. The American Occupational Therapy Association among others, also certifies various paraprofessional classifications.

Many people have expressed concern over the various requirements for the helping professions, the separate certifying functions of a large number of organizations, and the proliferation of new mental health fields. A now defunct group, called The Ad Hoc Committee on Behavioral Science Legislation, decided in 1971 that in order to encourage maximal cooperation between the behavioral science specializations, to provide maximal use of educational opportunities in all fields, and to offer the public protection from falsely titled or unqualified practitioners, legislation would be necessary. A proposed Behavioral Sciences Practice Act was drawn up. It created five professional levels within each specialization. These were:

—Supervisory professionals with a Doctoral degree in any of the behavioral sciences, or its equivalent; three years' experience; and 25 hours of training in supervision.

—Professionals with a Master's degree in any behavioral science, or its equivalent, and at least two years of supervised experience or a Doctoral degree and one year experience.

—Assistants with a Master's degree.

—Interns with a B.A. or Associate degree.

—Trainees with a certificate from an accredited institution or some equivalent.

Qualifying boards, which would be comprised of representatives from all levels in the profession, educators, human services organizations, and concerned lay people, would certify in each of nine specializations. Applicants could be licensed in as many behavioral sciences as they qualified for. This excellent proposal unfortunately was never enacted. The problems of certification and the provision of services still exist. What are the differences between the services provided by clergymen, lawyers, school counselors, psychologists, nurses, and bibliotherapists if all of them deal with troubled individuals? This concern was voiced by Howard Rome, a psychiatrist, who asks "If psychotherapy is not the exclusive purview of psychiatry, what is the difference between what they do and others do? And what are the safeguards for a gullible public?"[15]

Contracting for service. The most obvious protection for the public is that of the law, which judges the viability of the contract between client and practitioner by the process of licensing. One reason that the distinction between psychotherapy and other behavioral sciences, between doctor and nurse, between librarian and bibliotherapist, is so significant, lies in the differing codes of ethics and the varied responsibilities of each profession. The hierarchies of supervisor, professional, assistant, intern, and trainee are also based on the relative amounts of responsibility each classification requires.

These distinctions are perhaps most dramatic in institutional settings where the legal responsibilities are most pronounced. In an institution to which a person is legally committed (e.g., prison or mental hospital) all people working with the residents have legal responsibilities to them. But in a voluntary situation, the legal responsibilities are limited only to contracts between the individual client and a professional. Obviously, the vulnerability of the client (and the legal responsibility of the practitioner) is greater in the first instance. Thomas Szasz in *The Myth of Mental Illness* distinguishes two types of psychiatry. The first is "institutional psychiatry" which is practiced by physicians who are employed by the state and whose services are largely unsolicited by their appointed patients.[17] In *The Politics of Therapy*, Seymour Halleck has this to say about institutional psychiatry:

> The unhappy person becomes a psychiatric patient when he or his society decides he is behaving in an unreasonable manner. When the individual makes his own decision, it is usually based upon his experience of personal suffering . . . Such a person voluntarily seeks the psychiatrist's assistance in order to find a more trouble-free and meaningful existence. When society decides that a person is behaving unreasonably enough to be a psychiatric patient, it simply makes a judgment . . . as to the maladaptive basis of that person's conduct and assumes that the person who behaves in such a manner is troubled or unhappy. In some instances, the individual may not feel troubled; therefore he may be placed in a patient role involuntarily . . . It is important to note that the judgment of unreasonable suffering or behavior is always a value judgment . . .[5]

The second type of psychiatry delineated by Szasz is "contractual psychiatry" in which psychiatry is practiced with voluntary patients who actively contract for the therapist's help.[17]

It is important to consider the contractual basis for service when discussing certification and labelling of bibliotherapists. Lois Hinseth, a nurse and librarian, views bibliotherapy in two levels: that provided under an implicit contract and that provided under an explicit one. The first instance occurs when a person is able to contract for him or herself for assistance in self-actualization. The service may be provided by a "reader guidance-librarian, with a librarian-bibliotherapist, or with a licensed or unlicensed therapist of some other discipline. This is an implicit, nonlegal, transactional contract." In the second case, society contracts for the care of a person deemed incompetent. Only licensed individuals can provide such care under an "explicit, formal, legal contract (which) carries with it legal sanctions and liabilities."[7]

A bibliotherapy certification proposal. After having reviewed the bibliotherapy job descriptions now in existence, the examples set by po-

etry therapists in their curriculum proposal and certification requirements, the registration criteria for other mental health workers, and
the problems inherent in contracting for services, it seems reasonable
to propose a multi-level bibliotherapy certification program which requires education and experiential components and distinguishes between practitioners using bibliotherapy in various settings.

In the Introduction, three types of bibliotherapy were delineated:
institutional, clinical, and developmental. The first, "institutional,"
applies to bibliotherapy with individual clients who have been institutionalized by society or are patients in a psychiatrist/psychologist's
private practice. The institutional bibliotherapist would need an
extensive educational background and much prior experience because
of the nature of his/her clients and the settings in which s/he will work.
Often, institutional therapy is conducted by a team; in that case, none
of the individual team members needs to have all of the skills the team
requires.

For an institutional bibliotherapist working alone, rather than as
part of a team, these requirements are suggested:

1) Ph.D. in behavioral science, library science, counseling,
or nursing. Plus a set number of required clinical psychology, literature, and library science courses.

And 2) One year's experience working part time in a clinical
bibliotherapy situation, and one year of institutional
bibliotherapy part time under supervision.

And 3) One year's experience working full time in another
aspect of mental health, library science, or nursing.

For an institutional bibliotherapist working as a member of a team
(an "associate institutional bibliotherapist"):

1) M.L.S., or M.A. in behavioral sciences or nursing. Plus
a set number of required inter-disciplinary courses.

And 2) One year experience working part time as a bibliotherapist in a clinical or developmental situation.

And 3) One year experience working full time in another aspect
of library science, mental health, or nursing.

The second type of bibliotherapy discussed in chapter one was
termed "clinical" and applies to bibliotherapy as most practitioners
think of it—in group settings with clients who have emotional and/or
behavioral problems and are treated in either an institutional or a
community setting. Arleen Hynes' program is the best training for this
sort of work, but because there are few opportunities for such training
at this time, an alternative set of standards is offered:

1) M.L.S. or M.A. in behavioral sciences, nursing, counseling or education. Plus a set number of required courses

in the other fields. OR B.A. in one of these fields plus equivalent experience.

The third type of bibliotherapy, "developmental," referred to as group bibliotherapy with "normal" adults or children wishing to better understand themselves or their problems. These requirements are proposed:

      1) M.L.S. or B.A. in education, counseling, or education. Plus a required set of courses in library science, psychology, and literature.

And 2) One year part time experience as a bibliotherapist under supervision.

And 3) One year prior full time experience as a teacher, counselor, or librarian.

And 2) One year experience working part time as a bibliotherapist under supervision.

And 3) One year experience working full time in another aspect of library science, mental health, education, or nursing.

In order to implement the above requirements, a set curriculum, to be studied at any college or university, is necessary. The following courses are recommended in addition to any courses in bibliotherapy *per se* that may be available: surveys in psychology, literature, and library science, abnormal psychology, psychology of the personality, diagnostic testing, group dynamics, group leadership, book selection, reference, reading interests of adults (or children), program planning and evaluation, and language as behavior.

In addition, bibliotherapists who can supervise trainees, and an accrediting agency, are needed. Current bibliotherapy practitioners will have to be accepted as supervisors, under a "grandfather clause," until newly trained bibliotherapists are available. This problem has been solved in a similar fashion by other creative therapies when they were initiating certification standards. Even more difficult is the problem of establishing an accrediting agency. This author feels that an independent interdisciplinary association should be formed to promote bibliotherapy education and to certify qualified practitioners. The certification standards recommended in this chapter are but suggestions that hopefully will evoke reactions and discussion on a concern that is just now beginning to surface. Any standards will have to be revised by practitioners in the field and by the accrediting agency, but those presented here provide a starting point for future work.

Bibliotherapy has had a long history of development and growth, particularly in this country. The 1930's exemplified a surge in interest in the field similar to one experienced now. Yet, a great deal of research needs to be done in both the theory and the methods of bibliotherapy. Certification of practitioners and an independent and interdisciplinary bibliotherapy association are also urgent needs at this time, so that the many people expressing interest in bibliotherapy can work cooperatively to unify this special approach to literature and mental health.

REFERENCES

1. Alice I. Bryan, "The Psychology of the Reader," *Library Journal* 64:7-12 (January 1939).

2. Arthur W. Coombs, Donald L. Avila, and William W. Purkey, *Helping Relationships: Basic Concepts for the Helping Professions* (Boston: Allyn and Bacon, 1971).

3. Kenneth F. Edgar and Richard Hazley, "A Curriculum Proposal for Training Poetry Therapists," in Jack Leedy, ed., *Poetry Therapy* (Philadelphia: Lippincott, 1969).

4. Lucy F. Fairbanks, "Field: Activity Therapy," in William K. Beatty, ed., *Proceedings of the ALA Bibliotherapy Workshop in St. Louis June 25-27, 1964, A.H.I.L. Quarterly* (vol. 4, Summer 1964).

5. Seymour L. Halleck, *Politics of Therapy* (New York: Science House Inc. 1971).

6. Margaret Hannigan, "The Librarian in Bibliotherapy: Pharmacist or Bibliotherapist?," *Library Trends* 11:184-197 (October 1962).

7. Lois Hinseth, "Contract Considerations in the Practice of Bibliotherapy," *HRLSD Quarterly* 1:21-22 (October 1975).

8. Artemisia Junier, "Bibliotherapy: Projects and Studies with the Mentally Ill Patient," *Library Trends* 11:143 (October 1962).

9. Margaret Kinney, "The Bibliotherapy Program: Requirements for Training," *Library Trends* 11:129 (October 1962).

10. Arthur Lerner, "Poetry as Therapy," *American Psychological Monitor* 6:4-5 (August, 1975).

11. A. M. Miller, "The Reading Matter of Patients," *International Library Review* 4:374-375 (1972).

12. Pauline Opler, "The Origins and Trends of Bibliotherapy as a Device in American Mental Hospital Libraries," (M.S. Thesis, San Jose State College, 1969).

13. Victor C. Raimey, ed., *Training in Clinical Psychology* (New York: Prentice-Hall, 1950), p. 93 as quoted in *A.H.I.L. Quarterly* 4:42 (Summer 1964).

14. Carl R. Rogers, "The Necessary and Sufficient Conditions of Therapeutic Personality Change," *Journal of Consulting Psychology* 21:96 (April 1957).

15. Howard P. Rome, "Whence, Whither and Why? Psychiatry Circa 1964," *A.H.I.L. Quarterly* 4:32 (Summer 1964).

16. Louis A. Rongione, "Bibliotherapy: Its Nature and Uses," *Catholic Library World* 43:497-498 (May 1972).

17. Thomas S. Szasz, *The Myth of Mental Illness* (New York: Dell, 1967).

18. Ruth M. Tews, "The Role of the Librarian in Bibliotherapy," Unpublished speech given at the University of Wisconsin Library School, Madison, Wisconsin, (July 1968).

19. Ruth M. Tews, "The Role of the Librarian in the Interdisciplinary Team," in Margaret Monroe, ed., *Reading Guidance and Bibliotherapy in Public, Hospital, and Institution Libraries.* (Madison, Wisconsin: University of Wisconsin Library School, 1971).

Appendix I

Suggested Juvenile Materials For Bibliotherapy

This bibliography is only a sampling of currently available juvenile materials suitable for bibliotherapy. At the moment, such materials, though not referred to as bibliotherapeutic, are popular with publishers and producers. At least one publisher (Human Sciences Press) has begun a series of materials to "help children through normal developmental stages." One television network (ABC) has commissioned a series of television plays for children based on the understanding that "emotional dynamics build relationships; relationships build bonds, marriages, homes and families . . ." (quotations from promotional flyers). Perhaps it is becoming easier to find good bibliotherapeutic materials, but good indexing of them still does not exist.

It would be impossible to list here all the materials dealing with even one theme, such as death. Instead, a number of options are offered for each of the following themes: confinement, contemporary problems, death and old age, emotions, family, friends, identity and self-discovery, imagination and creativity, mental health, new experiences, physical handicaps, prejudice, privacy and sharing, responsibility and decision making, school, sexuality and love, and values. These broad categories are subdivided within each section of the bibliography. Although some cross-references are included, it is important to check under a number of headings to find the exact theme needed.

In order to limit the number of items included, 1960 was chosen as the borderline publication date; all of the works listed have been published since then and the emphasis is on materials produced during the past five years. Fiction and nonfiction materials are included although the emphasis is on the former since the author primarily uses creative materials for bibliotherapy. No biographies are listed because they are relatively simple to identify and categorize.

All works listed were read (or reread) for inclusion in this bibliography. The major criterion was the emotional impact of the work. Value decisions, rather than value judgments, are important components of bibliotherapeutic materials. Literary quality, *per se,* was not a criterion because often the most powerful works are not those that are award-winning or renowned. The list is very subjective and can only be used as a guide. Each bibliotherapist must create his or her own lists until appropriate indexes are available.

A few hints for using this bibliography: First and most important, do not feel that this list substitutes for reading and knowing the material well before attempting to use it. Secondly, note that a whole book or film need not be used. It could be that a chapter from a book or a scene from a play will work best. Whenever possible, materials are noted which, not necessarily good in themselves, include worthy sections. This again, is a personal decision.

For each item listed, full bibliographic information, reading and interest levels, and special notes are offered in addition to a short annotation. Cross-references are given when possible. The reading and interest levels used are: *preschool* (mostly to be read aloud, some picture books), *elementary* (first to third grade), *intermediate* (fourth to seventh), and *teen* (eighth grade to adult). These are merely descriptive, and not prescriptive; the individual child's reading and emotional level must be your guide. It should be noted that many books designated for intermediates, for example, could be read aloud to younger children if the theme is appropriate; conversely, a slow-reading older child may be able to enjoy a carefully selected easy book. The special notes added to some references serve to point out special qualities the material has which may be significant. For example, materials depicting Black or Chicano characters are marked; nonsexist materials are also noted. Attention is called to materials which vary in any way from the traditional all-White children's materials; a concerted effort was made to include as many of these new works as possible.

For the reader in need of other bibliographies, the following resources are suggested:

Adell, J. and Klein, H. *A Guide to Non-Sexist Children's Books* (Chicago: Academy Press, 1976).

Artel, Linda and Wengraf, Susan. *Positive Images: A Guide to Non-Sexist Films For Young People* (San Francisco: Booklegger Press, 1976).

Council on Interracial Books For Children. *Human (and Anti-Human) Values in Children's Books* (New York: CIBC, 1976).

Kelley, Marjorie E. *In Pursuit of Values: A Bibliography* (New York: Paulist Press, 1973).

Kircher, C. *Character Formation Through Books: A Bibliography* (Washington, D.C.: Catholic University, 1952).

Moody, M. and Limper, H. *Bibliotherapy: Methods and Materials* (Chicago: A.L.A., 1971).

Reid, V. *Reading Ladders for Human Relations.* 5th ed. (Washington, D.C.: American Council on Education, 1972).

Schultheis, Sister Miriam, *A Guidebook for Bibliotherapy* (Glenview, Illinois: Psychotechnics, Inc., 1973).

White, M. *High Interest/Easy Reading* (New York: Citation Press, 1972).

Zaccaria, J., and Moses H. *Facilitating Human Development Through Reading* (Champaign, Illinois: Stipes, 1968).

CONFINEMENT

Armstrong, William H. *Sounder* (New York: Harper, 1969).
Reading level: intermediate. Interest level: into early teen.
Note: Black family.

In this story of a Black sharecropper and his family, the son's reactions to, and acceptance of, his father's imprisonment are handled well. A strong family unity is depicted.

Cages. 9 minutes, Color, McGraw-Hill, Film.
Level: teen.

Animated film which shows prisons within prisons within prisons: We are all prisoners.

Cunningham, Julie. *Drop Dead* (New York: Random House, 1965).
Reading level: intermediate. Interest level: through teen.

A parable about control and confinement, told by Gilly Ground, an orphan. A difficult and disturbing book.

Kesey, Ken. *One Flew Over the Cuckoo's Nest.* (New York: Viking, 1962).
Reading and interest level: teen.

McMurphy is released from a penal farm by feigning insanity only to discover that the mental hospital is worse. The ward is controlled by a dictator, the "Big Nurse." McMurphy tries to get the ward's patients to absorb some of her power, but the hospital has all the weapons of confinement.

See also under other headings:

Green, Hannah. *I Never Promised You a Rose Garden.* Mental Illness.
Rubin, Theodore. *Jordi.* Mental Illness.
Sherbourne, Zoa. *Stranger In the House.* Mental Illness.

CONTEMPORARY PROBLEMS

This section includes materials dealing with drugs, gangs, juvenile delinquency, fighting, lying, pregnancy, and the difficulty of reconciling two lifestyles.

Alexander, Anne. *Trouble on Treat Street* (New York: Atheneum, 1974).
Reading and interest level: intermediate
Note: Interracial.

Gangs. Manolo, a Chicano in San Francisco and Clem, his new Black neighbor, disliked each other on first sight. But both of them had to contend with El Diablo and his gang. In so doing, they become almost-friends. Realistic, frightening.

Almost Everyone Does. 14 minutes, Color, Wombat Productions, Film.
Level: late intermediate and teen.

Drugs. Drug and alcohol problems discussed. Nonfiction.

Anonymous. *Go Ask Alice* (Englewood Cliffs, New Jersey: Prentice-Hall, 1971).
Reading and interest level: teen.

Drugs. The real diary, published by her parents posthumously, of a fifteen-year-old drug user.

Blue, Rose. *Nikki 108* (New York: Franklin Watts, 1972).
Reading level: easy intermediate. Interest level: intermediate.

Drugs. Eleven-year-old Nikki sees her Mom working hard all day for little money and her brother die of a heroin overdose. She takes a long look at his friends, and hers, and decides to avoid drugs and study to become a nurse.

Bonham, Frank. *Viva Chicano* (New York: Dutton, 1970).
Reading and interest level: teen.
Note: Chicano.

Juvenile Delinquency. Keeny (for Joaquin) doesn't see how he can avoid the Youth Authority considering his mother doesn't trust him, his Anglo stepfather is always out of work, and his Chicano pride gets him into trouble. One day, a cardboard dummy of Zapata gives him an idea and he turns his pride to work *for* him. Excellent. Good portrayal, too, of a parolee halfway house.

Brink, Carol Ryrie. *The Bad Times of Irma Baumlein* (New York: Macmillan, 1972).
Reading and interest level: intermediate.

Lying. Irma was new in town, had no siblings, no pets, a busy father, and a mother away at a health spa. What could she do to make friends except to lie and impress them? She claimed to have the biggest doll in the world and then had to produce it, which led to theft. The ending is very unrealistic, in that everyone—parents, authorities, and peers alike—are forgiving and understanding, but parts are good.

Byars, Betsy. *The Eighteenth Emergency* (New York: Viking, 1973).
Reading and interest level: intermediate.

Fighting. "Mouse" doesn't know how to evade the eighteenth emergency: Marv's threat of revenge. After a week of fear, he finds that he can't avoid the beating so he simply takes it and becomes the most honorable twelve-year-old around.

Childress, Alice. *A Hero Ain't Nothing But A Sandwich* (New York: Coward, McCann, and Geoghan, Inc., 1973).
Reading level: intermediate. Interest level: into teen.
Note: Black.

Drugs. Benjie Johnson is thirteen and hooked on heroin. This excellent story is told by Benjie; by Butler Craig, his stepfather; by Jimmy Lee Powell, his best friend; by Benjie's mother, Rose; and by Walter, the pusher, in turn. All sides are presented realistically and convincingly.

Clymer, Eleanor, *My Brother Stevie* (New York: Scholastic, 1967).
Reading and interest level: intermediate.

Juvenile delinquency. Written from Annie's perspective, this short book recounts her attempts to keep her brother Stevie out of trouble. They live with their grandmother, who is little help, because their mom's deserted them.

Craig, Jean. *New Boy on the Sidewalk* (New York: Norton, 1967).
Reading and interest level: elementary.

Fighting. A new boy moves into Joey's neighborhood; they immediately don't like each other. But when two bigger boys bully them, they have to stick together.

Fitzhugh, Louise, and Scoppettone, Sandra. *Bang Bang You're Dead* (New York: Harper, 1969).
Reading and interest level: intermediate.

Fighting. James, Timothy, Stanley, and Bert like to play "Bang, bang, you're dead." One day, Big Mike and his three friends try to overtake their hill, and the two groups have a real fight. Everyone is hurt; it is no fun. They resolve to share the hill and return to make-believe war.

Hinton, S. E. *The Outsiders* (New York: Viking, 1967).
Reading level: easy teen. Interest level: teen.

Gangs. This novel, written by a seventeen-year-old, is about the violence between two gangs, the Socials (the haves) and the Jets (the have-nots). It is told from the point of view of Ponyboy, a fourteen-year-old greaser, who has to witness three deaths before beginning to understand his brothers, his gang, and himself.

Jackson, Jesse. *Tessie* (New York: Harper, 1968).
Reading and interest level: intermediate.
Note: Black characters.

Two worlds. Tessie tries to reconcile her two worlds—home in

Harlem and an exclusive private school where she's a scholarship student.

Lucy. 14 minutes, Color, Pictura, Film.
Level: teen.
Note: Puerto Rican characters.

Pregnancy. The unwanted pregnancy of a sixteen-year-old.

Manuel from Puerto Rico. 14 minutes, Color, Encyclopaedia Brittanica, Film.
Level: intermediate.
Note: Puerto Rican.

Two Worlds. American born Manuel must learn to fit into Anglo society yet keep his Latino identity.

Peck, Richard. *Don't Look and It Won't Hurt* (New York: Holt, 1972).
Reading and interest level: teen.

Pregnancy. Title refers to advice given to Ellen about her pregnancy and giving the baby away. The book is written from her sister, Carol's, perspective.

Sachs, Marilyn. *Veronica Ganz* (New York: Doubleday, 1968).
Reading and interest level: intermediate.

Bully. Veronica is the biggest kid in her class, a "tomboy," and a bully. When one little kid outsmarts her, and other frustrations set in, she discovers that things must change.

Stolz, Mary. *Bully of Barkham Street* (New York: Harper, 1963).
Reading and interest level: intermediate.

Bully. Martin Hastings is a lonely eleven-year-old, both older and larger than his classmates. He pretends not to care that he has no friends; he shows his disappointment, though, by being hateful and irresponsible. After his beloved dog is taken from him, he realizes he has to change himself, but it's harder than he realized to live down a reputation.

Stolz, Mary. *A Dog on Barkham Street* (New York: Harper, 1960).
Reading and interest level: intermediate.

Bully. The same story as *Bully of Barkham Street* but written from the point of view of Edward, Martin's next door neighbor, who is constantly intimidated and tormented by Martin. Edward's chief desire (after getting rid of Martin) is to have a dog of his own.

Waltrip, Lela and Rufus. *Quiet Boy* (New York: Longmans, Green, & Co., 1961).
Reading and interest level: intermediate.
Note: Native American.

Two worlds. Quiet Boy is the head of his household after his father dies. He wants to follow his father's wishes and learn to live with the White man, but many of the other Navajos are opposed to dealing with the Whites. After an adventure and some sleuthing, Quiet Boy proves to himself, and others, the wisdom of borrowing from both worlds.

Zindel, Paul. *My Darling, My Hamburger* (New York: Harper, 1969). Reading and interest level: teen.

Pregnancy. Humorous story about the senior year of high school for Sean and Liz, and Dennis and Maggie. Liz gets pregnant and has an abortion; Maggie worries about her appearance, and other adolescent worries. Well done.

See also under other headings:

Alexander, Anne. *To Live A Lie*, Family.
Hinton, S. E. *That Was Then, This Is Now*, Responsibility and Decision-Making.

DEATH AND OLD AGE

Baldwin, Anne Norris. *Sunflowers for Tina* (New York: Four Winds Press, 1970).
Reading and interest level: elementary.
Note: Black characters.

Tina wished she could grow a garden outside her New York City apartment and admires the sunflowers in a vacant lot. Then she decides to become a sunflower herself to brighten up her grandmother's life.

Bawden, Nina. *Squib* (Philadelphia: Lippincott, 1971).
Reading and interest level: intermediate.

Kate (12) has never accepted the death of her father and only brother. She feels that Rupert is still alive somehow; so when she sees the mysterious Squib, her fantasy takes more concrete form. The book is very British and has an extremely unrealistic ending, but chapters of it could be used well.

Blue, Rose. *Grandma Didn't Wave Back* (New York: Franklin Watts, 1972).
Reading level: easy intermediate. Interest level: elementary through intermediate.
Note: Nonsexist.

Debbie lives with her lawyer-mother, father, two brothers, and grandma. Grandma becomes forgetful and strange and soon has to be taken to a nursing home. Excellent.

Borack, Barbara. *Someone Small* (New York: Harper, 1969).
Reading and interest level: elementary.

A nameless girl has a new baby sister and a new baby bird. Although she prefers the bird, she tries to be nice to her sister, too.

When the bird dies, both girls bury it before turning their attentions elsewhere.

Brown, Margaret Wise. *The Dead Bird* (New York: Young Scott Books, 1963).
Reading and interest level: elementary.

Some children find a dead bird and give it an elaborate funeral.

Cleaver, Vera and Bill. *Grover* (Philadelphia: Lippincott, 1970).
Reading and interest level: intermediate.

After Grover's mother kills herself to end a painful sickness, Grover has to deal with the neighbor's reactions, his own grief, and his father's unrealistic sorrow. Excellent.

Donovan, John. *Wild in the World* (New York: Harper, 1971).
Reading level: intermediate. Interest level: into teens.

John, a teenager, is left alone to take care of his home and himself after all of his family members die. He befriends a stray animal and the two of them plan a life elsewhere. At the end of the book, John dies of pneumonia. Basically an adventure-type story. This book is unsentimental.

Konigsburg, E. L. "The Night of the Leonids," in her *Altogether One At A Time* (New York: Atheneum, 1971).
Reading and interest level: intermediate.

Lewis and his grandmother, who get along remarkably well, go to see a shower of stars but the night is too cloudy to see. What Lewis does see is another side of his grandmother.

Lee, Virginia. *The Magic Moth* (New York: Seabury Press, 1972).
Reading level: intermediate. Interest level: elementary to intermediate.

A simple, touching short novel about the death of Maryanne from a heart defect. Marko (6), William, Julie, and Barbara (the eldest, 13) accept the death with the help of honest, intelligent parents.

Little, Jean. *Home From Far* (Boston: Little, Brown & Co., 1965).
Reading and interest level: intermediate.

Jenny has trouble accepting the death of her twin brother Michael in a car accident. When her parents take in two foster children including a boy named Mike, she has to change.

Miles, Miska. *Annie and the Old One* (Boston: Little, Brown & Co., 1971).
Reading and interest level: elementary.
Note: Native American.

Beautiful book about a Navajo family. Annie's grandmother announces that when the rug her daughter is weaving is done, she will die. Annie tries to delay her mother's weaving so that the Old

One won't die. Her grandmother teaches her that she cannot stop time or nature.

Orgel, Doris. *Mulberry Music* (New York: Harper, 1971).
Reading and interest level: intermediate.
Note: Inter-religious marriage depicted.

Libby has trouble accepting that Grandma Liz, her favorite relative is sick and in the hospital. Later, her death comes as no surprise and Libby helps with the funeral. Very realistic yet sympathetic.

Peck, Richard. *Dreamland Lake* (New York: Holt, 1973).
Reading and interest level: teen.

Flip and Bryan, both 13, discover a dead man in the woods and build up the episode into a great mystery. By the end of the book, Bryan has seen two more deaths and has a new perspective on death.

Smith, Doris Buchanan. *Taste of Blackberries* (New York: Crowell, 1973).
Reading and interest level: elementary to intermediate.

The narrator is a young boy who feels guilty when his friend, Jamie, dies of an allergic reaction to bee stings. He had assumed that Jamie was just playing another game when he died. Excellent; unsentimental and insightful. Takes the reader through Jamie's funeral and to the beginning of the child's recovery from his guilt feelings.

Viorst, Judith. *The Tenth Good Thing About Barney* (New York: Atheneum, 1972).
Reading and interest level: elementary.

Barney was a cat who died. His owner was very sad until he learned the tenth good thing about Barney—that he would help the new flowers to grow.

Warburg, Sandol Stoddard. *Growing Time* (Boston: Houghton-Mifflin, 1969).
Reading and interest level: elementary.

Jamie's dog, King, dies and his family helps him to understand death and life by getting him a new puppy.

Wojciechowska, Maja. *Hey, What's Wrong With This One?* (New York: Harper, 1969).
Reading level: intermediate. Interest level: elementary to intermediate.

When the book opens, the three brothers still remember their mother who has been dead for two years, but they'd like another mother. No housekeeper will stay because of their behavior, so they decide to find a new wife for their father. The youngest (7) finds a likely mom in the grocery store. Acceptance of death and need for change.

Zolotow, Charlotte. *My Grandson Lew* (New York: Harper, 1974).
Reading and interest level: elementary.

Lewis remembers his grandfather and tells his mother how he misses him. She shares some of her memories of her father, too, so they can remember him together and neither of them will be as lonely.

See also these titles under other headings:

Stolz, Mary. *By The Highway Home.* Family.
Winthrop, Elizabeth. *A Little Demonstration of Affection.* Love and Sexuality.

EMOTIONS

This category touches upon many emotional themes. Of course, other sections (especially family, death, friends, and prejudice) deal with the emotions involved with the problem or process being examined. Please look through the other sections for additional references.

Babbitt, Natalie. *The Something* (New York: Farrar, Straus, and Giroux, 1970).
Reading and interest level: preschool.

Fear. Mylo is afraid of the dark because a "something" may come in through the window. In an attempt to distract Mylo from this fear, his mother brings him modeling clay out of which he makes a statue of the "something." That night he is no longer afraid. Good story.

Berger, Terry. *I Have Feelings* (New York: Human Sciences Press, 1971).
Reading and interest level: preschool and elementary.

Emotions. Seventeen different feelings, both positive and negative, and the situations that precipitated each one are featured and illustrated with photographs, e.g., "This week I tried out for school band. I made it! I feel good! Now I'm glad I practiced everyday even though I missed some ball games. Sometimes you have to give up something to get something you want even more." Can be preachy in parts. One of a series of Human Sciences Press books designed by psychologists to help children through specific developmental stages.

Coatsworth, Elizabeth. *The Princess and the Lion* (New York: Pantheon, 1963).
Reading and interest level: intermediate.

Courage. Princess Miriam of Abyssinia has an adventurous

journey as she sets off across her country to find her brother Michael who is to be the next king. Her courage combined with rich historical and geographical details make a good story.

Conford, Ellen. *Why Can't I Be William?* (Boston: Little, Brown & Co., 1972).
Reading and interest level: elementary.

Envy. Jonathan wishes he could be William who has a room of his own, no pesty brother, can eat candy whenever he wants, and has great pets. But when Jonathan and his mother visit William's house, Jonathan decides he is happier being himself.

Cunningham, Julia. *Macaroon* (New York: Pantheon, 1962).
Reading and interest level: easy intermediate.

Temperament. Erika is a very disagreeable child until Macaroon, a raccoon, moves into her house for the winter.

Danijan, Mischa. *Atuk* (New York: Panetheon, 1964).
Reading and interest level: intermediate
Note: Eskimo characters.

Revenge. An Eskimo boy kills a wolf that has killed his dog, but finds that the revenge doesn't make him feel any better. He is still unhappy until he makes friends with a flower. Beautifully illustrated.

DeJong, Meindert. *Far Out The Long Canal* (New York: Harper, 1964).
Reading and interest level: intermediate.

Courage. Nine-year-old Moonta can't skate although nearly everyone else in his North Sea village does. When it finally ices over in the canal, Moonta learns to skate and has an adventure on skates.

Fitzhugh, Louise. *The Long Secret* (New York: Harper, 1965).
Reading and interest level: intermediate.

Anger. In this sequel to *Harriet the Spy*, Harriet remains the self-made detective, exuberant, loud, and very unladylike. Her friend, Beth Ellen, is timid until she explodes angrily and then is able to feel better and to act less shyly. She has to deal with the return of a mother she hasn't seen for a long time and a crush.

Gaeddert, Lou Ann. *Noisy Nancy Norris* (New York: Doubleday, 1965).
Reading and interest level: preschool and early elementary.

Cooperation. Nancy is noisy all the time until a neighbor warns her that they will have to move if she isn't quieter. It is very difficult for Nancy, but she tries to be cooperative.

Gallant Little Tailor. 10 minute, Black/White, Contemporary, Film.
Reading and interest level: preschool and elementary.

Courage. Based on the fairy tale, this is the story of a little tailor who gains courage by killing seven flies at one blow.

Green, Phyllis. *The Fastest Quitter in Town* (Reading, Massachusetts: Young Scott Books, 1972).
Reading and interest level: elementary.

Anger. Johnny always quits baseball games in anger. But when his great grandfather loses a ring, Johnny keeps searching and learns the value of not giving up.

Hoban, Russell. *Harvey's Hideout* (New York: Parents Magazine Press, 1969).
Reading and interest level: elementary.

Loneliness. Harvey and Mildred Muskrat argue all summer. Then Harvey decides to build a secret hideout and Mildred starts going to secret parties. When each finds out that the other is as lonely as himself, they decide to share their summer plans.

Hoban, Russell. *The Little Brute Family* (New York: Macmillan, 1966).
Reading and interest level: elementary.

Temperament. Great story of the Brute family members who growl at each other, and are sullen and unhappy, until Baby Brute finds a "wandering lost good feeling" and takes it home. Soon everyone has a good feeling and the family changes its name to the Nice Family.

Hodges, Elizabeth Jamison. *Free As A Frog* (Reading, Massachusetts: Addison-Wesley Pub. Co., 1969).
Reading and interest level: elementary.

Shyness. John Frederick Allen is six years old, has a slight lisp, and is very shy until he finds a frog one day. He shares it at show and tell and then puts it back in the pond.

Lexau, Joan M. *Benjie* (New York: Dial Press, 1964).
Reading and interest level: elementary.
Note: Black characters.

Shyness. Benjie is so shy that he can't talk to anyone except his grandma. Then one day she loses her special earring and he has to find it for her—and overcome his shyness.

Lexau, Joan M. *I Should Have Stayed in Bed* (New York: Harper, 1965).
Reading and interest level: elementary.

Frustration. Some days *everything* goes wrong. On one of those days, Sam goes back to bed to start the day over again.

Ness, Evaline. *A Gift for Sula Sula* (New York: Scribner's, 1963).
Reading and interest level: elementary.

Envy. Miki, a pelican, is jealous of Sula Sula, a new orange bird who has everyone's attention. But when he finds that he is the only one who can solve a problem of hers, he begins to feel good about himself again.

Ness, Evaline. *Pavo and the Princess* (New York: Scribner's, 1964).
Reading and interest level: elementary.

Crying. Phoebe was a beautiful princess who never cried—until her father's favorite peacock flew away. Then she cried and cried until he returned. Sometimes she cried even after that; "on special occasions they cried just for the joy of it."

Norris, Gunilla B. *Time For Watching* (New York: Knopf, 1969).
Reading and interest level: intermediate.

Curiosity. Jachim is curious about everything, especially about the mechanical workings of objects. But his parents and neighbors think he is just selfish and a troublemaker because he'll do anything to see how things work and how his neighbor, the watchmaker, fixes them.

Schlein, Miriam. *The Girl Who Would Rather Climb Trees* (New York: Harcourt, 1975.)
Reading and interest level: elementary.
Note: Nonsexist.

Sensitivity to others. When Melissa is given a doll and a baby carriage, she doesn't know what to do. She hates dolls but doesn't want to hurt anyone's feelings.

Surowiecki, Sandra L. *Joshua's Day* (Chapel Hill, North Carolina: Lollipop Power, Inc. 1972).
Reading and interest level: preschool and early elementary.

Anger. One day when Joshua is at the daycare center (mother works; no father) and his tower of blocks is knocked over, he gets very angry. It takes friends and Mommy to make him feel better again.

Tadpole Tale. 16 minutes, Color, Universal, Film.
Reading and interest level: elementary to intermediate.

Acceptance. A little boy unable to have a pet catches a tadpole in Central Park. He takes it home to take care of it and to watch it. When it grows into a frog, he realizes that it needs water and returns it to the lake. Film is done without narration.

Taylor, Theodore. *The Cay* (Garden City, New York: Doubleday, 1969).
Reading level: intermediate. Interest level: into teen.
Note: Interracial.

Dependence. Philip and his parents are Americans living in Curacao at the onset of World War II. When Philip and his mother try to return to the US, their ship is torpedoed. Philip finds himself saved by Timothy, an old Black man, on whom he is totally dependent. Philip is temporarily blinded so becomes even more tied to Timothy. When the old man dies, Philip survives on the island until he is rescued. Great adventure story that deals with dependence, and racism, very well.

Updike, John. "Tomorrow and Tomorrow and So Forth," in Charlotte Zolotow, *An Overpraised Season* (New York: Harper 1973). Short story.
Reading and interest level: intermediate to early teen.

Cruelty. A high school class finds the subtlest and cruelest joke to play on their teacher who mistakenly feels that he understands them perfectly.

Viorst, Judith. *My Mamma Says There Aren't Any Zombies, Ghosts, Vampires, Creatures, Demons, Monsters, Fiends, Goblins, or Things* (New York: Atheneum, 1973).
Reading and interest level: preschool and elementary.

Fears. Sometimes Mama makes mistakes, but not about zombies, ghosts, vampires, etc.

Wagner, Jane, *JT* (New York: Dell, 1969). (Also a TV special)
Reading and interest level: intermediate.
Note: Black characters.

Frustration. JT is a ten year old kid living in the inner city. His frustrations erupt into lies and thefts until he finds a stray cat which he is able to love and care for.

Williams, Jay. *The Question Box* (New York: Norton and Co., 1965).
Reading and interest level: intermediate.

Curiosity. Maria was a question box, always asking questions which people couldn't answer. Her mother said that girls shouldn't be so curious. But because of her curiosity, she discovered the secret to the town's great clock and saved it from sabotage.

Zolotow, Charlotte. *The Hating Book* (New York: Harper, 1969).
Reading and interest level: preschool and elementary.

Hate. Hurt feelings, based on a misunderstanding, almost turn a liking-relationship into a hating one. Excellent.

Zolotow, Charlotte. *The Unfriendly Book* (New York: Harper, 1975).
Reading and interest level: preschool and elementary.

Jealousy. Bertha is jealous when Judy plays with other friends and decides she doesn't like any of them. Judy's response is a surprise—and a good discussion starter.

Also see these titles under other headings:

Arthur, Ruth. *My Daughter Nicola.* Identity and Self-Discovery.
Cleaver, Vera and Bill. *Grover.* Death and Old Age.
Coatsworth, Elizabeth. *Lonely Maria.* Fantasy and Imagination/Creativity.

Desbartes, Peter. *Gabrielle and Selena.* Friends.

Donovan, John. *Remove Protective Coating . . . A Little at a Time.* Identity and Self-Discovery.

Greene, Bette. *Philip Hall Likes Me.* Friends.

Griese, Arnold A. *At the Mouth of the Luckiest River.* Physical Disabilities.

Hazen, Nancy. *Grownups Cry, Too.* Identity and Self-Discovery.

Holland, Isabelle. *Amanda's Choice.* Responsibility and Decision-Making.

Hutchins, Pat. *Tom and Sam.* Friends.

Johnson, Annabel. *The Grizzly.* Family.

Lionni, Leo. *Tico and the Golden Wings.* Friends.

Norris, Gunilla. *If You Listen.* Family.

Southall, Ivan, *Ash Road.* Responsibility and Decision-Making.

Please also check other headings for the emotional content of the event or situation the category implies.

FAMILY

This section includes family relationships, sibling rivalry, single parent families (including divorce and separation), foster families, and orphans.

Adams, Florence. *Mushy Eggs* (New York: G. P. Putnam's Sons, 1973).
Reading and interest level: elementary.
Note: Nonsexist.

Divorce. The story of two little boys who live with their mom who is a computer worker, and Fanny who is their baby-sitter. A realistic story and one with an excellent female role model.

Alexander, Anne. *To Live a Lie* (New York: Atheneum, 1975).
Reading and interest level: intermediate.

Divorce. Jennifer lives with her dad after her parents are divorced, but she finds it easier to tell people that her mother is dead. Lies always seem easier to Jennifer until she is found out.

Alexander, Martha. *Nobody Asked Me If I Wanted A Baby Sister* (New York: Dial Press, 1971).
Reading and interest level: preschool and elementary.

Sibling Rivalry. Oliver can't stand all the fuss over Bonnie, his new baby sister so he tries to give her away. He finds out that she wants *him*—and then she doesn't seem so bad anymore.

Bawden, Nina. *Runaway Summer* (Philadelphia: Lippincott, 1969).
Reading and interest level: intermediate.

Divorce. Mary (11) is angry and resentful that her parents are divorced. She wants to be bad, but even being rude, lying, making ugly faces, and stealing candy bars doesn't help. As she gets involved in a real adventure, she learns that she can't run away from her situation. At the end she decides to stay with Aunt Alice and Grampy instead of her newly divorced mom.

Blue, Rose. *A Month of Sundays* (New York: Franklin Watts, 1972).
Reading and interest level: intermediate.

Divorce. When ten-year-old Jeff's parents decide to get a divorce, he decides that it is his fault. He has to deal with his own guilt feelings, a move to New York City, and only seeing his dad on Sundays. Honest, outspoken portrayal.

Blume, Judy. *It's Not the End of the World* (Scarsdale, New York: Bradbury Press, 1972).
Reading and interest level: intermediate.

Divorce. Twelve-year-old Karen is bewildered and anxious about her parents' upcoming divorce. She and her brother would do anything to prevent the divorce; her brother Jeff even runs away. But the problem remains.

The Bridge of Adam Rush. 47 minutes, Color, Time/Life, Film.
Level: intermediate into teen.

Adam and his new stepfather don't get along until they have to. When necessity brings them together, they even learn to like each other.

Byars, Betsy. *Go and Hush the Baby* (New York: Viking, 1971).
Reading and interest level: preschool and elementary.

Will tries everything he can to keep the baby entertained while his mother is painting. He creates a story that is so good that he remains interested in it even after the baby is asleep.

Byars, Betsy. *The House of Wings* (New York: Viking, 1972).
Reading and interest level: intermediate.

Sammy tries to run away from his grandfather when he discovers that he's been left at his grandfather's by his parents who have gone on to Detroit without him. But when they find a wounded crane and nurse it back to health, Sammy begins to feel comfortable with himself and his grandfather.

Caines, Jeanette. *Abby* (New York: Harper and Row, 1973).
Reading and interest level: preschool and elementary.
Note: Black family.

Adoption. Abby likes to ask questions about when she was born and when she was adopted. Her brother Kevin even takes her to school for show-and-tell. Loving book and illustrations.

Cameron, Eleanor. *A Room Made Of Windows* (Boston: Atlantic-Little, 1971).
Reading and interest level: intermediate.

Remarriage. Julie is a writer. Her room—enclosed by windows—is essential for her to write, as are her friends and neighbors. But her mother wants to remarry and to move; Julie would lose all of what she treasures. Julie learns a lot about her neighbors and herself during this trying period.

Carlson, Natalie Savage. *Ann Aurelia and Dorothy* (New York: Harper, 1968).
Reading and interest level: intermediate.

Foster parents. The adventures of Ann Aurelia and her friend Dorothy. Ann Aurelia lives with Mrs. Heicken, a foster mother whom she loves. When her real mother returns, it is a difficult decision for Ann Aurelia.

Cleaver, Vera and Bill. *I Would Rather Be A Turnip* (Philadelphia: Lippincott, 1971).
Reading level: later intermediate. Interest level: into teen.

Illegitimacy. Twelve-year-old Annie Jelks is angry when her father agrees to let seven-year-old Calvin, her sister's illegitimate son, live with them. She also feels betrayed and at the end of the book is only beginning to recover.

Corcoran, Barbara. *Trick of Light* (New York: Atheneum, 1972).
Reading and interest level: intermediate.

Sibling rivalry; twins. Cassandra and her brother Paige were especially close because they were twins. When Paige begins to hang around with the boys, Cass feels left out. Hunting for their pet dog, and losing him, helps Cassandra to learn that growing up and apart doesn't mean having to grow away from one another.

Crawford, Eleanor. *Luke Was There* (New York: Holt, 1973).
Reading and interest level: intermediate.

Abandonment. Ten-year-old Julius tells the story of how he and his brother Danny are abandoned by their father, step-father, mother (who is hospitalized) and then by Luke, their friend at the Children's Shelter. Julius runs away and learns about trust while searching New York City for his family and himself.

Cozzens, James Gould. "Total Stranger," in Charlotte Zolotow. *An Overpraised Season* (New York: Harper, 1973).
Reading and interest level: intermediate.

Father. When John meets a beautiful, sophisticated woman whom his father used to know, he begins to see his father differently.

Crawford, Sue H. *Minoo's Family* (Canadian Women's Educational Press, 1974).
Reading and interest level: elementary.
Note: Nonsexist.

Separation. Minoo's parents fight a lot and then decide to separate. Minoo has mixed feelings about living alone with her mother, but discovers that she is still able to see her daddy and make new friends.

Engebrecht, Patricia A. *Under the Haystack* (New York: Nelson, 1973). Reading and interest level: teen.

Desertion. Thirteen-year-old Sandy discovers that her mother and step-father have deserted her and her two younger sisters. She shields them from that knowledge and keeps them together on the debt-ridden farm.

Ewing, Kathryn. *A Private Matter* (New York: Harcourt, 1975). Reading and interest level: intermediate.

Divorce. Nine-year-old Marcy becomes very attached ("Too attached" according to her mother) to Mr. Endicott next door because she misses her dad.

Fitzhugh, Louise. *Nobody's Family Is Going to Change* (New York: Farrar, Straus, and Giroux, 1974). Reading level: late intermediate. Interest: through teen. Note: Black family.

Family expectations. Their middle class father wants Willie (7) to become a lawyer like himself and Emma (11) to be a housewife. But both kids are talented and stubborn—Willie wants to be a dancer like his Uncle Dipsey and Emma wants to be a lawyer. Emma goes so far as to join a "Children's Army" and to take an interest in women's liberation. She finally realizes that her parents aren't going to change, but rather that she and her friends will have to stop expecting approval from their parents. Very intricate book covering many issues humorously and well.

Fox, Paula. *Blowfish Live in the Sea* (Scarsdale, New York: Bradbury Press, 1970). Reading and interest level: intermediate.

Divorce. Rediscovery of natural father. Carrie doesn't understand her brother's preoccupation with blowfish or his growing alienation from the family. Then, unexpectedly, Ben's father (by their mutual mother's former marriage) writes to ask to meet him. Ben discovers that he's a drunkard and a liar, but chooses to live with him anyway.

Geoffrey, Bernice. *Irene's Idea* (Waterloo, Ontario: Canadian Women's Educational Press). Reading and interest level: elementary.

Fatherless. Irene comes up with an idea of what to do while the other kids—who have fathers—draw father's day cards at school.

Gerber, Merrill Joan. "How Love Came to Grandmother," in Charlotte Zolotow. *An Overpraised Season* (New York: Harper 1973). Short Story. Reading and interest level: intermediate.

Family history. Mattie likes hearing about how her parents met and how her grandparents met. But she surprises her mother one night by re-telling the history in a very different way based on her aunt's version.

Gill, Joan. *Hush Jon* (Garden City, New York: Doubleday, 1968).
Reading and interest level: elementary.

Sibling Rivalry. When school was out for the summer and Jon had to play quietly all day because of his baby sister Samantha, he began to resent her. But since she laughed at his faces and liked him so much, he decided he could stand having a baby sister.

Goff, Beth. *Where Is Daddy?* (Boston: Beacon Press, 1969).
Reading level: preschool. Interest level: through elementary.

Divorce. Excellent psychologically sound and touching story about Janeydear's anger and confusion when her parents get divorced.

Greenfield, Eloise. *She Come Bringing Me That Little Baby Girl* (Philadelphia: Lippincott, 1974).
Reading and interest level: elementary.
Note: Black family.

Sibling rivalry. A child is angry and jealous of his new baby sister until he discovers how important big brothers are. Excellent.

Gustar, Susan Wakeling. *When I Visit Daddy or Daddy Visits Me* (Waterloo, Ontario: Canadian Women's Educational Press).
Reading and interest level: elementary and preschool.

Separation. A child talks about the fun things he does with Daddy on their visits. During the week, the child is in a daycare center.

Heide, Florence Perry. *The Key* (New York: Atheneum, 1971).
Reading and interest level: late intermediate into teen.

Family relationships. Three short stories, each dealing with an unusual family situation. "The Key" is about an orphan; "Wild Bird" is about an Indian boy and his grandfather trying to exist in a big city; and "Let Down Your Golden Hair" is about a girl with an alcoholic mother and retarded sister. All difficult stories.

Hoban, Russell. *A Baby Sister For Frances* (New York: Harper, 1964).
Reading and Interest level: preschool.

Sibling rivalry. Frances decides that the baby makes her house not as nice to live in so she runs away—under the dining room table. But she hears her parents talking about how much they miss her and how important big sisters are, so she comes back. Wonderful tale.

Johnson, Annabel and Edgar. *The Grizzly* (New York: Harper, 1964).
Reading level: easy intermediate. Interest level: intermediate.

Separation. Eleven-year-old David is concerned about pleasing his father who is separated from his mother. When a grizzly bear injures Dad, David finds a new courage and self-understanding besides earning the needed respect.

Keats, Ezra Jack. *Peter's Chair* (New York: Harper, 1967).
Reading and interest level: preschool and elementary.

Sibling rivalry. Peter doesn't want his parents to paint his chair pink the way they painted his crib and high chair for the new baby. But when he sits in his chair, ne discovers that he is much too big for it, and decides to paint it after all.

Klein, Norma. *Confessions of an Only Child* (New York: Pantheon, 1974).
Reading and interest level: intermediate.

Sibling rivalry. Toe (Antonia) doesn't want her parents to have a baby because she likes being an only child. But when the baby dies right after it is born, Toe begins to see her mother's side and to feel guilty that she'd not wanted the baby. At the end of this excellent book, Mom has another baby and Toe learns that it isn't so terrible after all.

Klein, Norma. *Blue Trees, Red Sky* (New York: Pantheon, 1975).
Reading and interest level: elementary.

Widowed mother; sibling rivalry. Valerie wishes her mother didn't have to work so Mr. Weiss, who favors her brother, wouldn't have to take care of them.

Klein, Norma. *Mom, The Wolfman, and Me* (New York: Pantheon, 1972).
Reading and interest level: intermediate into teen.

Unmarried mother. An unusual, funny, and frank novel of a girl, Brett, living with her mom and her mom's male friend, whom Brett is afraid her mother will marry. Nonjudgmental, nonsexist presentation.

Klein, Norma. *Taking Sides* (New York: Pantheon, 1975).
Reading and interest level: intermediate into teen.

Divorce. Twelve-year-old Nell and her little brother live with their dad's new girlfriend and are worried about him. But she enjoys the weekends and vacations spent with her mom and her friend in the country. Excellent book for its attitude toward divorce, alternative lifestyles, and female role models.

Kraus, Robert. *Whose Mouse Are You?* (New York: Macmillan, 1970).
Reading and interest level: preschool.

Family relationships. Very simple story about a mouse discovering that a family is made up of its members.

Lasker, Joe. *Mothers Can Do Anything* (Chicago: Albert Whitman, 1972).

Reading and interest level: preschool and elementary.

Mothers. Traditional and nontraditional jobs and avocations for mothers.

Lexau, Joan M. *Emily and the Klunky Baby and the Next Door Dog* (New York: Dial Press, 1972).
Reading and interest level: elementary.

Divorce. Emily's Mom has to do the taxes now that she's divorced and Dad doesn't do them anymore. So Emily must be quiet and keep the klunky baby quiet, too. Instead, she decides to run away with the baby to Daddy's house. They never find it, but they do find their way back home.

Lexau, Joan M. *Me Day* (New York: Dial Press, 1971).
Reading and interest level: elementary.
Note: Black family.

Divorce. The story of Rafer's birthday when he gets the best present ever: a surprise visit from his dad. Black slang used. Excellent.

Little, Jean. *Look Through My Window* (New York: Harper, 1970).
Reading and interest level: intermediate.

Only child. Emily is very upset when she finds herself, an only child, sharing her house with her four cousins. She finds that sharing, and friends, turn out to be very rewarding.

Mann, Peggy. *My Dad Lives In A Downtown Hotel* (Garden City, New York: Doubleday, 1973).
Reading and interest level: elementary into intermediate.

Divorce. This excellent book has already been made into a TV special. Joey feels that it must be his fault that his parents are separated and getting divorced. Both his parents try to convince him that it isn't his fault but it is hard for him to believe. It is also hard to see that things might be better this way.

Merriam, Eve. *Mommies At Work* (New York: Scholastic, 1961).
Reading and interest level: preschool and easy elementary.

Mothers. Mommies are shown at all kinds of jobs, professional and nonprofessional. The book stresses that no matter what job a mommy does, she still is happy to be a mommy, too.

Norris, Gunilla B. *If You Listen* (New York: Atheneum, 1971).
Reading and interest level: intermediate.

Family problems. For Lia, life is lonely whether her family is in its winter city house or summer country house. Mother's on pills, her brother entertains himself, and her father is rarely at home. Lia finally makes an unexpected friend and develops the courage to tell her family that no one listens to anyone else at their house.

Ogan, Margaret and George. *Number One Son* (New York: Funk and Wagnalls, 1969).
Reading and interest level: intermediate.
Note: Asian-American family; interracial friendship.

Sibling rivalry. Fouteen-year-old Paddy wishes he were the number one son rather than his brother Jerry. He gets his chance to help his dad on the fishingboat, and after an adventure, proves to his father that he has two number one sons.

Sachs, Marilyn. *Amy and Laura* (Garden City, New York: Doubleday, 1966).
Reading and interest level: intermediate.

Sibling rivalry. Dorrie O'Brien is very unhappy when her mother has triplets and the family has to move.

Schick, Eleanor. *Peggy's New Brother* (New York: Atheneum, 1970).
Reading and interest level: elementary.
Note: Interracial pictures.

Sibling rivalry. Peggy isn't happy about her baby brother Peter. She tries to be a helper but always does things wrong—until she finds that she can make him laugh. That becomes her special job and both she and Peter like it.

Scott, Ann Herbert. *On Mother's Lap* (New York: McGraw-Hill, 1972).
Reading and interest level: preschool.
Note: Eskimo family.

Sibling rivalry. Michael, a small Eskimo boy, learns that there's room on his mother's lap for him and the baby, too.

Scott, Ann Herbert. *Sam* (New York: McGraw-Hill, 1967).
Reading and interest level: preschool through elementary.
Note: Black family.

Family support. Sam is lonely because everyone in his family is too busy for him—until they see how sad he is and give him the support he needs.

The Son. 10 minute, Black/White, McGraw-Hill, Film.
Level: teen.

Alienation based on the "generation gap."

Sonnenborn, Ruth A. *Friday Night is Papa Night* (New York: Viking, 1970).
Reading and interest level: elementary.
Note: Latin American family

Father working nights. Pedro's papa works two jobs, so he only comes home one night a week—Friday night—which becomes a festive occasion for the family.

Stolz, Mary. *By The Highway Home* (New York: Harper, 1971).
Reading level: intermediate. Interest level: into teen.

Family adjustment. When Catty's brother dies in Vietnam, her family becomes tense, her Dad loses his job, and they have to move.

Stolz, Mary. *Juan.* (New York: Harper, 1970).
Reading level: intermediate.
Note: Chicano

Orphan. Juan insists, to others and to himself, that he is not an orphan although he lives in a Mexican orphanage.

Taylor, Elizabeth, "Red Letter Day," in Charlotte Zolotow. *An Overpraised Season* (New York: Harper, 1973). Short Story.
Reading and interest level: intermediate.

Mother/son alienation. Both Edward and his mother dread visiting day at his boarding school and are relieved when it is over. It is not that they don't care for each other, but that they do not know how to act toward one another.

Zolotow, Charlotte. *A Father Like That* (New York: Harper, 1971).
Reading and interest level: elementary.

Fatherless child. Small boy without a father tries to imagine what his father would be like.

Also see these titles under other headings:
Armstrong, William. *Sounder.* Confinement.
Borack, Barbara. *Someone Small.* Death and Old Age.
Burch, Robert. *Simon and the Game of Chance.* Mental Illness.
Campbell, Hope. *Why Not Join the Giraffes?* Identity and Self-Discovery.
Cleaver, Vera and Bill. *Ellen Grae.* Responsibility and Decision-Making.
Clymer, Eleanor. *My Brother Stevie.* Contemporary Problem.
Donovan, John. *I'll Get There. It Better be Worth the Trip.* Love and Sexuality.
Donovan, John. *Remove Protective Coating A Little At A Time.* Identity and Self-Discovery.
Fox, Paula. *How Many Miles to Babylon?* Fantasy and Imagination/Creativity.
Hoban, Russell. *The Little Brute Family.* Emotions.
Kerr, M. E. *Dinky Hocker Shoots Smack.* Physical Disability.
Little, Jean. *Home From Far.* Death and Old Age.
Neville, Emily. *Garden of Broken Glass.* Friends.
Platt, Kin. *Chloris and the Creeps.* Mental Illness.
Rich, Louise. *Three of a Kind.* Physical Disabilities.
Sachs, Marilyn. *Laura's Luck.* New Experiences.
West, Jessamyn. "Crimson Ramblers of the World, Farewell." Love and Sexuality.
Wojciechowska, Maja. *Hey, What's Wrong with this One?* Death and Old Age.

FANTASY AND IMAGINATION/CREATIVITY

Afternoon of Alice McClure. 28 minutes, Sepia and Color, Phoenix, Film. Level: elementary through intermediate.

Instead of returning to a bleak lonely apartment after school, Alice imagines a deserted house into a living situation more to her liking.

Anderson, Mary. *I'm Nobody! Who Are You?* (New York: Atheneum, 1974).
Reading and interest level: intermediate.

Stephanie lives with her divorced father in New York. On her first day at the new school, she befriends fat four-eyed Ellie and the two become close friends, bound together by Stephanie's psychic powers.

Bulla, Clyde Robert. *The Moon Singer* (New York: Crowell, 1969).
Reading and interest level: elementary.

A hard-working boy goes deep into the woods at night to sing. Some villagers thought he was mad; some thought he was gifted. He could only sing alone and at night, despite the queen's interest in having him sing at court. Unusual book.

Burn, Doris. *Andrew Henry's Meadow* (New York: Coward-McCann, 1965).
Reading level: elementary.   Interest level: into intermediate.

Andrew Henry liked to build things but no one appreciated his hobby. So one day he packed up and moved to a meadow where he could build as much as he liked. Soon, six other children with unappreciated talents move there, too. After four days, their parents make them move back home, but at least they've found recognition for their creativity.

Coatsworth, Elizabeth. *Lonely Maria* (New York: Pantheon, 1960).
Reading and interest level: elementary.
Note: Black characters.

Maria was an only child who lived on an island in the West Indies. One day when she was lonely she drew pictures in the sand and created friends for herself. When a storm washed them away, she had to create some new ones. She learned that her imagination was her most reliable friend.

Fox, Paula. *How Many Miles to Babylon?* (New York: David White Co., 1967).
Reading level: intermediate. Interest level: into early teen.
Note: Black characters.

Ten-year-old James lives in Brooklyn with his three aunts because his father is gone and his mother is in a mental hospital—or so he is told. He fantasizes that his mother is an African queen and he is a prince who soon will return to his native land. One day, while acting out his fantasy, he's caught by three tough kids who kidnap him to help with their dog theft scheme. After a long and terrifying day, James gets away and returns home to meet his real mother. Excellent.

Freeman, Don. *A Rainbow of My Own* (New York: Viking, 1966).
Reading and interest level: preschool.

A boy sees a rainbow and wishes he could have one of his own. And he does—that is made by the reflection off his fish bowl.

Hall, Lynn. *Ride A Wild Dream* (Chicago: Follett, 1970).
Reading level: intermediate. Interest level: into teens.

Twelve-year old Jon wants a horse more than anything else and finally earns the money to buy one—his dream horse, a gold Palomino he names Sun God. But the horse is too rough for him; he is hurt repeatedly yet won't listen to his older brother's advice. He won't abandon his dream of the horse finally loving and obeying him. Only after a serious accident, will he admit to himself that Sun God is not his dream-come-true.

Hanson, Joan. *The Monster's Nose Was Cold* (Minneapolis: Carolrhoda Books, 1971).
Reading and interest level: preschool.

A little boy tells of a friendly, fuzzy monster who sleeps with him, tells him stories, and is his friend. Then a baby brother is born and the monster disappears as the brother becomes his friend.

Keith, Eros. *A Small Lot* (Englewood Cliffs, New Jersey: Bradbury Press, 1968).
Reading and interest level: elementary.

Bob and Jay live beside a small empty lot. Although grown-ups say it is too small to use for anything, the boys find it just the right size to be whatever they imagine it to be. Well illustrated with black and white pictures for reality and colored ones to represent the imagination.

Ness, Evaline. *Sam, Bangs, and Moonshine* (New York: Harper, 1966).
Reading and interest level: elementary.

Sam lives with her father and Bangs, her cat. She tells stories of a mermaid mother and a pet kangaroo. No one believes her tales except Thomas who is hurt in a sudden storm which forces Sam to draw a line between moonshine and reality.

Raskin, Ellen. *Franklin Stein* (New York: Atheneum, 1972).
Reading and interest level: elementary.

Franklin Stein doesn't mind that he has no friends because he is too busy making a friend, Fred, out of coat hangers, mops, and all sorts of things. He doesn't care either that most people don't appreciate Fred, because he finds that some important people do.

Sachs, Marilyn. *The Truth About Mary Rose* (Garden City, New York: Doubleday, 1973).
Reading level: late intermediate. Interest level: into early teen.
Note: Interracial marriage depicted.

Mary Rose Ramirez is proud to be named after her aunt who was a child heroine. She spends a lot of time pretending to be the other Mary Rose and looking for clues to her past. What she overhears about her aunt, who actually had been a typical, selfish child rather than heroic, makes her rethink her own identity.

Sendak, Maurice. *In The Night Kitchen* (New York: Harper, 1970).
Reading and interest level: preschool.

When Mickey can't sleep because he hears a strange noise, he has an adventure (dream) in the night kitchen.

Sendak, Maurice. *Where the Wild Things Are* (New York: Harper, 1963).
Reading and interest level: preschool.

Max is sent to bed without supper for misbehaving. He dreams of sailing to where the wild things are and being their king. But since he wants to be where someone loves him, he sails back to his own room, and supper.

Snyder, Zilpha Keatley. *The Egypt Game* (New York: Atheneum, 1968).
Reading level: intermediate. Interest level: into teen.
Note: Interracial friendship

April Hall is sent by her actress Mom to stay with her grandmother. April puts on a lot of Hollywood airs, but Melanie (a neighbor) still likes her. The two build a secret land of Egypt in an abandoned storage yard and create a private world intruded upon only by a murder in the neighborhood and an oracle's predictions.

Turkle, Brinton. *Adventures of Obadiah* (New York: Viking, 1972).
Reading and interest level: elementary.

Obadiah, a young Quaker boy, likes to tell wild tales. One day a real adventure, wilder than his imaginary ones, happens to him.

Zolotow, Charlotte. *Someday* (New York: Harper, 1965).
Reading and interest level: preschool.

A young girl fantasizes about what will happen someday, e.g., "I'm going to catch a high ball and my team will win because I did it." Fun, but realistic, nonsexist fantasies.

Zolotow, Charlotte. *The Three Funny Friends* (New York: Harper, 1961).
Reading and interest level: preschool and early elementary.

A little girl moves to a new house and doesn't know anyone. But she creates three imaginary friends to keep her company until she meets Tony, a real live friend.

Also see these titles under other headings:

Babbit, N. *The Something*. Emotions.

Bawden, Nina. *Squib*. Death and Old Age.

Bonham, Frank. *Viva Chicano*. Contemporary Problems.

Fitzhugh, Louise. *Bang, Bang, You're Dead*. Contemporary Problems.

Green, Hannah. *I Never Promised You A Rose Garden*. Mental Illness.

Hamilton, Virginia. *Zeely*. Identity and Self-Discovery.

Konigsburg, E. L. *Jennifer, Hectate, Macbeth, William McKinley, and Me, Elizabeth*. Identity and Self-Discovery.

Platt, Kin. *Chloris and the Creeps*. Mental Illness.

Sachs, Marilyn. *Marv*. Identity and Self-Discovery.

Shura, Mary F. *The Seven Stone*. Identity and Self-Discovery.

Snyder, Zilpha Keatley. *Witches of Worm*. Responsibility and Decision-Making.

Stolz, Mary. *Juan*. Family.

FRIENDS

Cohen, Miriam. *Will I Have A Friend?* (New York: Macmillan, 1967). Reading and interest level: preschool.
Note: Interracial pictures and friendships.

Jim's first day at school is lonely; there is no one for him to show his clay man to. At the end of the day, though, he makes a new friend.

Cohen, Miriam. *Best Friends* (New York: Macmillan, 1968). Reading level: preschool. Interest level: through third grade.

Jim and Paul cope with an emergency in the school incubator and become best friends. Sequel to *Will I Have A Friend?*

Delton, Judy. *Two Good Friends* (New York: Crown Publisher, 1974). Reading level: easy elementary. Interest level: preschool through third grade.

Bear and Duck are an "odd couple" of friends. One is so busy cleaning that he has no time to cook; one bakes and doesn't clean. The two friends finally share their talents and both are happy.

Desbartes, Peter. *Gabrielle and Selena* (New York: Harcourt, 1968). Reading and interest level: elementary.
Note: Interracial illustrations and friendship.

Gabrielle and Salena are best friends. When they become bored with their everyday routines, and envious of each other's lives, they decide to switch families.

Greene, Bette. *Philip Hall Likes Me. I Reckon Maybe* (New York: Dial Press, 1974).

Reading and interest level: intermediate.
Note: Black; nonsexist.

Beth reckons that Philip likes her. But competition—in school, in clubs, and in the County Fair—makes it hard for them to be friends. Especially since Philip has trouble losing to a girl.

Hoban, Russell. *Best Friends for Frances* (New York: Harper, 1969).
Reading level: Preschool. Interest level: through third grade.
Note: Nonsexist.

Frances befriends her little sister, Gloria, when Albert and the boys don't want to play with her. She teaches Albert—and herself—about friends when she has a 'best friends outing' for the girls only.

Hoffman, Phyllis. *Steffie and Me* (New York: Harper, 1970).
Reading and interest level: elementary.
Note: Interracial friendship.

A story of good friends and the things they do together.

Hutchins, Pat. *Tom and Sam* (New York: Macmillan, 1968).
Reading level: preschool. Interest level: through elementary.

Tom and Sam were best friends until Tom digs a lake in his garden. To compete, Sam builds a tower, Tom plants trees, Sam plants hedges, etc. The men are still envious of each other, though, until they exchange gifts and stop competing.

Lionni, Leo. *Tico and the Golden Wings* (New York: Pantheon, 1964).
Reading and interest level: preschool through elementary.

Tico, a bird, wishes he had golden wings. But when his wish comes true, his friends don't like him anymore. He comes up with a solution so he can use his wings to make people happy and regain his friends.

Morgan, Alison. *A Boy Called Fish* (New York: Harper, 1973).
Reading and interest level: Intermediate.

No one likes Fish—especially after he finds Floss, a stray dog others accuse of killing sheep. But through his love for Floss, Fish finally makes a friend.

Neville, Emily Cheney. *Garden of Broken Glass* (New York: Delacorte Press, 1975).
Reading and interest level: teen

Thirteen-year-old Brian's home situation is awful—he has no father, an alcoholic mother, and is one of the only Whites in his neighborhood. But when he makes friends with Fat Martha, Dwayne, and Melivita, he is able to see beyond his unhappy situation.

Nordstrom, Ursula. *Secret Language* (New York: Harper, 1960).
Reading and interest level: easy intermediate.

Victoria is lonely at boarding school until Martha befriends her and teaches her about the secret language and about friendship.

Shecter, Ben. *The Toughest and Meanest Kid on the Block* (New York: Putnam, 1973).
Reading and interest level: preschool and elementary.

Henry changes when he discovers the importance of having friends.

Steptoe, John. *Uptown* (New York: Harper, 1970).
Reading level: elementary. Interest level: into intermediate.
Note: Black.

A very sophisticated children's book dealing with two best friends in Harlem trying to decide what they want to be when they grow up. The options they see are: junkies, cops, hippies, karate experts, etc.

Stolz, Mary. *The Noonday Friends* (New York: Harper, 1965).
Reading and interest level: intermediate.

Eleven-year-old Franny is a "noonday friend" with Simone; she can rarely see her at other times because she must baby-sit her younger brother. The book includes an excellent section on a fight and reconciliation between the two friends.

Stolz, Mary. *Wonderful, Horrible Time* (New York: Harper, 1967).
Reading and interest level: intermediate.
Note: Black.

Mady and Sue Ellen are given an unexpected trip to camp which turns out to be a wonderful (for Mady) and horrible (for Sue Ellen) time.

Viorst, Judith. *Rosie and Michael* (New York: Atheneum, 1975).
Reading and interest level: preschool.

Realistic story about two friends who like each other even though it doesn't always seem so, e.g., "Just because I call her Gorilla Face doesn't mean Rosie's not my friend."

Wojciechowska, Maja. *Don't Play Dead Before You Have To* (New York: Harper, 1970).
Reading level: intermediate. Interest level: intermediate and older.

An unusual friendship develops between teen-aged Byron and 5-year old Charlie. It began as a baby-sitting job for Byron and develops into a substitute sibling relationship and then a friendship.

Also see these titles under other headings:

Anderson, Mary. *I'm Nobody. Who Are You?* Fantasy and Imagination/ Creativity.

Carlson, Natalie S. *Ann Aurelia and Dorothy.* Family.

Donovan, John. *I'll Get There. It Better Be Worth The Trip.* Love and Sexuality.

Hamilton, Virginia. *The Planet of Junior Brown.* Responsibility and Decision-Making.

Little, Jean. *Take Wing.* Physical Disabilities.

Sachs, Marilyn. *Amy Moves In.* New Experiences.

Sachs, Marilyn. *Peter and Veronica.* Prejudice.

Snyder, Zilpha Keatley. *The Egypt Game.* Fantasy and Imagination/Creativity.

Zolotow, Charlotte. *The Hating Book.* Emotions.

Zolotow, Charlotte. *The Three Funny Friends.* Fantasy and Imagination/Creativity.

Zolotow, Charlotte. *The Unfriendly Book.* Emotions.

IDENTITY AND SELF-DISCOVERY

This category includes self-acceptance, adolescence, conformity, individuality, role models, competition, and growing up.

Arthur, Ruth M. *My Daughter Nicola* (New York: Atheneum, 1965). Reading level: intermediate. Interest level: into teen.

Female roles. Nicola wants to prove to her father that she is as brave and adventurous as any boy, because in her small Swiss town, having a son is very important. She's a real "tomboy" and does win her father's respect.

Babbitt, Natalie. *Phoebe's Revolt* (New York: Farrar, Straus, and Giroux, 1968). Reading and interest level: elementary.

Females roles. Phoebe lived at the turn of the century but her problem is a contemporary one—she dislikes the curls, bows, frills, and lace she's expected to wear. She says that she'd rather wear her father's clothes, but that doesn't work out either. Her father solves the problem rationally and happily.

Bates, H. E. "The Small Portion," in Charlotte Zolotow, *An Overpraised Season* (New York: Harper, 1973). Short Story. Reading level: intermediate. Interest level: into teen.

The title of this story refers to Josephine's mother's view of life which is adopted by Josephine until a small incident with someone else allows her to see the world differently.

Blume, Judy. *And Then Again, Maybe I Won't* (Scarsdale, New York: Bradbury Press, 1971). Reading level: late intermediate. Interest level: early teen.

Adolescence. Tony is thirteen years old and gets stomach aches from all the worrying he has to do. He's concerned about wet dreams, erections, his friends' pickpocketing, the changes in his family now that they are wealthy, and the changes in his brother.

Blume, Judy. *Are You There, God, It's Me Margaret* (Scarsdale, New York: Bradbury Press, 1970).
Reading level: late intermediate. Interest level: early teen.
Note: Parents have an interreligious marriage.

Adolescence. Humorous story, popular with young women, about twelve-year-old Margaret who pleads to God to make her "normal" by giving her breasts and having her menstruate. She is also concerned about choosing a religion since one of her parents is Christian and one Jewish.

Blume, Judy. *Freckle Juice* (New York: Four Winds Press, 1971).
Reading and interest level: elementary.

Andrew will do anything to have freckles—even buy Sharon's secret formula.

Campbell, Hope. *Why Not Join the Giraffes?* (New York: Norton, 1968).
Reading level: intermediate. Interest level: into teen.

Conformity. Suzie Henderson wanted to have a family life similar to that of her friends instead of the unusual one she and her artist-parents and musician-brother lead. But she learns that "when you're really yourself, you can be free *for* other people, not just free *from* them." She tries out a number of lifestyles before choosing her very own.

Cleaver, Vera and Bill. *Lady Ellen Grae* (Philadelphia: Lippincott, 1968).
Reading and interest level: intermediate.

Female roles. Ellen Grae's divorced parents decide she should give up her tomboy ways and become a lady, so they send her to Seattle to live with her ladylike Aunt Eleanor and Cousin Laura. But not for long!

Cone, Molly. *Simon* (Boston: Houghton-Mifflin, 1970).
Reading level: intermediate. Interest level: through teen.

Adolescence. Simon decides to spend the summer escaping from his parents' expectations and rules, so he spends each day in an abandoned old car he calls "the cave." Important people in his life are Julia, a retarded neighbor, and an old blind man who accidentally discovers "the cave."

Confort, Ellen. *Impossible, Possum* (Boston: Little, Brown, & Co., 1971).
Reading level: elementary. Interest level: preschool, too.

Randolph does not hang by his tail like other possums. He would rather sleep in the leaves. But one winter his sister tricks him into thinking he *can* hang upside down—and she's right.

Cretan, Gladys. *All Except Sammy* (Boston: Little, Brown, and Co., 1966).
Reading and interest level: elementary.

Individuality. Everyone in Sammy's family is musical except for Sammy. One day he finds that he has another talent—drawing—and then doesn't feel left out of his artistic family.

DePoix, Carol. *Jo, Flo, and Yolanda* (Chapel Hill, North Carolina: Lollipop Power, Inc., 1973).
Reading and interest level: elementary.

The three girls are triplets and share almost everything, but still they find they are different from each other and from everyone else.

Dr. Seuss on the Loose: The Sneetches, The Zax, Green Eggs and Ham. 40 minutes, Color, BFA Educational Media, Film.
Reading and interest level: preschool and elementary.

The first of these three films deals with conformity, the second with change, and the third with appearance vs. reality.

Donovan, John. *Remove Protective Coating . . . A Little At A Time* (New York: Harper, 1973).
Reading and interest level: teen.

Harry does not come from a poor or broken home; rather, his parents were childhood sweethearts now grown up, eighteen years older than their son, and wealthy. They are interested in him and his problems, but Toots (Mom) has an identity crisis and Bud (Dad) reacts to it, so Harry is very lonely. Good portrayal of his fourteenth summer when he is infatuated with a set of twins at camp. Also of his friendship with an eccentric old lady.

Duvoisin, Roger. *What Is Right for Tulip* (New York: Knopf, 1969).
Reading and interest level: preschool and early elementary.

What is right for Tulip, a polar bear, may not be right for everyone else. Bathing, eating, sleeping, etc. are touched upon.

Fitzhugh, Louise. *Harriet the Spy* (New York: Harper, 1964).
Reading and interest level: intermediate.

Nonconformity. Wonderful story of Harriet who wants to be a spy, carries a notebook with her at all times, and learns as much as possible. Of course, this is not 'suitable' for a girl, but that doesn't stop Harriet.

Free to Be . . . You and Me. 42 minutes, Color, McGraw-Hill, Film.
Reading and interest level: elementary on up.

Sex roles. Marlo Thomas, Alan Alda et al. star in this adaptation of the book which deals with children and people being what they choose to be, unbound by sex stereotyping.

George, Jean C. *Julie of the Wolves* (New York: Harper, 1972).
Reading and interest level: intermediate.

Miyax (alias Julie) rebels against her home situation and runs away. A pack of wolves becomes her family when she gets lost.

George, Jean C. *The Summer of the Falcon* (New York: Crowell, 1962).
Reading level: intermediate. Interest level: into early teens.

June (13) learns about responsibility and self-respect when training her own falcon.

Gilbert, Nan. *Champions Don't Cry* (New York: Harper, 1960).
Reading and interest level: intermediate.

Sally (13) is determined to be a tennis champion but doesn't like to discipline herself. Her determination to succeed helps her through many trying matches until she does become "almost-a-champion."

Goffstein, M. B. *Two Piano Tuners* (New York: Farrar, Straus and Giroux, 1970).
Reading and interest level: elementary.

Debbie's grandfather is a piano tuner and she wants to be one, too. But he wants her to be a pianist instead.

Hamilton, Virginia. *Zeely* (New York: MacMillan, 1967).
Reading and interest level: intermediate.
Note: Black.

During a summer on her uncle's farm, Elizabeth discovers that who she is depends on what's inside of her, not on what she's called or does. Zeely—the mysterious woman who seems like an African queen to Elizabeth, helps her to understand this.

Hazen, Nancy. *Grownups Cry Too* (Chapel Hill, North Carolina: Lollipop Press, 1973).
Reading level: elementary. Interest level: preschool and elementary.

Stanley Cramer knows that crying is to let feelings out—happy ones, sad ones, hurt ones, angry ones, and scared ones.

Henry—Boy of the Barrio. 30 minutes, Black/White, Atlantic Prod., Film.
Level: intermediate through teen.

Documentary of a Chicano's search for identity. He has an Indian mother, a Mexican heritage, and lives in Anglo society.

Hentoff, Nat. *I'm Really Dragged, But Nothing Gets Me Down* (New York: Simon and Schuster, 1968).
Reading and interest level: teen.

Frank novel about Jeremy's decision about the draft, personal freedom, cowardice, family, and himself.

Hentoff, Nat. *Jazz Country* (New York: Harper, 1965).
Reading and interest level: teen.

Tom, a White high school senior, tries to cross the color line to be a jazz musician but finds racism. He has to decide about his career as a musician and about himself.

Katz, Bobbi. *The Manifesto and Me—Meg* (New York: Franklin Watts, 1974).
Reading level: intermediate. Interest level: into early teen.

Meg decides that kids should have consciousness-raising groups so that they won't need them when they grow up. She starts one (that is hilarious) and learns a lot about women's liberation and people.

Keats, Ezra Jack. *Whistle for Willie* (New York: Viking, 1964).
Reading and interest level: preschool.

Peter wants very badly to be able to whistle for Willie, his dog. He tries and tries and practices until he finally can do it.

Kerr, M. E. *The Son of Someone Famous* (New York: Harper, 1974).
Reading and interest level: teen.

Sixteen-year-old Adam tries to escape from being only the son of a famous father by living with his grandfather and using his name. But his grandfather's name has a reputation, too. In a hilarious year, he learns what his past does and does not have to mean.

Klein, Norma. *It's Not What You Expect* (New York: Pantheon, 1973).
Reading and interest level: teen.

Carla and Oliver, fourteen-year-old twins, rearrange their summer so that they can be with their mom who is temporarily separated from their dad. While they run a summer-only French restaurant, the two learn about people—a neighbor who returns from a mental hospital, their brother's girlfriend who has an abortion, and themselves. Excellent. Told from Carla's point of view.

Konigsburg, E. L. *Jennifer, Hectate, Macbeth, William McKinley, and Me, Elizabeth* (New York: Atheneum, 1967.)
Reading and interest level: intermediate.

When Elizabeth meets Jennifer, who claims to be a witch, she isn't lonely anymore. Instead, she's busy trying to become a witch, too. Until one day when the two friends stop pretending and begin to enjoy what and whom they really are.

Kraus, Robert. *Leo the Late Bloomer* (New York: Windmill, 1971).
Reading and interest level: preschool and early elementary.

Leo the tiger cub seems hopelessly behind his animal friends. But one day he utters his first words: "I made it!"

Lessing, Doris, "Flight," in Charlotte Zolotow, *An Overpraised Season* (New York: Harper, 1973), Short story.
Reading and interest level: teen.

Alice's grandfather lets loose one of his doves, and lets Alice go, too. A story about the struggle of the generations and what it means to leave home.

Lexau, Joan M. *Benjie on His Own* (New York: Dial Press, 1970).
Reading and interest level: elementary.
Note: Black characters.

Shyness. Benjie is old enough to go to school, but his grandmother always walks him there and back. When she becomes ill, he must overcome his shyness and handle the crisis himself with the help of good neighbors.

Marshall, James. "Someone Is Talking About Hortense" and "Snake," in his *Four Little Troubles* (New York: Houghton-Mifflin, 1975), Short stories.
Reading and interest level: preschool.

The first story shows Hortense worrying about being a toadstool in the school play; then she discovers that even with a minor role, she is important. The second story is about Snake who worries about conforming to everyone else.

Miss Esta Maude's Secret. 10 minutes, Color, McGraw-Hill, Film.
Level: elementary through intermediate.

Miss Esta Maude, a school teacher, reveals her secret passion for fancy clothes and cars, only late at night.

Morey, Walt. *Deep Trouble* (New York: Dutton, 1971).
Reading level: late intermediate. Interest level: through teen.

Joey has to support his family after his Dad dies and decides to do so by becoming a diver like his Dad was. Fresh out of high school, he learns about work, friends, loyalty, and himself.

Myers, Bernice. *Not This Bear* (New York: Scholastic, 1967).
Reading and interest level: elementary.

Herman, all dressed up in a long, warm, furry coat and hat, looks just like a bear. And it takes a lot of work on his part to convince a family of bears that he really is a boy.

Perl, Lila. *Me and Fat Glenda* (New York: Seabury Press, 1972).
Reading and interest level: intermediate.

Nonconformity. Sara's family is unusual—both her parents are artists, eat special diets, sleep on the floor, etc. When they move to conservative Havenhurst, they have some problems. Not as many, though, as Fat Glenda who lives next door. Sara and Glenda have an unusual and good friendship.

Randall, Florence Engel, *The Almost Year* (New York: Atheneum, 1971).
Reading and interest level: teen.
Note: Interracial.

Insightful portrayal of a Black adolescent girl's problems living in a White family's house. She feels like an unloved witch and all the resentment and hate in the house becomes a Poltergeist, a mystery to them all.

Rinkoff, Barbara. *I Need Some Time* (New York: Seabury Press, 1970).
Reading level: intermediate. Interest level: through early teens.

Scott (16) disagrees with his businessman father who wants him to start working toward a career. All Scott wants is to play his guitar. Once he is accepted by a band, he is confronted with Greenwich Village, a fellow musician dying of an overdose, and two types of women. At the end of the book, Scott returns home to try to reconcile with his parents and to think things out.

Rodgers, Mary. *Freaky Friday* (New York: Harper, 1972).
Reading and interest level: intermediate.

Very funny but insightful book about Annabel who wakes up one morning in her mother's body and *is* her mother for a long, hectic day before they switch places and bodies again.

Rookie of the Year. 47 minutes, Color, Time/Life Multimedia, Film.
Level: intermediate.
Note: Nonsexist.

Young female rookie is treated hostilely by the boy players, including her brother who is on the team. Then her girlfriends, too, begin to treat her unfairly. But she doesn't give up.

Rudolph, Marguerita. *The Sneaky Machine* (New York: McGraw-Hill, 1974).
Reading level: elementary. Interest level: some intermediate.
Note: Nonsexist.

Henry liked machines; his favorite was Grandmother's vacuum until his friends laughed at him for doing "Mommy's work." After awhile, they envy him for being able to run the sneaky machine.

Sachs, Marilyn. *Marv* (Garden City, New York: Doubleday, 1970).
Reading and interest level: intermediate.

Creative Marv loves to build things and often does. But only one teacher has ever admired his work; everyone else considers him a failure. He wants especially to impress his older sister Frances, but never can. He remains, however, optimistic.

Saroyan, William. "Seventeen," from *Points of Departure* (New York: Dell, 1967), Short story.
Reading and interest level: teen.

Sex roles. Boy learns that the masculine role he's adopted isn't working out.

Shotwell, Louisa R. *Magdalena* (New York: Viking, 1971).
Reading and interest level: intermediate.

Note: Latino characters.

Conformity. Magdalena was the only girl in her class to have long braids; her Puerto Rican grandmother insists upon them. Magdalena cuts them off anyway and that is the start of new adventures and a new self-concept.

Shura, Mary Francis. *The Seven Stone* (New York: Holiday House, 1972).
Reading and interest level: intermediate.

Maggie's miserable day at school is worse than ever when she is assigned to show Tibbie, the new girl, around. No one likes Tibbie because she is a "hippie" and claims to be a witch. But Maggie and Tibbie become good friends despite the other kids.

Townsend, John Rowe. *Good Night, Prof, Dear* (Philadelphia: Lippincott, 1971).
Reading and interest level: teen.

Graham refuses to go on a vacation with his middle class parents. Thus begins a long trip, many adventures, and self-discovery.

Uchida, Yoshiko. *In Between Miya* (New York: Scribner's, 1967).
Reading and interest level: intermediate.
Note: Asian-American characters.

Miya doesn't like being twelve years old, the in-between child, living a simple peasant life. But a trip to a wealthy Uncle's in Tokyo and the events that follow her trip, make her rethink her priorities.

Walker, Mary Alexander. *Year of the Cafeteria* (Indianapolis: Bobbs-Merrill, 1971).
Reading and interest level: teen.
Note: Black characters.

Azure moves from Breaux Bridge, Louisiana to Chicago in order to be with her grandmother and to help her run the school cafeteria. It is a difficult transition, but Azure learns a lot and realizes it when her grandmother dies.

Walter, Mildred Pitts. *Little of Watts: A Birthday Discovery* (Los Angeles: Ward Ritchie Press, 1969).
Reading and interest level: intermediate.
Note: Black characters.

Lillie (11) is looking forward to her birthday but everything possible goes wrong—she ruins her sweater and her Mother won't take her along to the Rich Lady's house where she works. And then out of fear of cats, she loses her mother's employer's cat. Strong family support is depicted.

Wersba, Barbara. *The Dream Watcher* (New York: Atheneum, 1973).
Reading Level: intermediate. Interest level: into teen.

Albert Scully, an adolescent misfit, becomes friends with Mrs.

Woodfin, an elderly eccentric who claims to have been a star. Their friendship, her death, and his resultant discoveries teaches Albert a lot about himself.

Wojciechowska, Maja. *The Shadow of the Bull* (New York: Atheneum, 1964).
Reading and interest level: intermediate to early teen.

Manolo has to struggle to maintain his own identity; everyone assumes he will become a matador like his father. It is a difficult decision to become a doctor instead.

Women in Careers. 15 minutes, Color, Doubleday Multimedia, Film.
Level: teen.

The changing values for women and their work.

Women of the Toubou. 25 minutes, Color, Phoenix, Film.
Level: teen.

The Toubous in the Sahara have equality for women. Good as a discussion starter.

Zolotow, Charlotte. *William's Doll* (New York: Harper, 1972).
Reading level: preschool. Interest level: into elementary.
Note: Nonsexist.

Though his brother said he was a creep, the neighbors called him a sissy, and his father kept bringing him other toys, William wanted a doll. Finally, his grandmother brings him one.

Also see these titles under other headings:

Beckett, Hilary. *My Brother Angel.* Responsibility and Decision-Making.
Bonham, Frank. *Viva Chicano.* Contemporary Problems.
Craig, Margaret Maze. *It Could Happen to Anyone.* Love and Sexuality.
Fitzhugh, Louise. *Nobody's Family Is Going To Change.* Family.
Heide, Florence Perry. *The Key.* Family.
Hinton, S. E. *The Outsiders.* Contemporary Problems.
Williams, Jay. *The Question Box.* Emotions.

LOVE AND SEXUALITY

Brown, Rita Mae. *Rubyfruit Jungle* (Plainfield, Vermont: Daughters, Inc., 1973).
Reading and interest level: mature teen.
Note: Lesbianism.

This autobiographical novel of a young girl first discovering sexuality and developing a lesbian awareness in high school is the only book of its kind. It is well written and fascinating with most of the sex scenes only partially explicit.

Craig, Margaret Maze. *It Could Happen to Anyone* (New York: Crowell, 1961).
Reading and interest level: teen.

Jean's senior year in high school is exciting as she and Andy grow to love each other and go steady. But a classmate's pregnancy makes Jean re-examine her own attitudes and feelings on love and sex.

Hall, Lynn. *Sticks and Stones* (Chicago: Follett, 1972).
Reading and interest level: teen.
Note: Homosexuality.

Excellent story of Tom who is new to the small town and becomes friends with Ward, a suspected homosexual. Rumors about Tom begin and he loses friends. Although the stories are unfounded, they nearly destroy Tom who must sort out for himself the meaning of sexuality.

Holland, Isabelle. *The Man Without a Face* (Philadelphia: Lippincott, 1972).
Reading and interest level: teen.
Note: Homosexuality.

When Charles decides he needs tutoring for an entrance exam, he approaches Justin MacLeod, the strange solitary man who had half his face burnt away in an accident. Surprisingly, they become friends, with Justin alternately playing surrogate father, teacher, and friend. One night Charles realizes that he wants to touch Justin and becomes fearful of homosexuality. Justin admits that he is a homosexual but that that has nothing to do with Charles' affection for him. Excellently handled.

Donovan, John. *I'll Get There. It Better Be Worth The Trip* (New York: Harper, 1969).
Reading and interest level: teen.
Note: Homosexuality.

Danny (13) and his dog are uprooted when his grandmother dies. He goes to live with his divorced mother whom he barely knows. His new friend, Altschuler, has similar problems at home. Their close friendship heightens to a brief homosexual moment, which they discuss and accept. They remain platonic friends.

Kerr, M. E. *If I Love You, Am I Trapped Forever?* (New York: Harper, 1973).
Reading and interest level: teen.

Alan Bennett's senior year in high school is nearly ruined by Duncan Stein who, surprisingly, steals his girlfriend and captivates the school. Alan has to deal with many kinds of love—going steady, pity/love for a father who abandoned him, and the startling love affair between Mrs. Stein and the football coach.

Velveteen Rabbit. 19 minutes, Color, LSB Productions, Film.
Level: elementary through intermediate.

The velveteen rabbit learns from another toy, the Skin Horse, that one seems beautiful only when one is loved. Based on a children's story by Margery Williams.

West, Jessamyn. "Crimson Ramblers of the World, Farewell," in Charlotte Zolotow, *An Overpraised Season* (New York: Harper, 1973). Short story.
Reading level: intermediate. Interest level: into teen.

Elizabeth (13) tries to please her Dad, but it is impossible. Even her beloved mother misunderstands her. Her great dream—a ride on Crimson Rambler's motorcycle—is ruined by a comment by her mother which causes her to feel that sexual curiosity is perverse and that affection from another source must be rebuffed.

Winthrop, Elizabeth. *A Little Demonstration of Affection* (New York: Harper, 1975).
Reading and interest level: early teen.
Note: Incest.

Excellent novel about Jenny's relationship with her older brother within the context of their unaffectionate family. A long hug causes Jenny pleasure, worry, and jealousy until she can learn to accept it as it was meant. Good section on the death of Charley's dog, also.

Also see under other headings:

Blume, Judy. *Are You There, God, It's Me Margaret.* Identity and Self-Discovery.
Blume, Judy. *And Then Again, Maybe I Won't.* Identity and Self-Discovery.

MENTAL ILLNESS/MENTAL HEALTH

Burch, Robert. *Simon and the Game of Chance* (New York: Viking, 1970).
Reading and interest level: intermediate.

Simon's big family was happy until his Mom had to be institutionalized. Then just when he was getting used to Clarissa, the eldest, always being there, she announces that she is getting married. Simon resents it. When her fiance dies suddenly the day of the wedding, Simon feels guilty and responsible. Excellent.

Green, Hannah. *I Never Promised You A Rose Garden* (New York: NAL, 1964).
Reading and interest level: mature teen.

Psychotic sixteen-year-old Deborah lives in an imaginary kingdom of Yr to avoid reality. She is hospitalized for three years during which each world punishes her for her involvement in the other. Powerful.

Platt, Kin. *The Boy Who Could Make Himself Disappear* (Philadelphia: Chilton, 1968).
Reading and interest level: teen.

Roger can't speak "R"s, both because his tongue was burned as a baby and because of the unloving parents he had to contend with. A good story of a boy on the edge of a schizoid withdrawal. At the end, he does withdraw ("Makes himself disappear") and only returns because of the sensitivity of two friends.

Platt, Kin. *Chloris and the Creeps* (Philadelphia: Chilton, 1975).
Reading and interest level: intermediate.
Note: Interracial marriage depicted.

Eight-year-old Jenny tells this story of her sister Chloris' hostile reactions to the "creeps" their divorced mother dates. Chloris is especially negative about Fidel, the man who becomes their new father. Chloris is obsessed with unrealistic fantasies about their natural father and tries to make Fidel leave. The ending may be overdone—she sets fire to Fidel's studio, sees a psychiatrist, and recovers—but parts are excellent.

Rubin, Theodore Isaac. *Jordi* (New York: Macmillan, 1960).
Reading and interest level: teen.

Short story based on case studies of a severely disturbed boy.

Rubin, Theodore Isaac. *Lisa and David* (New York: Macmillan, 1961).
Reading and interest level: mature teen.

Two mentally ill adolescents move toward health with the help of each other. This is really a love story, but between two disturbed people. A combination of novel and case study.

Sherbourne, Zoa. *Stranger in the House* (New York: William Morrow, 1963).
Reading and interest level: teen.

When Kathleen's mother returns from a nine year stay in a mental hospital, she is a stranger. This book is a popular one about accepting new roles.

Silent Snow, Secret Snow. 17 minutes, Black/White, Brandon films, Film.
Level: Mature teens.

Based on Conrad Aiken's short story of a boy who withdraws into a land of fantasy and eventual schizophrenia.

Also see these titles under other headings:

Hollard, Isabelle. *Amanda's Choice.* Responsibility and Decision-Making.

Kesey, Ken. *One Flew Over the Cuckoo's Nest.* Confinement.
Wojciechowska, Maja. *Don't Play Dead Before You Have To.* Friends.

NEW EXPERIENCES

This category includes starting school, going to camp and moving.

Brown, Myra. *Pip Moves Away* (San Carlos, California: Golden Gate Junior Books, 1967).
Reading and interest level: preschool and elementary.

Pip Potter and his family move across town to a new house—and new friends.

Caudill, Rebecca. *Pocketful of Cricket* (New York: Holt, 1964).
Reading and interest level: elementary.

Jay is a young farm boy who can't resist taking his cricket to school with him on his first day. The teacher lets Jay share his friend with the rest of the class.

Cleary, Beverly. *Ramona the Pest* (New York: William Morrow, 1968).
Reading and interest level: elementary.

Ramona's sister thinks she's a pest and so do the neighbors. But it's not until she starts kindergarten that she really makes trouble—for herself!

Cohen, Miriam. *The New Teacher* (New York: Macmillan, 1972).
Reading and interest level: elementary.

Despite their fears, the first graders find that the new teacher is fun. The third book about Jim and his classmates.

Coles, Robert. *Dead End School* (Boston: Little, Brown and Co., 1968).
Reading and interest level: intermediate.
Note: Black.

When Jim's family moves, he has to go to a new school. Jim has trouble adjusting to it, and as soon as he does, he's moved again—to a White school where everything's different.

Marshall, James. "Eugene," in his *Four Little Troubles* (Boston: Houghton-Mifflin, 1975).
Level: preschool.

Beginning school is frightening for Eugene.

Rogers, Fred. *Mr. Rogers Talks About* . . . (New York: Platt and Munk, 1974).
Level: preschool.

The introduction to this realistic book states that its purpose is to lead to open communication about important new experiences. Included are: going to the doctor, going to school, the new baby, haircuts, moving, and fighting. Illustrated with nonsexist, interracial photographs. Based on the TV shows.

Sachs, Marilyn. *Amy Moves In* (New York: Doubleday, 1964).
Reading and interest level: intermediate.

Amy moves, makes friends, loses some, and stands up for someone shyer than herself. One of the series about Amy and Laura.

Sachs, Marilyn. *Laura's Luck* (New York: Doubleday, 1971).
Reading and interest level: intermediate.

In this part of the series, Amy and Laura go to camp because their Mom's hospitalized. Amy wants to go, likes sports, and is popular. Laura is a bookworm and dreads camp. Despite everything, Laura makes a friend and has not too bad a time.

Talbot, Toby. *I Am Maria* (New York: Cowles Book Co., 1969).
Reading and interest level: elementary.
Note: Latino characters.

Maria, 9, has just moved to New York and is scared both of the city and of English which is difficult and new for her. But when she's needed by the crippled lady in the building, she ventures her first English words.

Also see these titles under other headings:

Baum, Betty. *Patricia Crosses Town.* Prejudice.
Cleaver, Vera and Bill. *Mimosa Tree.* Responsibility and Decision-Making.
Justus, May. *New Boy in School.* Prejudice.
Little, Jean. *From Anna.* Physical Disabilities.
Little, Jean. *Mine for Keeps.* Physical Disabilities.
Nordstrom, Ursula. *Secret Language.* Friends.
Stolz, Mary. *Wonderful, Horrible Time.* Friends.

PHYSICAL DISABILITIES

This section includes language and hearing problems, obesity, diseases, mental retardation, eyesight problems, and other disabilities.

Byars, Betsy. *After the Goat Man* (New York: Viking, 1974).
Reading and interest level: intermediate.

Obesity. Howard V. Coleman is fat and unhappy with both his diet and himself. Playing Monopoly with his friends Ada and Figgy helps some, but going after the goat man really made him forget his problems. Very funny book.

Byars, Betsy. *Summer of the Swans* (New York: Viking, 1970).
Reading and interest level: intermediate.

Retardation. Fourteen year old Sara is having a difficult summer. But when her mentally retarded brother disappears, nothing else matters to her until he is found.

Cleaver, Vera and Bill. *Me Too* (Philadelphia: Lippincott, 1973).

Reading level: intermediate. Interest level: into teens.

Retardation. Lydia has to care for Lorna, her twelve-year-old retarded twin sister when her parents separate. She tries to teach Lorna, and to fight neighborhood prejudice against her sister.

Corbin, William. *The Day Willie Wasn't* (New York: Coward McCann, 1971).
Reading and interest level: elementary.

Obesity. Willie was very fat. Determined to lose weight, he became so skinny that he disappeared.

Cunningham, Julia. *Burnish Me Bright* (New York: Pantheon Books, 1970), and *Far In The Day* (New York: Pantheon Books, 1972).

Mute. Two stories about Auguste, a mute boy who learns to express himself through mime. His adventures are a bit unrealistic, but the prejudices against him because of his muteness, and the magic of mime are well presented.

DuBois, William P. *Porko von Popbutton* (New York: Harper, 1968).
Reading and interest level: intermediate.

Obesity. A very funny novel about Porko—whose real name is Pat. He is 13-years-old and 274 pounds when he's sent off to boarding school. The climax of the comedy is a Canada/U.S. hockey match in which Porko unexpectedly gets to play. Once hockey wins his heart and soul, he loses weight.

Friis-Baastad, Babbis. *Don't Take Teddy* (New York: Scribner's, 1967).
Reading and interest level: intermediate.

Retardation. Mikkel tries to take full responsibility for his retarded brother, Teddy, but learns about his limitations, Teddy's problems, and his family's solution when the two boys run away.

Greenburg, Joanne. *In This Sign* (New York: Holt, 1972).
Reading and interest level: teen.

Deaf. Moving novel of two deaf young people who fall in love and leave the institution in which they've lived. Their adjustments and fears, and the adjustments of their children (hearing) are sympathetically and realistically drawn.

Griese, Arnold A. *At The Mouth of the Luckiest River* (New York: Thomas Y. Crowell Co., 1969).
Reading and interest level: intermediate.
Note: Native American characters.

Lame. Tatlek, an Athabascan Indian boy with a lame foot shows enough courage to confront his tribe's most powerful member—the medicine man—about his lies. Tatlek prevents a battle between the Indians and their neighbors, the Eskimos.

Kerr, M. E. *Dinky Hocker Shoots Smack* (New York: Harper and Row, 1972).

Reading level: late intermediate. Interest level: into teens.

Obesity. She doesn't really shoot smack, she just paints that expression on streets and walls to embarrass her mother who is getting an award for helping drug addicts. Her mother is a "good citizen" who has time to help lots of groups, but has no understanding of her fat daughter. Dinky's ploy works—her parents take her on a trip with them to try to resolve some of their conflicts.

Konigsburg, A. L. "Camp Fat," in her *Altogether One At A Time* (New York: Atheneum, 1971).
Reading and interest level: intermediate.

Obesity. Clara doesn't like Camp ToKeRoNo ("Camp Fat") and doesn't feel it is any help to her at all until she meets the mysterious Miss Natasha who teaches her something about being fat.

Konigsburg, A. L. "Inviting Jason," in *Ibid.*
Reading and interest level: intermediate.

Dyslexia. Stanley didn't want to invite Jason to his birthday party because Jason was a drip and had dyslexia, besides. But his mother insists he invite Jason and everything turns out quite unexpectedly for Stanley.

Little, Jean. *From Anna* (New York: Harper and Row, 1972).
Reading and interest level: intermediate.

Eyesight. In 1933, Anna and her family leave Germany to come to America. Everyone seems to adjust quickly except awkward Anna who was always slow and clumsy. But when Dr. Schumacher discovers that Anna needs glasses and special classes, she discovers new abilities in herself and has to teach them to her family.

Little, Jean. *Mine for Keeps* (Boston: Little, Brown and Co., 1962).
Reading and interest level: intermediate.

Cerebral Palsy. Sally has lived in a residential school for handicapped children for five years because she has cerebral palsy. When she's moved back home, she's excited but also scared—and the adjustment is difficult.

Little, Jean. *Take Wing* (Boston: Little, Brown and Co., 1968).
Reading and interest level: intermediate.

Retardation. Laurie is the only one in her family to fully realize that James is "different": he is mentally retarded. She helps her parents to find out what the problem is and to do something to help him. Meanwhile, relieved of some of the responsibility for James, she is able to develop a friendship with Elspeth, her cousin.

Norris, Gunilla B. *Top Step* (New York: Atheneum, 1970).
Reading and interest level: intermediate.

Asthma. Mikkel is asthmatic and finds that it causes him more than physical pain. His father expects him to be like other normal boys and that is too much to expect; his mother is overprotective and expects too little. Out of desperation, he decides to try the dangerous ice-jumping to prove himself to his father.

Platt, Kin. *Hey, Dummy!* (Philadelphia: Chilton Book Co., 1971).
Reading level: late intermediate. Interest level: into teen.

Retardation. Neil befriends Alan, a retarded boy nicknamed "the dummy" and becomes involved with his troubled and poor family life, his troubles at school, and finally a murder blamed unjustly on Alan. Before each chapter written from Neil's point of view is a page written from Alan's which helps the reader to see as he does. This is a difficult book with an unrealistic ending which may not be suitable for use—Neil decides to "turn off" and to become a dummy, too. Other parts of the book, however, are excellent.

Rich, Louise Dickinson. *Three of a Kind* (New York: Franklin Watts, Inc., 1970).
Reading and interest level: intermediate.

Autistic. Sally is a ward of the state living on an island with the Coopers. Their grandson, Benjie, comes to stay with them. She resents his coming until she realizes that because he is autistic, he needs her love. She also discovers how important it is to be needed.

Raskin, Ellen. *Spectacles* (New York: Atheneum, 1968).
Reading and interest level: elementary.

Eyesight. Excellent book about Iris who sees a dragon (instead of an aunt) and all kinds of other things which other people don't see. Then her mother takes her to a blue elephant (an optometrist) who gives her glasses, so she has the option of seeing things in two different ways. Great illustrations.

Robinson, Veronica. *David in Silence* (Philadelphia: Lippincott, 1965).
Reading and interest level: intermediate.

Deaf. David, who is deaf, adjusts to a new town and the neighbors learn to adjust to him. His older brother, Eric, and a neighbor, Michael, are the mouthpieces for the author to tell the reader some facts about deafness. But the emotional trauma of being deaf comes across best from David himself.

Slote, Alfred. *Hang Tough, Paul Mather* (Philadelphia: Lippincott, 1973).
Reading and interest level: intermediate.

Leukemia. An unusual sports story. Paul is a good ballplayer but has leukemia. Despite his parents' overprotection, he plays ball once too often and ends up in a hospital. His doctor, Tom, a sympathetic sports enthusiast, and the guys on the team help him to adjust to his bedridden state.

Southall, Ivan. *Let the Balloon Go* (New York: St. Martins Press, 1968).
Reading and interest level: intermediate.

Cerebral Palsy. John Sumner is a twelve-year-old boy like all others except that he has a mild case of cerebral palsy which causes spasms. Being spastic, however, is not as much of a problem for John as the reactions of his peers and the overprotection of his mother. The Australian author uses a lot of Briticisms.

Weik, Mary Hays. *Jazz Man* (New York: Atheneum, 1967).
Reading level: elementary. Interest level: into intermediate.
Note: Black family.

Clubfoot. Zeke and his parents live in Harlem and the happiest part of their day is listening to the jazz man play across the alley. But Zeke's Mom leaves them and soon his Dad stops coming home, too. And Zeke doesn't like leaving the house because of his clubfoot. Even the jazz man stops playing. Finally his parents both return. Perhaps the ending is too good to be true, but the book is a beautiful account of the effects of music on people.

Wojciechowska, Maja. *Single Light* (New York: Harper, 1968).
Reading and interest level: intermediate.

Deaf mute. The girl called "the dummy" cannot hear or talk and she is the village scapegoat. But she can understand and can love—she finds a valuable art piece that she loves. When an art collector comes to buy it, the girl is crushed. Both the artist and the priest realize her value to the village.

See also these titles under other headings:

Cleaver, Vera and Bill. *Mimosa Tree.* Responsibility and Decision-Making.
Heide, Florence Perry. *The Key.* Family.
Hodges, Elizabeth. *Free As A Frog.* Emotions.
Taylor, Theodore. *The Cay.* Emotions.

PREJUDICE

This category includes racism, integration, anti-semitism, and prejudice based on superstition.

Ball, Dorothy Whitney. *Don't Drive Up A Dirt Road* (New York: Lion Press, 1970).
Reading and interest level: intermediate.

Racism. Dicky Boy and his family move north after a series of lynchings and other violent episodes down south. They find that racism is rampant in the north, too, but in different formats.

Baum, Betty. *Patricia Crosses Town* (New York: Knopf, 1965).
Reading and interest level: intermediate.
Note: Term "Negro" is used.

Integration. Pat Marley, a Black fifth grader is one of a few Blacks to be bussed to a White school. She is not a crusader, but a normal twelve-year-old girl with real fears about integration. Sarah and Deborah, two White girls, have problems with integration, too, as Debby chooses to be Pat's friend and Sarah is allowed to see her only at school.

Blue, Rose. *The Preacher's Kid* (New York: Franklin Watts, Inc., 1975). Reading and interest level: intermediate.

Integration. Excellent book with no sugary interracial message but difficult decision making on everyone's part. Linda's father, a minister, supports bussing and his congregation asks him to leave. Linda's friends turn against her when she decides to attend the integrated school. She finds that she must re-examine her own friendships and prejudices.

Burch, Robert. *Queenie Peavy* (New York: Viking Press, 1966). Reading and interest level: intermediate.

Prejudice. Queenie is a thirteen-year-old girl in Georgia during the Depression. She's defiant, mean, and angry. Her father's in prison and no one will let her forget it.

Everyday People. Eight 30 minute segments, Color, PBS, Films. Level: preschool and elementary.

Each episode deals with another human difference and prejudices about them. Included are: size, race, age, sex, handicap, religion, occupational, and cultural prejudices.

Eye of the Storm. 25 minutes, Color, Xerox, Film. Level: intermediate.

Third graders learn about prejudice when a creative teacher allows discrimination to occur on the basis of eye color.

Grund, Josef Carl. *You Have A Friend Pietro* (Boston: Little, 1966). Reading and interest level: intermediate.

Vendetta. Pietro is the victim of Corsica's superstitions about the evil eye and its tradition of the vendetta or blood revenge. An old stonecutter helps the boys of the village to understand that the evil eye is only fear in the eyes of the one who is tormented, and that Pietro is only a scapegoat for the town.

Hamilton, Virginia. *M. C. Higgins, the Great* (New York: Macmillan, 1974). Reading and interest level: teen. Note: Black characters.

MC and his family are fearful of the Kilbourns who live in the next hill because they have six fingers on each hand and must therefore be "witchy." MC learns that they aren't, as he learns about himself, when two strangers come to their hill.

Ik, Kim Yong. *Blue in the Seed* (Boston: Little, Brown & Co., 1964).
Reading and interest level: intermediate.

Superstition. Chun Bok is called "Fish Eye" and is tormented and beaten because he is different from his peers in his Korean town; he has blue eyes rather than the customary black ones.

Justus, May. *New Boy In School* (New York: Hastings House Pub., 1963).
Reading and interest level: elementary.

Integration. When Lennie is seven, his family moves to Nashville in the middle of the school year. He must learn to adjust to a new school where everyone in the class is White.

Konigsburg, A. L. "Momma at the Pearly Gates," in her *Altogether One At A Time* (New York: Atheneum, 1971).
Reading and interest level: intermediate.

Racism. Momma's story of what happened to her when she was bussed to a White school as a child. It was the beginning of her career as an artist and of her classmate's acceptance of her.

The Lottery. 18 minutes, Color, Encyclopaedia Britannica, Film.
Level: mature teens.

Scapegoat. The film is faithful to Shirley Jackson's story of a small town's gathering for the annual lottery to decide who is to be stoned.

Neville, Emily C. *Berries Goodman* (New York: Harper, 1965).
Reading level: intermediate. Interest level: into teen.

Anti-Semitism. When Berries' family moves, he meets Sidney who is also an outsider—because he is Jewish. When Sidney has a near-fatal accident, Berries sees the intensity and resultant bitterness of such prejudice.

Rose, Karen. *A Single Trail* (Chicago: Follett, 1969).
Reading and interest level: intermediate.

Racism. Earl is Black and Ricky is White, but both are twelve and good at sports. Though they go to the same school and like the same teacher, they live very differently and very apart because of community prejudices against the Blacks. The book is written from the point of view of Ricky who is new to the neighborhood. It is realistic and unsentimental.

Sachs, Marilyn. *Peter and Veronica* (Garden City, New York: Doubleday, 1969).
Reading and interest level: intermediate.

Anti-Semitism. Peter and Veronica discover how difficult friendship can be when parents are prejudiced about their children's friends. A sequel to *Veronica Ganz*.

Also see these titles under other headings:

Cleaver, Vera and Bill. *Me Too.* Physical Disabilities.
Coles, Robert. *Dead End School.* New Experiences.
Hall, Lynn. *Sticks and Stones.* Love and Sexuality.
Hentoff, Nat. *Jazz Country.* Identity and Self-Discovery.
Randall, Florence. *The Almost Year.* Identity and Self-Discovery.
Robinson, Veronica. *David in Silence.* Physical Disabilities.
Rookie of the Year. Identity and Self-Discovery.
Taylor, Theodore. *The Cay.* Emotions.
Wojiechowska, Maja. *Single Light.* Physical Disabilities.

RESPONSIBILITY AND DECISION-MAKING

Arora, Shirley L. *What Then, Ramon?* (Chicago: Follett, 1960).
     Reading and interest level: intermediate.

   Ramon is the best reader in the Indian village school, but he must
   leave to help earn money for his family. While working he meets
   an American woman who teaches him that his schooling carries a
   responsibility; he must teach others to read also. A bit preachy.

Beckett, Hilary. *My Brother Angel* (New York: Dodd, Mead and Co.,
     1971).
     Reading level: intermediate. Interest level: into teen.
     Note: Chicano characters.

   Thirteen-year-old Carlos is left to care for his five-year-old
   brother, Angel. Carlos learns about himself and about responsibility as he learns the respect of his brother.

Cleaver, Vera and Bill. *Ellen Grae* (Philadelphia: Lippincott, 1967).
     Reading and interest level: intermediate.

   Ellen Grae is a loveable nonconformist with a rich imagination—
   she likes to tell wild stories. But one tale, dismissed by others as
   another fiction, she knows to be true. She must decide what to do
   with her retarded friend Ira's terrible secret without getting him
   into trouble. First of a series of Ellen Grae Derryberry novels, in
   which she lives with the McGruders during the school year because her parents are divorced.

Cleaver, Vera and Bill. *Mimosa Tree* (Philadelphia: Lippincott, 1970).
     Reading level: late intermediate. Interest level: into teen.

   Marvella and her "hillbilly" family, including her blind father,
   move to Chicago. The change is a shock but things get even worse
   when their stepmother abandons them and fourteen-year-old Marvella with her ten-year-old brother must steal in order for the family to eat. Finally, Marvella decides that the family must return to
   the country rather than sacrifice their pride to the city.

Cleaver, Vera and Bill. *The Mock Revolt* (Philadelphia: Lippincott, 1971).
Reading and interest level: intermediate and early teen.

Ussy, 13, decides that he wants to be different from the "deadlies" in his town, so he decides to make enough money to run away. The problem is that Luke Wilder, the son of a poor migrant worker, needs the money and wants it. Ussy turns out to be different from other people, but not quite in the way he'd anticipated. Set in the 1930's. Not their best book.

Follow the North Star. 47 minutes, Color, Time/Life, Film.
Level: intermediate.

Benji, a White boy, helps a slave boy to escape via the underground railway.

Hamilton, Virginia. *The Planet of Junior Brown* (New York: Macmillan, 1971).
Reading level: late intermediate. Interest level: into teens.

A very unusual story of Junior Brown, an obese would-be musician with a large imagination and his friend, Buddy Clark, a homeless man-child who takes responsibility for a number of people "because we have to learn to live for each other." Excellent.

Hazen, Barbara Shook. *The Gorilla Did It* (New York: Atheneum, 1974).
Reading and interest level: preschool.

The gorilla made the mess, ate the food, and generally disturbed things. Who else would have done that?

Hinton, S. E. *That Was Then, This Is Now* (New York: Viking, 1971).
Reading and interest level: teen.

A powerful and disturbin; novel about two "brothers," drugs, conscience, and betrayal. Bryon has to make a very difficult decision about his best friend, Mark.

Hoban, Russell and Lillian. *The Sorely Trying Day* (New York: Harper, 1964).
Reading and interest level: elementary.

Once the mouse admits his part in the family uproar, the dog, and then all four kids admit their participation.

Holland, Isabelle. *Amanda's Choice* (Philadelphia: Lippincott, 1970).
Reading and interest level: intermediate.

Amanda (12) is angry because she feels abandoned. No one else realizes that, however; they think she isujust a discipline problem or emotionally disturbed. She tells her father "What's the use? When I'm good, you don't know I'm there. When I'm bad, you do, even if you hate me." When she makes an unexpected friend, she finds she has to decide whether to act more acceptably or not.

Holm, Ann. *North to Freedom* (New York: Harcourt, 1965).
Reading and interest level: Late intermediate and early teen.

Twelve-year-old David escapes from a prison camp in Eastern Europe into a world where freedom brings responsibility, decisions, pain, and personal identity.

Millions of Cats. 10 minutes, Black/White, Weston, Film.
Level: preschool and elementary.

Animated film about choosing a cat.

Ness, Evaline. *Josefina February* (New York: Scribner's, 1963).
Reading and interest level: elementary.

In order to get a pair of real leather shoes for his grandfather's birthday present, Josefina has to sell the little burro she had found and loved.

Sachs, Marilyn. *The Bear's House* (New York: Doubleday, 1971).
Reading and interest level: early intermediate.

Fran Ellen's escape mechanism from her unhappy family situation is her teacher's dolls' house at school. It seems real to her, especially when she sucks her thumb. When her teacher tells her that she must make a decision, she stops sucking her thumb in order to win the doll's house.

Snyder, Zilpha Keatley. *Witches of Worm* (New York: Atheneum, 1973).
Reading and interest level: late intermediate.

Jessica feels abandoned by her Mom and friends. Once she finds Worm, a kitten, she starts doing mean, terrible things to people. Of course it is because Worm is a witch and is forcing her into these activities. Or is it?

Southall, Ivan. *Ash Road* (New York: St. Martin's Press, 1965).
Reading and interest level: late intermediate into teen.

Gripping story of three boys on a camping trip. They accidentally start a serious brush fire. How they deal with their fear and guilt, and how the residents of Ash Road deal with the fire and crisis, fill the story.

Zindel, Paul. *The Pigman* (New York: Harper, 1968).
Reading and interest level: teen.

Lorraine and John, two high school sophomores, record their friendship with a lonely old man. The experiences which develop out of the relationship teach them that they alone are responsible for their lives.

See also these titles under other headings:

Blue, Rose. *The Preacher's Kid.* Prejudice.
Nikki 108. Contemporary Problems.

Burch, Robert. *Simon and the Game of Chance.* Mental Illness.
Cleaver, Vera and Bill. *I Would Rather Be A Turnip.* Family.
Duvoisin, Roger. *What Is Right for Tulip.* Identity and Self-Discovery.
Gilbert, Nan. *Champions Don't Cry.* Identity and Self-Discovery.
Hentoff, Nat. *I'm Really Dragged, but Nothing Gets Me Down.* Identity and Self-Discovery.
Platt, Kin. *Hey, Dummy!* Physical Disabilities.
Sachs, Marilyn. *The Bear's House.* Responsibility and Decision-Making.

SHARING AND PRIVACY

Hill, Elizabeth Starr. *Evan's Corner* (New York: Holt, 1967). Also in film version 23 min. Color BFA.
Reading and interest level: elementary and preschool.

Evan's apartment is crowded and he wants space and privacy. So he sets up his own corner in which to waste time, enjoy peace and quiet, and be lonely. He finds he still needs to share and have friends, that both privacy and sharing are important.

Ness, Evaline. *Exactly Alike* (New York: Scribner's, 1964).
Reading and interest level: preschool.

In trying to decide which of her four quadruplet brothers is which, Elizabeth learns an important lesson about give and take.

Udry, Janice May. *What Mary Jo Shared* (Chicago: Albert Whitman, 1966).
Reading and interest level: elementary.
Note: Interracial.

Mary Jo never participates in Show and Tell because she can't think of anything that no one else has shared — until she decides to share her father with the class.

Also see these titles under other headings:

Delton, Judy. *Two Good Friends.* Friends.
Hoban, Russell. *Harvey's Hideout.* Emotions.
Lionni, Leo. *Tico and the Golden Wings.* Friends.
Little, Jean. *Look Through My Window.* Family.

VALUES

Aaron, Chester. *Better Than Laughter* (New York: Harcourt, 1972).
Reading level: intermediate. Interest level: into teens.

Allan (12) and Sam (10) run away, but can't escape the selfish, insensitive values of their parents' generation. At the end of the book, they resort to violence to protect a value of theirs. Well done.

Krumgold, Joseph. *Henry Three* (New York: Atheneum, 1967).
Reading and interest level: teen.

Henry struggles to determine his own values in contrast to those of the adults in his suburb and in his father's business executive world. A natural disaster throws people together temporarily, and Henry wants to know why they can't always be cooperative. Excellent.

Vonnegut, Kurt. "The Lie," in Charlotte Zolotow. *An Overpraised Season* (New York: Harper, 1973).
Reading and interest level: intermediate.

Dr. Remenzel tells his wife and his son, Ben, that he doesn't believe in special treatment because of their wealth and prestige. But he proves his value of equal treatment a lie when Ben isn't accepted at his Alma Mater.

See also these titles under other headings:

Donovan, John. *Remove Protective Coating . . . A Little At A Time.* Identity and Self-Discovery.
Hall, Lynn. *Sticks and Stones.* Love and Sexuality.
Lionni, Leo. *Tico and the Golden Wings.* Friends.

Appendix II

Adult Bibliotherapy Discussion Group Bibliography

by Clara E. Lack

This bibliography represents many experiments in attempting to match needs and interests of a wide variety of clientele in bibliotherapy groups led weekly by the author and Mr. Bruce Bettencourt, Bibliotherapist I. All items listed have been used successfully at least twice with different groups in the last two years. Successful use is defined as a favorable response to the material by the group and whether or not a discussion is stimulated. (See Bates Scale of Group Member Response cited in Chapter Two).

Some considerations in the selection process of literature to be used with groups are: Is the length and clarity sufficient to present and discuss in one and one-half hours? Does the material have enough content to stimulate comments and discussion? Does the selection very quickly involve the reader or viewer emotionally? Has the group or individuals in the group shown any interest in the subject? Has a staff member at a facility indicated that a particular topic should be explored for the benefit of a group member? Will the material expand the awareness of the group, amuse, stimulate intellectually, inform? Will the group be able to identify with the characters and the situation? Is it relevant? Obviously, some selections included will only qualify for one reason. Several selections are used in the course of a bibliotherapy group with residents of convalescent hospitals.

Much of the material has been used with a variety of groups at psychiatric, drug or alcohol units and detention facilities. But the material used at convalescent hospitals is rarely used with other groups, except for riddles and a few movies. The generation gap is real.

Sometimes, the generation gap is bridged with movies, e.g., *Replay*, or with poetry, but the differences in age, ability, and interest are very wide. Convalescent groups prefer materials of information, humor, and nostalgia. Biography and familiar poetry are well liked. Many older people are offended by the lack of restraint in much modern literature.

The reader will note that no mention has been made about literary or production standards or aesthetics. These are criteria in selection, but interest is the first consideration. The bibliotherapist must be vigilant in order not to impose his/her tastes and interests, or, idiomatically, not to "lay a trip" onto the group. The goal of bibliotherapy, as in other therapy, is to help free the individual sufficiently to be able to make her/his own choices.

ACCEPTANCE

Bond, Ruskin. "The Crooked Tree." *Short Story International* January 1965. Joy and sorrow of two young men in India. (Short story)

Frost, Robert. "Acceptance." (Poem)

Steinbeck, John. "Breakfast." *Turning Point. Fourteen Great Tales of Daring and Decision.* (New York: Dell, 1965). A simple act of kindness extends human warmth. (Short Story)

ADOLESCENCE

The Game. 28 minutes, Black/White, 1966. Boy-girl-peer relationships, macho. (Film)

Stafford, William. "Fifteen." Adolescence. (Poem)

ALCOHOLISM/DRUGS

Brautigan, Richard. "The World War I Los Angeles Airplane." *Revenge on the Lawn* (New York: Simon and Schuster, 1971). A man uses sweet wine as substitute for living. (Short Story)

Ciardi, John. "Dragons." *In The Stoneworks* (New Brunswick, New Jersey: Rutgers University Press, 1961). (Poem)

Inge, William. "I'm A Star." *This Is My Best in the Third Quarter of the Century* (New York: Doubleday, 1970). Dominance-Dependence: roles played by two women who live together. (Play)

Lawrence, Jerome. "Live Spelled Backwards." (A Moral Immorality Play). *The Best Short Plays of 1972* (Radnor, Pa.: Chilton Book Company, 1972). A bartender tricks his customers into examining the nature of their reality. (Play)

That Other Guy. Part I and II. Color. Drift into alcoholism, "It couldn't happen to me." (Film)

Vonnegut, Kurt, Jr. "The Euphio Question." *Welcome to the Monkey House* (New York: Dell, 1970). The drug-induced state of mind compared to the straight. (Short Story)

ANGER

Blake, William. "A Poison Tree." (Poem)

Bradbury, Ray. "The Town Where No One Got Off," *A Medicine for Melancholy* (New York: Doubleday, 1959). Displayed hostility and aggression. Plan to even the score of a lifetime's frustration on an unknown victim. (Short Story)

Bradbury, Ray. "The Smile." *Ibid.* Displayed anger. Importance of beauty to the human spirit. (Short Story)

Bukowski, Charles. "The Loser." (Poem)

Ciardi, John. "In Place of a Curse." (Poem)

Ciardi, John. "Why Nobody Pets the Lion at the Zoo." (Poem)

Ellison, Harlan. "Along the Scenic Route," *Deathbird Stories* (New York: Harper and Row, 1975). Aggression. Science Fiction. Two highway duelists. (Short Story)

Hemingway, Ernest. "The Doctor and the Doctor's Wife." *The Short Stories of Ernest Hemingway* (New York: Charles Scribner's Sons, 1953). Family. Avoidance of expressing hostility. (Short Story)

Joans, Ted. "It is Time." (Poem)

Lamb, Charles and Mary. "Anger." (Poem)

Masters, Edgar Lee. "Dorcas Gustine." (Poem)

Moore, Merrill. "Henry Tripp." *What she did in the morning, I wouldn't know, she was seated there in the midst of her resiliant symptoms, always.* (Poem)

Reddy, Helen. "The Last Blues Song" and "Hit the Road Jack" (Song lyrics)

Rubin, Theodore Isaac. *The Angry Book* (New York: Collier, 1969). When you lose your temper honestly, it can be good for you, according to Dr. Rubin. (Nonfiction)

Swenson, May. "Fable For When There's No Way Out." (Poem)

ANIMAL/PETS

About Cats. 11 minutes, Color, Films, Inc. (Film)

Boone, John Allen. *The Language of Silence* (New York: Harper, 1970). Nonverbal communication between animals and man. Unity of all life.

___*Kinship With all Life* (New York: Harper, 1954). Oneness of life, nonverbal communication.

Brown Wolf. 26 minutes, Color, Learning Corp. of America. Based on Jack London story of the conflict of *Call of the Wild* and civilization. (Film)

Ciardi, John. "Why Nobody Pets the Lion at the Zoo." Inner Conflicts. (Poem)

Durden, Kent. *Gifts of an Eagle* (New York: Simon and Schuster, 1972). Training of a wild eagle. (Nonfiction)

Eliot, T. S. "Growltiger's Last Stand." (Poem)

Phillip and the White Colt. 23 minutes, Color, Learning Corp. The love of a boy and a wild colt. (Film)

Stafford, William. "Traveling Through the Dark." (Poem)

Whitman, Walt. "Animals." (Poem)

World of the Beaver. 32 minutes, Color, Holt. (Film)

Zlatch the Goat. 20 minutes, Color, Weston Wood. Because of a bad year, a boy must sell his pet goat, but a blizzard intervenes. Based on a story by Isaac Bashevis Singer. (Film)

APHORISMS

Hoffer, Eric. *The Passionate State of Mind and Other Aphorisms* (New York: Perennial Library, 1968). Useful as discussion starters.

ART

Art Is. 28 minutes, Color, Sterling Films. What is art? Everyone has his own answer. (Film)

Currier and Ives. 11 minutes, Color. Examples of prints with folk songs as background. No biographic information. (Film)

Hailstones and Halibut Bones. 6 minutes, Color. Sterling. Celeste Holm reads Mary O'Neil's poetry as accompaniment to changing kaleidoscopes. (Film)

Hess, LaRena. *How to Paint with Natural Earth and Sands* (Happy Camp, California: Naturegraph, 1968). Techniques and philosophy of author. (Essay)

Lapis. 10 minutes, Color. Kaleidoscope of color and shape moves to sitar music. (Film)

Peters, Harry. *Currier and Ives; Printmakers to the American People* (New York: Doubleday, 1942). U. S. History. (Biography)

Pratt, John L. *Currier and Ives Chronicles of America* (Maplewood, New Jersey: Hammond, 1968) U. S. History. (Biography)

Searching Eye. 18 minutes, Color, Pyramid. The art of seeing, observation, and imagination; fantasy. (Film)

Why Man Creates. 25 minutes, Color, Pyramid. Series of explorations and comments on creativity. (Film)

World of Andrew Wyeth. 26 minutes, Color, 1968. Biographical information and examples of his work. (Film)

BIOGRAPHY

"Ah-one and Ah-two." Interview with Lawrence Welk. *The Christian Science Monitor.* September 25, 1974.

Cather, Willa. *Collected Short Fiction 1892-1912* (Rev. ed. Lincoln: University of Nebraska Press, 1970). Includes biographical sketch by Mildred R. Bennett.

Cookley, Mary Lewis. *Mister Music Maker, Lawrence Welk* (New York: Doubleday, 1958).

Cutter, John H. *Ed Brooke, Biography of a Senator* (Indianapolis: Bobbs-Merrill; 1972).

Desmond, James. *Nelson Rockefeller: A Political Biography* (New York: Macmillan, 1964). Politics.

Dunbar, Janet. *Mrs. G.B.S. A Portrait* (New York: Harper, 1963). Charlotte served G. B. Shaw's genius; was never intimidated by it.

Krents, Harold. *To Race The Wind* (New York: Putnam, 1972). An autobiography which inspired the play "Butterflies are Free," about blindness.

Lindbergh, Anne Morrow. *Hour of Gold, Hour of Lead; Diaries and Letters 1929-1932* (New York: Harcourt-Brace, 1973). Grief, loss.

Logsdon, Gene. *Wyeth People* (New York: Doubleday, 1971). A portrait as seen by friends and neighbors.

Martin, Ralph G. *Jennie: The Life of Lady Randolph Churchill 1854-1895* (New American Library, 1969), and *Jennie, Volume II: The Life of Lady Randolph Churchill, The Dramatic Years 1895-1921* (New York: New American Library, 1969). A beautiful transplanted American scandalized England and raised a powerful son.

Meyer, Lewis. *Off the Sauce* (New York: Doubleday, 1967). Useful concepts for nonalcoholics also.

Sheehan, Susan. "Washington's Wittiest Woman." *McCalls* (January 1974) Alice Roosevelt Longworth.

Thomas, Piri. *Down These Mean Streets* (New York: New American Library, 1967). Poverty, race-relations, crime.

Vestal, Bud. *Jerry Ford Up Close* (Berkeley: Medallion, 1974).

Welk, Lawrence with Bernice McGeehan *Wunnerful, Wunnerful* (Englewood Cliffs, New Jersey: Prentice Hall, 1971).

CHANGE

Bukowski, Charles. "The Loser." (Poem)

Experimental. 13 minutes, Color, Phoenix. The excitement and perseverance involved in man's learning to fly. (Film)

Jackson, Shirley. "My Life with R. H. Macy." *The Lottery* (New York: Avon, 1960). Confusion of a new job. (Short Story)

Koertge, Ron. "Modifications." (Poem)

Moore, Merrill. "The Noise that Time Makes." (Poem)

Nash, Ogden. "Don't Look for the Silver Lining, Just Wait for It." (Poem)

Pryor, Hubert. "New Ideas for America." *Modern Maturity*, vol. 18 (August-September 1975) #8. Spend money to make money. (Essay)

The Real West. 54 minutes, Black/White, McGraw-Hill. Misfits were the ones who endured hardship to search for a new chance. Narrated by Gary Cooper from historical documents. (Film)

Toffler, Alvin. *Future Shock* (New York: Bantam, 1970). (Nonfiction). Also 42 minutes, Color, McGraw-Hill. Coping with and planning for rapid change. (Film)

Vidal, Gore. "Visit to a Small Planet." *Ten Short Plays* (New York: Dell, 1965). Fantasy, ethics, humor. What is power? (Play)

CHRISTMAS

Berkeley Christmas. 47 minutes, Color, Time-Life. Man-woman relationships. Values. Humorous tale of a "square" student and a "flower child" who is nine months pregnant and unmarried. (Film)

Broun, Heywood. "A Shepherd." *Eleanor Roosevelt's Christmas Book* (New York: Dodd, Mead, 1963). "I will stay with the sheep."

A Christmas Carol. 26 minutes, Color, Xerox. Dickens' poignant tale in animation with voices of Michael Redgrave and Alistair Sims. (Film)

Ferlinghetti, Lawrence. "Christ Climbed Down." *Garlands for Christmas* (New York: Macmillan, 1965). Against the commercialism and for the reconception of Christmas. (Poem)

Frost, Robert. "In the Clearing." (Poem)

Glaspell, Susan. "Cherished and Shared of Old." *The Light of Christmas* (New York: Dutton, 1964). Two children and a dog bring reconciliation to feuding neighbors. (Short Story)

Hardy, Thomas. "The Oxen." (Poem)

McCabe, Charles. "Giving and Taking." *San Francisco Chronicle.* November 30, 1973. Unconscious motivations and feelings in giving and receiving. (Essay)

Steffens, Lincoln. "A Miserable Merry Christmas." *The Autobiography of Lincoln Steffens* (New York: Harcourt, Brace, 1931). Despair to ecstasy in a few short hours.

COMMUNICATION

Connell, Evan S. "The Corset." *At the Crossroads* (New York: Simon and Schuster, 1961). Man-woman relationship, living up to expectations. (Short Story)

A Fable. 18 minutes, Color, Xerox. Marcel Marceau mimes the story of a man erecting walls for protection and discovering he has imprisoned himself. (Film)

Frost, Robert. "The Wood Pile." (Poem)

Gibson, Walker. "Advice to Travelers." (Poem)

Hay, Sara Henderson. "The Builders." (Poem)

Replay. 8 minutes, Color, McGraw-Hill. Generation Gap, humorous: Flashbacks to dances and movies in the 20's that were similar to now. (Film)

Robinson, Edwin Arlington. "Richard Cory." (Poem)

Rukeyser, Muriel. "Effort at Speech Between Two People." (Poem)

Saxe, John Godfrey. "The Blind Men and the Elephant." (Poem)

Simon, Paul and Art Garfunkel. "Sounds of Silence." *Sounds of Silence* (Lyric)

Williams, William Carlos. "This Is Just to Say." (Poem)

COURAGE

"The Merchant and the Genie." *Arabian Nights* (New York: David McKay, 1946). Merchant settles his debts and keeps his word even in danger of his life. (Short Story)

"Scheherazade" in *Ibid.* An early storyteller and bibliotherapist. (Short Story)

CURIOSITIES

Batchelor, Julie Forsythe and Claudia de Lya. *Superstitious? Here's Why!* (New York: Harcourt, Brace, 1954).

Sann, Paul. *Fads, Follies and Delusions* (New York: Crown, 1967).

Storer, Doug. *Amazing but True Stories about People, Places and Things* (New York: Pocket Books, 1973). (Short Stories)

DANCE

Pas de Deux. 14 minutes, Black/White, National Film Board of Canada. Two dancers perform with stroboscopic photography and optical printing. A visual jewel. (Film)

DEATH

An Occurrence at Owl Creek Bridge. 27 minutes, Black/White, Fantasy.

Ambrose Bierce's Civil War story of a man about to be executed. (Film)

DECISION MAKING

Bukowski, Charles. "The Loser." (Poem)

Frost, Robert. "Stopping by Woods on a Snowy Evening," "The Road Not Taken," "Acceptance," and "Minor Bird." (Poems)

Stafford, William. "Fifteen" and "Freedom." (Poems)

Stockton, Frank R. "The Lady or the Tiger." *Masterpieces of Surprise* (New York: Hart, 1966). (Short Story)

DESPAIR

Henry, O. "The Cap and the Anthem." *The Best Short Stories of O. Henry* (New York: Modern Library, 1973). There is also hope. (Short Story)

ECOLOGY/CONSERVATION

Don't. 19 minutes, Color, Phoenix. A butterfly's struggle for life. (Film)

Enduring Wilderness. 28 minutes, Color, Sterling. The need to create and maintain natural preserves. (Film)

Grand Canyon. 26 minutes, Color, Sierra Club. (Film)

Nature's Half Acre. 33 minutes, Color, Walt Disney Productions. Continuity of life and interdependence of birds, plants and insects. (Film)

The Redwoods. 20 minutes, Color, CCM. Helped in creation of Redwoods National Park. (Film)

FAMILY

Bradbury, Ray. "Heavy-Set." *I Sing the Body Electric* (New York: Alfred A. Knopf, 1969). Mother-son relationship when apron strings remain tied. (Short Story)

Connell, Evan S. *Mr. Bridge* (New York: Alfred A. Knopf, 1969). A "good" man out of touch with his feelings.

—— *Mrs. Bridge* (New York: Dell, 1958). Relationships in middle class family. Short chapters useful as individual short stories.

Eskimo: Fight for Life. 51 minutes, Color, EDC. Stuggle and celebration of survival. (Film)

Family of Man. 26 minutes, Black/White, 1966. Human portrait of rural Polish family. (Film)

Friedman, Edward. "Blood Photo." *The Best Short Plays of 1969.* (Radnor, Pennsylvania: Chilton Book, 1969). One girl in a feuding family manages to live her own life. (Play)

Gill, Brendan. "Truth and Consequences." *Fifty-five Stories from the New Yorker* (New York: Simon and Schuster, 1949). Mother-son relationship. Eighteen-year-old boy is shaken by his meeting with an honest girl. (Short Story)

Gilroy, Frank. "The Subject Was Roses." *The Best Plays of 1964-65* (New York: Dodd, 1965). Mother finds it difficult to let son grow up. (Play)

Hughes, Langston. "Mother to Son." (Poem)

Jackson, Shirley. "Charles." *The Lottery* (New York: Avon, 1960). Humor, child projection. (Short Story)

Jong, Erica. "Mother." (Poem)

Miller, Arthur. "The Price." *The Best Plays of 1967-68* (New York: Dodd Mead, 1968). Security and duty vs. self-actualization. (Play)

Sandhi, Kuldip. "With Strings." *Ten One-Act Plays* (Heinemann Educational Books. Ltd., 1968). The generation gap. Social change in modern Kenya. Interracial marriage. (Play)

Wilder, Thornton. "Our Town." *Three Plays by Thornton Wilder* (New York: Bantam, 1958). Idyllic life in early 1900's. (Play)

FANTASY

"Big Rock Candy Mountain." (Poem)

Brake Free. 7 minutes, Color, A.C.I. A joyous ride on the last steam driven cog railway in New Hampshire. (Film)

Brautigan, Richard. "Blackberry Motorist." *Revenge on the Lawn* (New York: Pocket Book, 1972). Blackberry-picking enhanced. (Short Story)

Castles Made of Sand. 8 minutes, Color, Pyramid. A castle building contest with a touch of fantasy. (Film)

Driscoll, Louise. "Hold Fast Your Dreams." (Poem)

Hollywood, the Dream Factory. 52 minutes, Color, Films, Inc. (Film)

Hoyt, Helen. "Ellis Park." (Poem)

Hughes, Langston. "Dreams." (Poem)

Kelso, Peter. "Poems." *Miracles*

Parker, Dorothy. "The Standard of Living." *The World's Best Short, Short Stories* (New York: Bantam, 1967). Familiar daydreams, "What would you buy if . . . . . ?" (Short Story)

Poe, Edgar Allan. "The Raven." (Poem)

Swenson, May. "At Breakfast." (Poem)

Vonnegut, Kurt, Jr. "Who Am I This Time?" *Welcome to the Monkey House* (New York: Dell, 1950). Self-concept: Search for identity through play-acting. (Short Story)

FASHION

Anspach, Karlyne. *The Why of Fashion* (Ames, Iowa: Iowa University Press, 1967).

Rosencranz, Mary Lou. *Clothing Concepts, A Social Psychological Approach* (New York: Macmillan, 1972).

FEAR

Blyth, Myrns. "Get Well Soon." *Ms.* February, 1974. A woman unwilling to risk involvement. (Short Story)

Jong, Erica. "Paper Cuts." (Poem)

Legend of Sleepy Hollow. 13 minutes, Color, Stephen Bosustow Productions. Supernatural, animated version of Washington Irving's tale. (Film)

Nash, Ogden. "The Tale of Custard the Dragon." *Poems to Read Aloud* ed. by Edward Hodnett. (New York: W. W. Norton, 1967). Humorous. Even dragons are sometimes afraid. (Poem)

Open Window. 12 minutes, Color. Based on Saki's short story of the same title. (Film)

Perkins, Elizabeth. "A Squeaking of Rats." *Six One Act Plays* (St. Lucia, Queenland, Australia: University of Australia Press, 1970). Four young adults in crisis are given shelter and acceptance. (Play)

Romanith, Olga. "Scared to Life." *Famous Short, Short Stories* (New York: New American Library, 1966). Fear of a "haunting" causes the community people to come together to make music. (Short Story)

Schisgal, Murray. "Fragments." *Five One Act Plays* (New York: Dramatist Play Service, Inc. 1968). Fear of loneliness, failure and relationship briefly bring three men and a girl together. (Play)

The Will to Win. 27 minutes, Color, Pyramid. Do men compete to win or to prove they are not afraid? (Film)

The Witches of Salem: The Horror and the Hope. 35 minutes, Color, Learning Corp. (Film)

FOLKLORE

Coffin, Tristram Potter and Hennig Cohen, eds. *Folklore from the Working Folk of America* (New York: Doubleday, 1973). Home medications and riddles especially popular.

FREEDOM

Aichinger, Ilse. "The Bound Man." *Turning Point* (New York: Dell, 1965). Questions pertaining to inner and outer freedom. (Short Story)

Hang Gliding: The New Freedom. 15 minutes, Color, Oxford Films. The feel and challenge of flying like a bird. (Film)

Solzhenitsyn, Alexander. "Freedom to Breathe." *Stories and Prose Poems.* (New York: Farrar, Straus and Giroux, 1970). Air outside of prison smells different.

Stafford, William. "Freedom." (Poem)

GOVERNMENT

League of Women Voters Analysis of Ballot Propositions.

Somehow It Works. 54 minutes, Color. Light-hearted, but critical look at campaign politics. (Film)

Wieck, Paul R. "Fred Harris: The Oklahoma Preacher." *New Republic* (June 21, 1975) 14-17.

HISTORY

Bangs, Edward. "The Yankees' Return from Camp." (Poem)

Hemans, Felicia. "The Landing of the Pilgrim Fathers." (Poem)

Longfellow, Henry Wadsworth. "Paul Revere's Ride." (Poem)

Time. Special 1776 Issue 105: entire issue, 1975.

HOLIDAYS

Bradbury, Ray. "Tricks, Treats, Gangway!" *Reader's Digest* October 1975, p. 129. Halloween: A nostalgic look at the holiday and boyhood. (Short Story)

Lee, Ruth Webb. *A History of Valentines* (Wellesley Hill, Massachusetts: Lee Publication, 1952).

McGinley, Phyllis. "Halloween." (Poem)

HUMAN INTEREST

Case, Victoria. *Applesauce Needs Sugar* (New York: Doubleday, 1960). Humor; women; life with large family on Canadian farm in early 20th century.

Rondon, Feodora. "The Alley." Unpublished typewritten manuscript, 1960. Life among Italian immigrants.

HUMOR

Adler, Bill, ed. *Dear Dating Computer* (Indianapolis, Indiana: Bobbs-Merrill, 1968). Man/woman relationships.

Carroll, Lewis. "Jabberwocky." *The Family Book of Best Loved Poems* David L. George ed. (New York: Doubleday, 1952). Fantasy. (Poem)

Carroll, Lewis, "The Walrus and the Carpenter." *The Best Loved Poems of the American People* Hazel Felleman ed. (New York: Doubleday, 1936). Fantasy. (Poem)

Cerf, Bennett. *Bennett Cerf's the Sound of Laughter* (New York: Doubleday, 1970).

Cerf, Bennett. *Stories To Make You Feel Better* (New York: Random House, 1972).

Charlie McCarthy Show (Glenview, Illinois: National Recording Co.). (Tape)

Chrystie, Frances, comp. *Riddle Me This* (New York: Henry Z. Walck, 1968).

Emerson, Ralph Waldo. "The Mountain and the Squirrel." Differences, power, humor. (Poem)

Fibber McGee & Molly. *Fibber Plans a Magic Act for the Elk's Club Smoker* (Glenview, Illinois: National Recording Co.). (Tape)

Fibber McGee & Molly. *Mysterious McGee the Mental Marvel* (Glenview, Illinois: National Recording Co.). (Tape)

Gallico, Paul. *Mrs. 'arris Goes to New York* (New York: Doubleday, 1960). When Mrs. 'arris wanted to go to New York, not even the State Department daunted her.

Gardner, Hy. *So What Else Is New* (Englewood Cliffs, New Jersey: Prentice-Hall, 1959). Short fillers on varied subjects.

Gilman, Dorothy. *The Unexpected Mrs. Pollifax* (New York: Fawcett, 1966). She volunteers her services to the C.I.A.

The Great Radio Comedians. Three reels, Black/White and Color. McGraw-Hill. Edgar Bergen, W. C. Fields, George Burns, Jack Benny, Fred Allen, Fibber McGee & Molly. (Film)

Henry, O. "The Ransom of Red Chief." *The Best Short Stories of O. Henry* (New York: The Modern Library, 1945). Crime doesn't pay. (Short Story)

Hudson, Virginia Cary. *O Ye Jigs and Juleps!* (New York: Macmillan, 1962). Precocious child of the South in early 1900's.

Lancaster, Hal. "Villains Everywhere Beware! Capt. Sticky Tries to Gum Up Evil." *Wall Street Journal,* February 11, 1975, Page 1. Good/evil.

Lear, Edward. *The Complete Nonsense Book* (New York: Dodd, Mead & Co., 1912).

Leeming, Joseph, sel. *Riddles, Riddles, Riddles* (New York: Franklin Watts, 1953). Useful as attention grabbers.

Linkletter, Art. *A Child's Garden of Misinformation* (New York: Bernard Geis Assoc., 1965).

Lowney, Paul B. *Gleeb* (New York: Dodd, Mead & Co., 1968).

Milne, A. A. "The Ugly Duckling." *Twenty Four Favorite One Act Plays.* (New York: Doubleday, 1965). Fantasy, marriage, beauty vs. character in a mythical kingdom where one princess is not beautiful. (Play)

Nash, Ogden. *Verses from 1929 On* (New York: Modern Library, 1959).

Nicol, Eric & Peter Whalley. *Say Uncle, a Completely Uncalled for History of the U.S.* (New York: Harper, 1961). Written by two Canadians.

People Soup. 13 minutes, Color, Learning Corporation of America. Fantasy, change, two brothers experiment with chemistry. (Film)

Price, Jonathan. "Ice Cream." (Poem)

Savage, George. "A Small Down Payment." *Short Plays for Modern Players* (New York: D. Appleton & Co., 1931). (Play)

Smith, Elinor Goulding. *The Complete Book of Absolute Perfect Housekeeping* (Curtis, 1956). How to make the average housewife feel better.

Smith, H. Allen. *Write Me a Poem, Baby* (Boston: Little, Brown, 1956). Teacher's memories.

Twain, Mark. "The Adventures of Tom Sawyer." *Radio Plays of Famous Short Stories* (Boston: Boston Plays, Inc., 1956). Parent-child relationships. Feelings of rejection. Death.

Twain, Mark. "A Connecticut Yankee in King Arthur's Court." *Radio Plays of Famous Stories* (Boston: Boston Plays Inc., 1956). Resistance to change.

Wiesner, William, Coll. *A Pocketful of Riddles* (New York: E. P. Dutton, 1966).

INFLATION

Brautigan, Richard. "The Last Chapters of Trout Fishing in America: Rembrandt Creek and Catherage Sink." *Revenge on the Lawn* (New York: Pocket Book, 1972). A parable: various reactions to the oversized ego of a river.

JUSTICE

Rose, Reginald, "Twelve Angry Men." *Great Television Plays* (New York: Dell, 1969). Am I my brother's keeper? (Play)

Hayden, Robert, "The Whipping." (Poem)

Nebel, Frederick. "Back in Town." *Famous Short Short Stories* (New York: New American Library, 1966). Facing the hometown after jail. (Short Story)

LONELINESS

A Boy Alone. 13 minutes, Color, McGraw Hill. Gauche behavior repels some people. Unable to respond to friendly gestures of others. No narration. (Film)

A Fable. 18 minutes, Color, Xerox. Marcel Marceau mimes building a wall around his bit of paradise only to discover it is a prison. (Film)

Gibran, Kahlil. "Of Life" from The Voice of the Master in *A Second Treasury of Kahlil Gibran* (New York: Citadel, 1968). Solitude— only way of finding self-identity.

Jenkins, Brooks. "Loneliness." (Poem)

Moustakas, Clark E. *Loneliness* (Englewood Cliffs, New Jersey: Prentice-Hall, 1961). Some positive aspects.

Moustakas, Clark E. *Portraits of Loneliness and Love* (Englewood Cliffs, New Jersey: Prentice-Hall, 1974).

Rosenbaum, Jean and Veryl Rosenbaum. *Conquering Loneliness* (New York: Hawthorne Books, 1973). Self-help book in layman's language. (Nonfiction)

String Bean. 17 minutes, Black/White, McGraw-Hill. No narration. Parisian elder finds release from loneliness in loving care of bean plant. (Film)

Tanner, Ira J. *Loneliness: The Fear of Love* (New York: Harper & Row, 1973). Applied psychology, transactional analysis. (Nonfiction)

Williams, Tennessee. "The Strangest Kind of Romance." *27 Wagons Full of Cotton and Other Plays* (New York: New Directions, 1945). A loser's involvement with a cat and other boarders. (Play)

LOVE

Bradbury, Ray. "A Medicine for Melancholy." *A Medicine for Melancholy* (New York: Bantam Books, 1960). A story of romantic love. (Short Story)

Brooks, Gwendolyn. "To Be in Love" and "The Sonnet Ballad" in Richard Peck, ed. *Sounds and Silences*, 1970. (Poems)

Devadasi. "The Day of the Sufi Dancing." *Redbook.* November 1974. (144, No. 1) Man/woman relationship. Facing pain of rejection and the healing process beginning. (Short Story)

Dryden, John. "Song." from "Secret Love." (Poem)

Ferlinghetti, Lawrence. "Number 7." Self-Insight (Poem)

Gordon, George (Lord Byron). "She Walks in Beauty." (Poem)

Gotlieb, Phyllis. "First Person Demonstrative." (Poem)

Housman, A. E. "When I was one-and-twenty." Humorous. Learning from experience. (Poem)

Ian, Janis. *Who Really Cares* (New York: Dial, 1969).

Inge, William. "The Mall." *Summer Brave and Eleven Short Plays* (New York: Random House, 1950). Love and friendship in many costumes. (Play)

Lamson, David. "School Teachers Don't Know Everything. *Once in My Saddle* (New York: Charles Scribners' Sons, 1940). Man/woman relationship; dominance.

Loneliness and Loving. 17 minutes, Color, Learning Corporation of America, 1973. Man/woman relationship. A segment from the movie *Five Easy Pieces* which asks what is involved in searching for fulfillment in human relationships. (Film)

McCabe, Charles. "I Accept You Madly" *San Francisco Chronicle,* March 8, 1974. Man-woman relationships. Acceptance is a better word than love. (Essay)

McKinney, G. "Ivory Tower." *New One-Act Plays.* (Baylor University Press, 1948). Perfectionism. Can love conquer all? Surprise ending. (Play)

McKuen, Rod. *Listen to the Warm* (New York: Random House, 1970). (Poems)

McKuen, Rod. *Stanyan Street and Other Sorrows* (New York: Random House, 1954). (Poems)

McKuen, Rod. *Come to Me in Silence* (New York: Simon and Schuster, 1973). (Poems)

McWilliams, Peter. *Love Is Yes* (New York: Versemonger Press, 1973). (Poems)

Nimoy, Leonard. *You and I.* Celestial Arts, 1973.

Shakespeare, William, "As You Like It." *Radio Plays from Shakespeare* (Boston: Boston Plays, Inc. 1958). (Play)

Shakespeare, William, Sonnet's *CXVI* and *LXXIII.* (Poems)

Velveteen Rabbit. 19 minutes, Color, LSB Productions. A plaything becomes real when loved. Can be used with some adults as a parable. (Film)

Wyse, Lois. *Are You Sure You Love Me?* (Mountain View, California: The World Publishing Co., 1969).

MAN/WOMAN RELATIONSHIPS

Adams, Alice. "Ripped Off." *Prize Stories 1972: The O. Henry Awards.* (New York: Doubleday & Co., 1972). Living together. Hidden fears. (Short Story)

Being. 21 minutes, Color, A.C.I. A friendly girl shows a skeptical young man who is on crutches that she enjoys his company. (Film)

Braudy, Susan. "After the Marriage is Over: A Diary of the First 441 Days." *Ms.*, April, 1974. The pain and growth that can come from ending a relationship. (Nonfiction)

Cheever, John. "The Five-Forty-Eight." *Points of View* (New York: New American Library, 1966). Dominance-dependence. A secretary gets even with an office-Romeo. (Short Story)

Frayn, Michael. "Chinamen." *The Best Short Plays of 1973* (Radnor, Pennsylvania: Chilton Publishing Co., 1973). A mixed-up dinner party. (Play)

Giraudaux, Jean. "The Apollo of Bellac." *Fifteen International One-Act Plays* (New York: Washington Square Press, 1969). Is every man beautiful? Flattery will get you everywhere. (Play)

Harnick, Sheldon and Jerry Bock. *The Apple Tree* (New York: Random House, 1966). Based on Twain's *The Diary of Adam and Eve*, Stockton's *Lady and the Tiger*, Feiffer's *Passionella*. (Plays)

Harold and Cynthia. 10 minutes, Color, Eccentric Circle. Impact of advertising. (Film)

Inge, William. "Glory in the Flower." *Twenty-four Favorite One-Act Plays* (New York: Doubleday & Co., 1958). Childhood sweethearts meet after fifteen years. (Play)

—— "People in the Wind." *Summer Brave and Eleven Short Plays* (New York: Random House, 1950). Loneliness, alcoholism. Movie "Bus Stop" was enlarged version. (Play)

Jackson, Shirley. "Like Mother Used to Make." *The Lottery* (New York: Avon, 1949). Dominance. Manipulation, suppressed anger. (Short Story)

Jones, Leroi. "For Hettie." (Poem)

Owen, Alan. "Male of the Species." *Best Short Plays of the World Theatre 1968-1973* (New York: Crown, 1973). Influence of early conditioning on adult pairing. (Play)

Robinson, Charles Lee. "Mating Season." *Playboy's Short Shorts* (Chicago: Playboy Press, 1970). Youth, sex, and morality. (Short Story)

Sherwood, Robert. "Extra, Extra." *A Book of Modern Short Stories* (New York: Macmillan, 1928). Marriage/divorce. Doing your own thing. (Short Story)

Twain, Mark. "The Diary of Adam and Eve." *The Complete Short Stories of Mark Twain* (New York: Doubleday, 1957). Man/woman relationship when the world was fresh and new. (Short Story)

MENTAL HEALTH/MENTAL ILLNESS

Benet, Stephen Vincent. "Minor Litany." (Poem)

Dr. Jekyll and Mr. Hyde. 27 minutes, Black/White, Manbeck. First American horror film made in 1920 with John Barrymore. From the Robert Louis Stevenson Story. (Film)

Ensana, Joe. "Please No Flowers." *The Best Short Plays of 1968* (Radnor, Pennsylvania: Chilton Book Co., 1968). Suicide. The little things in life can make the difference between despair and joy. (Play)

Mitchell, Joni. "Trouble Child" and "Twisted." *Court and Spark.* (song lyrics)

Of Mice and Men. 90 minutes, Black/White, McGraw-Hill. The touching friendship of two migrant workers and its tragic end, from the John Steinbeck novel. (Film)

Rose, Reginald. "The Incredible World of Horace Ford." *Six Television Plays* (New York: Simon and Schuster, 1956). What are the signs? (Play)

MUSIC

Andres Segovia. 18 minutes, Black/White 1956. Great guitarist discusses his instrument and performs in his Paris studio. (Film)

Armstrong, Louis. "You'll Never Walk Alone," "Sunrise, Sunset," "I Will Wait for You." Brunswick. (Songs)

Beatles. *Let It Be* and *Rubber Soul* (songs)

—— "Within You Without You." *Sgt. Pepper's Lonely Hearts Club Band.* Self-actualization. (Song)

Carpenter, Karen and Richard. "Mr. Guder." *Close to You.* Change, conformity. (Song)

Cash, Johnny. *At San Quentin.* Harsh realities. (Songs)

—— *From Sea to Shining Sea.* (Songs)

Collins, Judy. "Turn, Turn, Turn!" *Recollections.* Change. (Song)

Diamond, Neil. *Jonathan Livingston Seagull.* Original motion picture soundtrack. Columbia, 1973.

Dylan, Bob. "Bringing It All Back Home" (Song)

—— "Chimes of Freedom." *Another Side of Bob Dylan.* Columbia. Freedom. (Songs)

—— "Don't Think Twice, It's All Right." *The Freewheeling Bob Dylan.* Columbia. Loss. (Song)

—— "Mixed Up Confusion." *Freewheeling Bob Dylan, Part II.* (Song)

Gershwin, George. *Porgy and Bess.* Columbia. (Soundtrack)

—— *Levant Plays Gershwin.* Columbia.

Grofe, Ferde. *Grand Canyon Suite.* Mercury.

The Guitar. 22 minutes, Color, 1966. John Williams illustrates with old and modern instruments. (Film)

Holst, Gustav. *The Planets.* Steinberg, Boston Symphony Orchestra, Cosmos.

Horn, Paul. *Inside.* NR Productions. Self-awareness.

Ives, Burl. *The Best of Burl's for Boys and Girls.* Decca.

Lawrence Welk Country Music's Greatest Hits.

Manhattan Street Band. 24 minutes, Color, Carousel Films. Intercultural. Savor New York with happy foot-tapping music made by young ghetto men. (Film)

McKuen, Rod. *Greatest Hits of Rod McKuen.* Seven Arts Records.

Mitch Miller and the Gang. *Night Time Sing Along.* Columbia

___ *Party Sing Along with Mitch.* Columbia.

Mitchell, Joni. "Help Me." *Court and Spark.* (Song)

___ "People's Parties." *Court and Spark.* Asylum Records. Feeling out of place. (Song)

Moody Blues. "Question." *A Question of Balance.* London. (Song)

Night on Bald Mountain. 8 minutes, Black/White, 1933. Halloween. Eerie animation to Mussorgsky's music. (Film)

1927. Vintage. Twenties heard again in original performances.

The Norman Luboff Choir. *"But Beautiful."* Columbia.

Reddy, Helen. "Hit the Road Jack." *I Am Woman.* Capitol, 1972. Anger. (Song)

___ "The Last Blues Song." *I Am Woman. Ibid.* Change. (Song)

___ "I Am Woman." *I Am Woman. Ibid.* Woman. (Song)

Ronstadt, Linda. "Different Drum." *Different Drum.* Capitol. (Song)

Seeger, Pete. *American Favorite Ballads.* Folkways.

Simon, Paul and Art Garfunkel. "The Sounds of Silence," "I Am A Rock" and "Richard Cory." *Sounds of Silence.* Columbia. Communication.

Smith, Kate. *Here and Now.*

The Sons. "Follow Your Heart." (Song)

Susan Reed Sings Old Airs. Elektra.

Tiomkin, Dimitri. *The Old Man and the Sea.* Warner Bros.

NATURE

Barrier Beach. 20 minutes, Color, ACI. Process of daily and seasonal change along Pacific shore line near San Francisco. (Film)

Beal, Merrill D. *Grand Canyon: The Story Behind the Scenery* (Las Vegas, Nevada: KC Publications, 1967). Brief survey of geologic forces that formed and are forming Grand Canyon. (Nonfiction)

Better Homes & Gardens. *House Plants for the Indoor Gardener* (Meredith, 1959). Humorous and practical.

Browning, Robert. "The Year's at the Spring." (Poem)

Coller's Hill. 14 minutes, Phoenix Productions. Grandeur of winter in Yellowstone Park. (Film)

Coatsworth, Elizabeth. *Country Poems* (New York: Macmillan, 1942).

Cummings, E. E. "In Time of Daffodils." *A Selection of Poems.* (Poem)

Cunningham, Allan. "A Sea-Song." (Poem)

The Day San Francisco Burned. 12 minutes. Black/White. Production Unlimited. Imaginative treatment of on-the-spot photographs of 1906 earthquake. (Film)

Don't. 19 minutes, Color, Phoenix Productions. A butterfly's struggle for life. (Film)

Dunes. 8 minutes, Color, Learning Corp. Shifting patterns in desert life. (Film)

Earthquake I: The Land. ABC Media. What and how of earthquake geology. (Film)

Gordon, George (Lord Byron). "The Sea." (Poem)

Hans, Marcie. "Fueled." (Poem)

Hanson, John and Avis Elkins. *Memories of San Francisco: 1906 Earthquake.* Oral History. Interviewed by Clara Lack. (Tape)

Heirtzler, J. R. "Project Famous. Man's First Voyages Down to the Mid-Atlantic Ride." *National Geographic.* May, 1975. Ocean floor. (Nonfiction)

Housman, A. E. "Loveliest of Trees, The Cherry Now." (Poem)

Koriyama, Naoski. "Unfolding Bud." (Poem)

Leaf. 8 minutes, Color, 1962, Holt. Journey of a single leaf with music. (Film)

Lindbergh, Anne Morrow. "Dogwood." (Poem)

Manley, Robert and Sean. *Beaches— Their Lives, Legends and Lore* (Radnor, Pennsylvania: Chilton, 1968).

Masefield, John. "Sea Fever." (Poem)

Masters, Marcia. "April." (Poem)

Ocean. 10 minutes, Color, 1970. Meditative mood held with shapes and hues of sea and Keats and Byron poetry. (Film)

Rainshowers. 14 minutes, Color, Churchill. Sights and sounds, beauty, rhythm of summer shower. (Film)

Secrets of the Plant World. 15 minutes, Color, Walt Disney Prod. Time-lapse photography reveals nature's many methods of planting seeds. Beautiful. (Film)

Secrets of the Underwater World. 16 minutes, Color, Walt Disney Prod. Oceans. (Film)

Shakespeare, William. "When Daffodils Begin to Peer." (Poem)

Tompkins, Peter and Christopher Bird. *The Secret Life of Plants* (San Francisco: Harper & Row, 1973). Metaphysics.

Waters of Yosemite. 10 minutes, Color, Holt. A visual poem of flowing waters. (Film)

Wordsworth, William. "I Wandered Lonely as a Cloud . . ." (Poem)

NOSTALGIA

Gross, Martin A. *The Nostalgia Quiz Book* (New York: New American Library, 1969).

Stations. 27 minutes. Roger Hagen Associates. How railroad stations have been saved from destruction throughout America. (Film)

This Fabulous Century. 1910-1920. vol. II Time-Life. 1969.

Valley of Hearts Delight. 28 minutes, Black/White, Monaco Laboratories. Scenes of San Jose, California and neighboring communities in 1922. (Film)

OLD AGE

Dr. Heidegger's Experiment. 22 minutes, Color, Encyclopaedia Britannica. Science fiction. Hawthorne's classic tale on turning back the clock. Would you make the same mistake? (Film)

Holmes, Oliver Wendell. "The Chambered Nautilus." (Poem)

Nahanni. 18 minutes, Color, Film Board of Canada, 1963. A 73 year old man searches for a lost gold mine in Canadian wilderness. (Film)

Passing Quietly Through. 26 minutes, Black/White, Grove. Death. Meaningful encounter between an old man who is dying and a nurse. (Film)

Peege. 28 minutes, Color, Phoenix. A grandson manages to break through his grandmother's isolation. (Film)

Sarton, May. "The Great Transparencies." (Poem)

Wild Goose. 18 minutes, Black/White, Films, Inc. A rebellious resident of a convalescent home makes his escape. (Film)

PARABLES

Shah, Indries. *The Pleasantries of the Incredible Mulla Nasrudin* (New York: Dutton, 1971). Humorous, nonsense, short, short stories.

PSYCHOLOGY

Childhood: The Enchanted Years. 50 minutes, Color, Films, Inc. Child psychology. Child's development from birth to first year at school. (Film)

Landers, Ann. *Ann Landers Says Truth Is Stranger* (Englewood Cliffs, New Jersey: Prentice-Hall, 1968). Applied psychology. (Nonfiction)

PURPOSE

Bach, Richard. *Jonathan Livingston Seagull* (New York: Macmillan, 1970). Perfection, skill, joy.

Hatfield, Mark O. "The Vulnerability of Leadership." *Christianity Today.* June 22, 1973. Temptation of power.

RELIGION

Catholic Encyclopedia. "John, Gospel of."

Gasztold, Carmen Bernos de. *Prayers from the Ark* (New York: Viking, 1962). (Poetry)

Ickis, Marguerite. *The Book of Religious Holidays and Celebrations* (New York: Dodd Mead and Co., 1966). Primarily Christian and Jewish festivals with short coverage of others. (Nonfiction)

Interpretors Bible. vol. 8. "John."

"John, Gospel of." *Good News for Modern Man.* American Bible Society, 1973. The New Testament in Today's English Version.

McGinley, Phyllis. "Martin Luther." Biography. (Poem)

Mishkin, Leonard C. "Yom Kippur." *World Book Encyclopedia.* Description of the Jewish Day of Atonement observed with fasting. Origin of the term "scapegoat."

Webb, Thomas H. B. "An Ancient Prayer." (Poem)

REVENGE

Gonzales, Jovita. "Don Tomas." *We Are Chicanos* (New York: Simon and Schuster, 1973). Supernatural.

SELF-ACTUALIZATION

Cather, Willa. *My Antonia* (New York: Houghton, 1918, 1954). Hardships and joys of pioneers in Nebraska.

Chayefsky, Paddy. "Marty." *Television Plays by Paddy Chayefsky* (New York: Simon and Schuster, 1955). An ugly man discovers his real worth and finds a girl. (Play)

Cockrell, Marian. *The Revolt of Sarah Perkins* (New York: David McKay, 1965). Resourceful school teacher in early Colorado.

Hughes, Langston. "Thank You, Ma'am." *Something in Common and Other Stories* (New York: Hill and Wang, 1963). Older woman shows understanding of would-be purse snatcher. (Short Story)

Johnson, Dorothy, *A Man Called Horse* (New York: Ballantine, 1976). Identity. While searching for adventure, a Boston man also finds self-respect.

Newman, Mildred and Bernard Berkowitz with Jean Owen. *How to Be Your Own Best Friend* (New York: Ballantine Books, 1974). Useful self-help book.

Prather, Hugh. *Notes to Myself* (Lafayette, California: Real People Press, 1970). Diary of an inner journey.

Sandray, Sheila Brown. "A Man of Dignity." *Short Story International.* January, 1965. Man-woman relationship: Emotional stages of shock, anger, revenge, self-affirmation in love triangle. Set in Africa. (Short Story)

Where All Things Belong. 28 minutes, Color, Essentia Prod. Rebirth and change. Setting new limits and taking risks to get more from life. (Film)

You Pack Your Own Chute. 29 minutes, Color, Rami Prod. How to avoid making excuses and get control of one's life. (Film)

Zunin, Leonard, M.D., with Natalie Zunin. *Contact: The First Four Minutes* (Plainview, New York: Nash, 1972). Some self-awareness games useful. (Nonfiction)

SELF-CONCEPT

Aichinger, Ilse. "The Bound Man." *Turning Point* (New York: Dell, 1965). Questions pertaining to inner and outer freedom. (Short Story).

Bradbury, Ray. "The Headpiece." *Medicine for Melancholy* (New York: Doubleday, 1959). Man-woman relationship. Dependency. Will a wig bring happiness? (Short Story)

—— "The Watchful Poker Chip of H. Matisse." *October Country.* (New York: Ballantine, 1956). Middle-aged identity crisis. (Short Story)

Casteneda, Carlos. "Erasing Personal History." *Journey to Ixtlan.* (New York: Pocket Books, 1972). Autonomy vs. cultural and familial identity. (Nonfiction)

Crawford, Karen. "Being Nobody." *Miracles.* (Poem)

Cullen, Countee. "Incident." (Poem)

Dickinson, Emily. "The Brain Is Wider Than the Sky" and "I'm Nobody! Who Are You?" (Poem)

Evans, Naur. *I Am a Black Woman* (New York: William Morrow Co., 1970). (Nonfiction)

Farrell, Warren. *The Liberated Man* (New York: Random House, 1974). The women's movement has sparked a growing awareness among men. (Nonfiction)

Fessier, Michael. "That's What Happened to Me." *Short Stories.* (New York: Oxford University Press, 1948). An attempt at inflation.

Foss, Sam Walter. "The House by the Side of the Road." (Poem)

Gibbs, Wolcott. "Declaration of Independence." (Poem)

Grosvenor, Verta Mae. "For Once in My Life (A Short Statement)." *We Be Word Sorcerers.* (New York: Bantam, 1973). A strong woman wants to be lean awhile.

Lifton, Betty Jean. "An Adopted Daughter Meets Her Natural Mother." *Ms.* December 1975. Mother and daughter look into the past despite fear and guilt. (Nonfiction)

McCullers, Carson. "Sucker." *Ten Modern American Short Stories.* (New York: Bantam, 1965). Displaced anger. Growing up, adolescence. A boy's idol has feet of clay. (Short Story)

Men's Lives. 43 minutes, Color, New Day Films. A documentary about masculinity in America. (Film)

Mortimer, John. "Call Me A Liar." *The Television Playwright* (New York: Hill and Wang, 1960). Man-woman relationship. Humor. A man embroiders the truth to make his life more interesting. (Play)

Nash, Ogden. "Adventures of Isabel." (Poem)

Rostand, Edmond. "Cyrano de Bergerac." *Radio Plays of Famous Stories* (Boston, Massachusetts: Boston Plays, Inc., 1956). Cyrano's self-evaluation does not coincide with the lady's estimation. (Play)

Saroyan, William. "Seventeen." *Point of Departure* (New York: Dell, 1967). A boy learns that the masculine role he has adopted does not work. (Short Story)

SELF-INSIGHT

Coffin, Robert P. Tristram. "Crystal Moment." (Poem)

Coleridge, Samuel Taylor. "Kubla Khan." (Poem)

Cummings, E. E. "A Total Stranger." Recognizing one's dark side. (Poem)

Dickinson, Emily. "Have You Got A Brook?" (Poem)

Francis, Robert. "Summons." (Poem)

Greenberg, Joanne. "The Length." *Summering.* (New York: Avon, 1974). An enemy's parting gesture brings dissatisfaction to her survivor. (Short Story)

___ "Two Annas." *Summering.* (New York: Avon, 1974). Deliberately becomes schizoid in order to survive in prison. (Short Story)

Guest, Edgar. "It Couldn't Be Done." (Poem)

Jerome, Judson. "Crabs." (Poem)

McGinley, Phyllis. "Reflections at Dawn." (Poem)

Merriam, Eve. "How to Eat a Poem." (Poem)

Millay, Edna St. Vincent. "Exiled." (Poem)

Moffett, John. "To Look at Any Thing." (Poem)

Nash, Ogden. "The Tale of Custard The Dragon." (Poem)

Oliver, Mary. "Stark Boughs on the Family Tree." (Poem)

Previn, Dory. "Listen," "Broken Soul (Schiz: Broken, Phrenas: Soul)" and "I Can't Go On." (Poems)

Sarton, May. "Moving In" and "Beyond the Question." (Poems)

Stafford, William. "Freedom." (Poem)

White, E. B. "I Paint What I See." (Poem)

SEXUALITY

Martin, Del and Phyllis Lyon. "Lesbian Mothers." *Ms.* August, 1973. Women with children, exploring new sexual identities. (Nonfiction)

Position of Faith. 18 minutes, Color, McGraw-Hill. Documentary on whether or not a gay minister should be ordained. (Film)

SLEEP

Hartman, Ernest. *Functions of Sleep* (New Haven, Connecticut: Yale University Press, 1973). Sleep research adds a little chemistry to the Bard's observation. (Nonfiction)

Pai, M. N. *Sleeping Without Pills* (Briarcliff Manor, New York: Stein and Day, 1966). Self-help for insomnia. (Nonfiction)

Steincrohn, Peter J. *How to Get a Good Night's Sleep* (Chicago: Henry Regnery, 1968). Popular writing. Excerpts from newspaper column.

SOCIAL CUSTOMS

Frayn, Michael. "Chinamen." *The Best Short Plays 1973* (Radnor, Pennsylvania: Chilton Book Co., 1973). Man-woman relationships, alcoholism, humor. (Play)

Jackson, Shirley. "The Lottery." *15 American One-Act Plays* (New York: Washington Square Press, 1961). Outmoded social institutions. Scapegoating. (Play)

SOCIAL SATIRE

Brautigan, Richard. *Revenge on the Lawn* (New York: Simon and Schuster, 1971). Short avant-garde pieces.

Brautigan, Richard. *The Pill vs. the Springhill Mine Disaster* (New York: Dell, 1968). (Poems)

SPORTS

Americans on Everest. 59 minutes, Color, Chomolongma Productions. Mountain climbing. (Film)

Fabulous Harlem Globetrotters. 9 minutes, Color, Creative Film Society. Basketball. (Film)

Mobius Flip. 28 minutes, Color, Summit. Fantasy: Skiing with cinematographic flips from color to black/white to positive to negative. (Film)

Ski the Outer Limits. 28 minutes, Color, Summit. (Film)

Solo. 15 minutes, Color, Pyramid. Mountain climbing. (Film)

The Surfers. 24 minutes, Color, Fleetwood Films. (Film)

SYMBOLISM

Brautigan, Richard. "Kool Aid Wino." *Trout Fishing in America* (New York: Dell, 1967). Need for ritual. (Short Story)

URBAN LIVING

Louis, Arthur M. "Utopia Revisited: America's Safest Cities." *Sundancer.* June 1975. Reprinted from Harpers, January 1975.

VALUES

Blake. 19 minutes, Color, McGraw-Hill. A Canadian flyer works only long enough at regular jobs to fly his one engine plane. (Film)

Blake, William. "Auguries of Innocence." (Poem)

Brautigan, Richard. "The Wild Birds of Heaven." *Revenge on the Lawn.* (New York: Pocket Book, 1972). Satire on TV, credit buying, advertising, etc. (Poem)

Dickinson, Emily. "The Brain Is Wider Than the Sky." (Poem)

Foss, Sam Walter. "The House by the Side of the Road." (Poem)

Freeman, Leonard. *The Answer* (Hollywood: Samuel French, 1958). Alcoholism. What is the meaning of life? (Play)

Gibran, Kahlil. *The Prophet* (New York: Alfred A. Knopf, 1923). (Poetry)

———. *Sand and Foam* (New York: Alfred A. Knopf, 1973). (Poetry)

Greenberg, Sidney. *A Treasury of the Art of Living* (Hartford: Hartman House, 1963). Wise quotations.

I Am Also A You. 13 minutes, Color, 1970. Famous quotations interpreted through the eyes of today. Love of humanity. (Film)

Ishi In Two Worlds. 19 minutes, Color, Contemporary Films. Found in Northern California in 1911, he is the sole survivor of his tribe. (Film)

The Old Man and the Devil. 17 minutes, Color, Perguson Films. Faust in modern dress. Old Age. (Film)

The Reason Why. 13 minutes, Color, BFA. Is man a violent animal who wants to kill? A one act allegory written by Arthur Miller. (Film)

Simon, Sidney; Leland Howe; Howard Kirschenbaum. *Values Clarification* (New York: Hart, 1972). Games and exercises to sort out what one considers important. (Nonfiction)

WOMAN

Anything You Want To Be. 8 minutes, Black/White, New Day Films. Girls guided only into certain careers. (Film)

Autobiography of Miss Jane Pittman. 116 minutes, Color, Learning Corp. of America. Profound and moving story of a black woman from childhood slavery to old age. (Film)

Bernikow, Louise, "Confessions of An Ex-Cheerleader." *Ms.* October 1973. The values women grew up with. (Nonfiction)

"The Bloody Side of Little Women." *San Francisco Chronicle.* August 13, 1975. Under pseudonym Louisa M. Alcott wrote stories of strong women angry at men. (Nonfiction)

Janie's Janie. 24 minutes, Black/White, Odeon. The story of a woman beginning to take responsibility for her own life. (Film)

Luce, Clare Booth. "Time to Grow Up." *Readers' Digest.* April 1975. Men, women, marriage, women's liberation, and the roles we all play. (Nonfiction)

No Lies. 17 minutes, Color, Phoenix. Young woman's story of rape compiled from actual reports of victims. (Film)

Owen, Alun. "Doreen." *The Best Short Plays 1971* (Radnor, Pennsylvania: Chilton Book, 1971). Battle of the sexes. The double standard. (Play)

Priestly, J. B. "Mother's Day." *English One-Act Plays of Today* (New York: Oxford University Press, 1962). Women's rights. Dominance, dependence. Humor. (Play)

Shakespeare, William. "Taming of the Shrew." *Radio Plays from Shakespeare* (Boston: Boston Plays, Inc., 1958). Dominance, dependence, marriage. (Play)

Shaw, George B. "The Man of Destiny." *Fifteen International One Act Plays* (New York: Washington Square Press, 1969). A mysterious woman matches wits with General Bonaparte. (Play)

Sylvia, Fran and Joy. 25 minutes, Color, Churchill. Three young women describe how they view themselves. (Film)

Appendix III A

Certification and the St. Elizabeths Hospital Bibliotherapy Training Program

by Arleen M. Hynes

Bibliotherapy is a word librarians have used since the early 1930's to describe the broad range of programs using literature therapeutically. As librarians began to include other visual and aural materials, the meaning of the word became less precise. Today films, tapes and records are other presentations of the same creative process and should also be included as tools for the liberation of the human spirit.

Lesta Burt, Ph.D., director of the Sam Houston State University Library School, pointed out in her doctoral thesis the confusion in library literature in the past over what was actually meant by the bibliotherapy process.[1] Sharon H. Sclabassi M.S.W. has also pointed out succinctly vagaries in the literature of the field.[2]

Bibliotherapy is a generic term for the continuum of activities which implies the potential for self-understanding, growth or healing through the use of literature or films. The essential process lies in the interaction among the triad made up of the individual, the materials and the facilitator. This interaction may occur on a one-to-one basis or in a group setting using either imaginative or didactic literary materials or creative writing. Poetry, drama, short stories, novels, films are all included as genre of imaginative literature. Personal encounters with beauty and the creative process are integral components of bibliotherapy. Didactic materials in bibliotherapy are used subjectively rather than intellectually. Complementary materials introduced by the facilitator or by the patrons, such as related visual images, objects or music, may be used to heighten the emotional impact of the literature or films to bring about better self-awareness.

The development of the St. Elizabeths training program was spurred by the publication of the "Standards for Certification of Poetry Therapists and Related Matters: A Proposal," by the Association for Poetry Therapy in the *Association of Hospital and Institution Libraries Quarterly,* Summer/Fall, 1973. The salient paragraphs follow:

> . . . Hereafter, no applicant may be granted a certificate as poetry therapist unless he meets one of the following requirements: (1) He presents evidence of holding the degree of doctor of medicine or a doctorate in clinical psychology or has been licensed to practice psychotherapy in the State of New York. (2) He has completed two years of supervised training under approved auspices — one year as trainee in poetry therapy and an additional year as intern in poetry therapy and has completed the course work hereafter.
>
> To obtain designation of trainee in poetry therapy the applicant (1) must present proof of graduation from an accredited college, (2) or achieve equivalence through other study programs and experience, and (3) must have been accepted as a volunteer or salaried employee in an educational, rehabilitation, or mental health facility where he will be trained in poetry therapy under the supervision of a psychiatrist or registered psychologist . . .
>
> After February 1, 1973 no person may represent himself as poetry therapist by adding the letters C.P.T. unless he has fulfilled all qualifications for certification, attested to by the signatures of the certification committee.[3]

These requirements set goals that could be achieved. Since poetry is the main tool used in the St. Elizabeths program and those who use poetry therapy recognize that they use only one aspect of bibliotherapy, we sought to develop a training program whose graduates could qualify for certification from the Association.

As long ago as 1962, *Library Trends* devoted an entire issue to bibliotherapy, so it isn't quite as new as it may seem. In that issue, Ms. Margaret Kinney, then as now, Chief Librarian in the Veterans Administration Hospital, the Bronx, N.Y., wrote a chapter entitled, "The Bibliotherapy Program: Requirements for Training." Hers was a chapter with vision, for in it she notes many of the relevant factors which must be taken into consideration in a training program. I quote:

> Experts in rehabilitation agree that up to this time the therapeutic process itself cannot be demonstrated to the student directly and cannot be reproduced experimentally, that many facets of the intricate human relationships which make up psychotherapy cannot be adequately presented to the trainee in a classroom setting. For this reason, field service training would be an important part of the bibliotherapy training program. Such a program would have to be organized in a manner similar to the practical work of social service, the supervised training in hospitals and clinics of clinical psychologists, and other on-the-job training.
>
> This part of the bibliotherapy training program would be designed to provide experience and to assist in the integration of principles learned in the more formal manner already discussed. This kind of participation would provide an opportunity to realize at first hand what the task is, what knowledge is required, how the program can be developed, and how to put into effect the necessary information received in the formal courses.[4]

Miss Kinney also described the qualities necessary for a bibliotherapist.

> To become a bibliotherapist, an individual needs the personal qualities, the emotional stability, the physical well-being, the character, and the personality necessary for him to work successfully with people. The work includes supervision and instruction of other personnel and co-workers, as well as a thorough understanding of the community. The demands of his work require a willingness to recognize the misfortunes of others and to react with sufficient facility to be of help. In addition, such a specialist has to understand the goal desired in each instance, be willing to accept responsibility for action taken, and be able to assume authority whenever necessary. Furthermore, it is necessary for the therapist to recognize and control personal prejudices, to be receptive to new learning, and to direct and channel personal feelings in a manner that would not impair his helpfulness to others. As a bibliotherapist such a person needs to assume responsibility for the selection of reading materials; his selections would be based upon the understanding of cause and effect as they relate to the physical, emotional and cultural factors related to the reader.
>
> An understanding of and a feeling for what goes on when one person talks and another listens are of primary importance to anyone understanding this aspect of librarianship. A thorough knowledge of disturbances in communication, whether distortions in perception (listening) or in transmission (speaking) and an ability to communicate with and feel a real interest in the other individual are of great value.[5]

SPECIFIC TRAINING NECESSARY TO BECOME A BIBILIOTHERAPIST

Experience in the bibliotherapy training program at St. Elizabeths has led us to ask ourselves why such a program is necessary for librarians and others from varied backgrounds. Primarily the reason is the development of new skills for use with special tools. Just as dance and body movement therapy uses the human body to release the self, just as art and music therapy uses each mode as a unique medium for self-expression and insight, so bibliotherapy uses written materials or films created by others (or created by the patrons themselves) to bring out uniquely personal feelings and emotions in the discussion that develops.

Training in psychotherapy, nursing or social work equips the individual with some clinical skills and knowledge but not with expertise in use of literature or films as therapeutic agents. The question needs to be raised and dealt with as to whether a psychiatrist, psychologist, or a social worker can automatically be a good bibliotherapist without further training.

The specific skills necessary to bibliotherapy seem to involve:
—Developing a sensitivity for the appropriate literature or films and learning to use them in an insightful or therapeutic way totally different from teaching, preaching or learning in the ordinary sense. We do not yet know whether this is an intuitive creative process or one for which hard and fast criteria will ultimately emerge. At present it seems

vital that trainees and interns, as well as practicing bibliotherapists, constantly review materials and use them with different groups and for different goals in order to gain this sensitivity.

—Understanding the process whereby literature or films encourages appropriate goals for individuals. These goals may range from pleasure to healthful opportunity for normal growth and self-understanding to self-affirmation through catharsis and insight. Much work needs to be done before this process is clarified.

—Gaining knowledge about oneself as a communicator of therapeutic literary materials and about the importance of the image one projects through expressive use of tone and diction, facial and body movement, so that the message is clarified. Sensing when the group members can communicate more effectively with each other than through the facilitator as the one who chooses materials and is the prime reader is an important second stage of this self-knowledge and moves the group into another phase of growth. The differences in dealing with mentally ill and with groups of ordinary people seeking normal growth will be highlighted here, for the role of the bibliotherapist as one who chooses the material and reads it aloud will vary considerably. Chronic patients or physically handicapped persons seem to need this kind of leadership at some point. Normal growth group members are less likely to.

—Mastering the art of directing the interaction process within the triad—the materials, the individual patron, and the facilitator. There is a further overlay when one adds the dimension of group dynamics and the interplay between the selected media and the group process. This is another area that demands further study.

—Learning to listen with the "third ear" in order to recognize the basic differences in responses to the literature, films or creative writing. One needs to learn whether the response is one of intellectualizing, judging, sermonizing, theorizing or refusing to deal in a feeling way. One also needs to gauge how to use that response to increase openness. One must learn how to encourage the open response without coercing or without endangering trust. At other times it will be necessary to know when overt adherence to the literature, films, or creative writing will be most productive of insight and when something seemingly tangential is of more significance.

—Each bibliotherapist is uniquely himself or herself and therefore there is no one acceptable way to lead a group. Through training and the resulting refinement of personal insight into the bibliotherapeutic process, each will come to the development of a therapeutic style.

All of this brings to mind the question as to whether a bibliotherapist is to be a mental health worker so trained that he could lay aside the tool and do therapy without the literary, film, creative writing materials. In the opinion of the author when a fully trained psychiatrist, psychologist, chaplain, social worker, or nurse wishes to lay aside this particular tool they may do so. However, the bibliotherapist, like the art, music or dance therapist, would not function as such without reliance on his unique tool.

THE TRAINING PROGRAM AT ST. ELIZABETHS

The on-going, two-year training program at St. Elizabeths has been conducted with a remarkable, dedicated group of nonstipended trainees who come for training, supervision and facilitating of groups after their regular work hours. These are the basic experiences that have gone into that program.

1. Class discussions based on assigned readings introduce the program. The librarian-bibliotherapist has gathered a body of materials for the necessary didactic presentations so that a basic understanding of bibliotherapy, its definition, goals, processes and techniques as well as relevant other materials can be presented. The books *Poetry Therapy* and *Poetry, the Healer,* edited by Dr. Leedy provide many provocative discussions.[6] There is a wide field of journal material on bibliotherapy and poetry as well as articles in the therapeutic field which add insights.

2. Simultaneously, from the very beginning, the trainees become a bibliotherapy group with the first sessions led by the bibliotherapist. Later, each trainee is involved as facilitator for this experiential bibliotherapy group. In all cases critiquing is done following each experience which continues throughout the two-year program. We find that didactic presentations alone do not sufficiently initiate trainees into the process. We believe our tool of bibliotherapy to be so effective we use it for our own self-growth and self-understanding during training.

3. Experience in facilitating bibliotherapy groups with patients is the major part of the training program. After the introductory formal training classes are completed each trainee is placed with a consultor, who is a psychotherapist who works on the ward to which the trainee has been assigned. The trainee will meet with the patient group for about one hour each week. Then he or she and the consultor will spend a half hour weekly discussing the patients' reactions and any procedural or therapeutic advice that would be of help to the trainee. In some cases the trainee and the consultor function as a team. As the trainee becomes comfortable with the situation, taping the session, with the permission of the patients, is encouraged so that listening to them will sharpen the awareness of what happened and what might have been overlooked. The individual short period weekly with the clinical liaison or consultor continues throughout the program.

(a) The continuity of meeting on the same ward, with the same consultor for the group session throughout the two years provides many advantages. The trainee learns much about herself or himself in terms of steadfastness and also gains familiarity with one ward's setting, a microcosm of the institution. The long term relationship allows the ward consultor or liaison, the group supervision supervisor and the bibliotherapist to learn much about the trainees' capacity for growth as progress is made through each one's own life as well as through the training program. All are thus better able to evaluate the trainee in the first year and the intern in the second year of the program. As time goes on there will be trained bibliotherapists serving on wards who will then become the ward consultor, just as now occupational, recreational and dance therapists help train their students.

(b) A second bibliotherapy group experience is required after the first half of the training program has been completed. This gives the intern an opportunity to work with another ward consultor and with patients whose problems are different from those of the first group. This breadth of guided experience is very beneficial.

4. Group supervision conducted by a psychiatrist, Kenneth Gorelick, M.D., Staff Psychiatrist, Dix Division, and the bibliotherapist is held for an hour and a half weekly throughout the entire program. Fortunately for the program, Dr. Gorelick, is providing group supervision of group therapy. He is also the consultor to the bibliotherapy training program and certifies the intern to the Association for Poetry Therapy at the end of the training program. During group supervision of group therapy what goes on in each trainee's group is reviewed with all present contributing observations and insights. Affirmation and validation of experiences are thus provided and deeper insights into more therapeutic facilitation is gained. The feelings of each trainee or intern in the situations that arise are also examined and reflected upon leading to greater self-awareness. Successful selections of materials are shared and changes in approach or materials used may be suggested.

5. An hour weekly with the bibliotherapist provides an opportunity for presentation and discussion of relevant didactic materials as well as for the periodic experiential bibliotherapy group meetings.

6. Reports are made by the trainees throughout the entire training program. At first the reports are for the bibliotherapist, the supervising psychiatrist and the ward consultant. The bibliotherapist counsels individually with the trainees and interns on the basis of the reports and group supervision. After the initial period, and where each trainee's or intern's schedule permits, they join in staff meetings. Reports are submitted for the patients' records near the end of the training program. Content of the reports needs further study and amplification.

7. Selection of effective and appropriate bibliotherapy materials is integral to proper training. Therefore, constant expansion of the range of materials chosen is part of the program. An ever-growing file of effective materials is kept in the Circulating Library. Each trainee also annotates each item she uses by noting on an index card with which kind of group the item was used, the general nature of the group response and any particularly valuable insight noted. A subject file with such headings as "Doors", "Forgiveness", "Loneliness",

"Sleep" is being developed. Each trainee finds out very early in the program that each must build a file of bibliotherapy materials as well as complementary items.

This ambitious training program at St. Elizabeths requires a minimum of 448 training hours over a two year period. The goal of the first year is that of becoming a volunteer bibliotherapy aide and that of the second year, professional bibliotherapy training. As of mid-1976 one intern has completed the program and, incidentally, has thereby met the requirements of and has been certified in the Association for Poetry Therapy. She has just become the first person hired by St. Elizabeths Hospital as a Bibliotherapist. Two of the first group of trainees are looking toward professional status, while three stopped at the pre-professional level (volunteer bibliotherapy aide) and two others broke off training. A second group has almost completed the first year and recruitment for the third class is in progress.

There is no national organization of bibliotherapists to grant certification. This needs to be created in the future. Poetry is the main tool used in the St. Elizabeths program. Poetry therapists recognize that they use only that one aspect of bibliotherapy. Since the Association for Poetry Therapy is the one body which has begun addressing standards and certification, we encourage our graduates to apply for the C.P.T., (certified poetry therapist).

Future planning envisions stipended bibliotherapy trainees in a full year's program at St. Elizabeths.

QUALIFICATIONS AND TRAINING EXPERIENCES

At St. Elizabeths we feel the basic qualifications for a bibliotherapist are the essential character traits and personal qualifications. In addition, we feel there must be facility with the tools, the literature and films used in a group setting. Familiarity with the management of groups and with the various liaison roles we play in an institutional setting are also essential.

The prerequisite character qualities we have identified include those essential for all people in the helping professions. In addition, specific training is needed to combine these characteristics with knowledge of literature and films and their resources and with the psychological skills to produce the bibliotherapist who can facilitate growth or healing.

The qualities of reliability, responsibility, consistency, nonexploitiveness, emotional stability and discretion in confidentiality are those which the budding bibliotherapist brings to the training program. It is these qualities as evidenced in the applicant's prior life experience and in his or her personal demeanor that will be sought out in the resume and personal interview. Over the two-year period it will also be evident that these qualities do persist.

As Ms. Kinney stated, a primary personal qualification is the necessity to relate to other individuals in a direct and personal way and to appreciate another's cognitive and emotional deficits as well as their strengths and be able to accept both.[6] With that goes the ability to evaluate the rest of the environment and its influences on responses.

Correlative qualifications include the ability to seek and use supervision and consultation so that the bibliotherapist will be able to know himself or herself. Group supervision, study of the reports by all consultors and supervisors, analysis of audio or visual tapes used in the ward groups and the evaluating interviews throughout the program will help the clinical supervisors and the bibliotherapist gauge this highly significant ability. In the trainee's or intern's ability to use supervision will lie the insight to more wisely perceive personal needs and feelings and the impact of these on the group. The problems of egocentrism, misuse of counter-transference and the pitfalls of saviorism can be modified and minimized through acceptance of wise guidance by the various members of the supervising team. If guidance and supervision cannot be accepted, the problems will remain and the person should not become a bibliotherapist.

The bibliotherapy experience base will be deepened in our training program by the addition of a second ward group in the second year of training. This will include working with a second ward consultor. The further experience will provide other opportunities to deal with charged moments resulting from the patient's psychosis or hostility. There will also be another consultor's insights into how to capably handle the realities of apathy, withdrawal, silence or avoidance.

Management of the group is an area of training that is necessary, although it is certainly possible to use bibliotherapy effectively on a one-to-one basis. Group activity has its own therapeutic advantages that work very well in combination with literature written by others or by group members or with films. In institutional or library settings the group will very likely continue to be the most common mode of procedure.

The trainees and interns need to learn how to relate to the group as a whole as a therapeutic agent, to individual members, and how to establish a group climate of trust built on the personal worth of each group member. In short, the trainee must learn to form, to maintain, to terminate a group and must be familiar in detail with these phases.

Bibliotherapists also need to learn about various leadership styles, when and how they might vary and how to identify their own unique styles within these variations. They also need to learn facilitating techniques and to adapt them to the use of literature and films. Training is needed to develop the skill of drawing out feeling response to literary input. Another fundamental of bibliotherapy is that it is not coercive and thus the trainee needs to gain facility in recognizing the group needs at the moment and be prepared to accommodate. How to compensate for and best utilize differences between chronic and acute patients, differences between people with different personalities and different problems must be learned in relation to group selection and mix.

From the very beginning of training the goals of the group and of the use of literature or films is stressed. Training is needed to develop a refinement of insight in identifying appropriate goals with different groups and at different times in the group life. At times sheer fun and aesthetic enjoyment may bring the best results: at some, recognition of the here and now issues may be indicated: at others, socialization and building strong group cohesion may be the best therapy; self-awareness and self-understanding leading to normal growth may be appropriate for other groups. Insight and catharsis may underlie and overlap all of these.

At the present state of the art, whenever a bibliotherapist deals with the mentally ill, he or she must operate under institutional oversight of the hospital, correctional institution, a community mental health center or supervising psychiatrist or psychologist. It is legitimate for a trained person to use bibliotherapy in a public library, a church group or retirement home when normal growth and self-understanding are clearly set as the goals. Training in a hospital setting would help the bibliotherapist to deal with normal and distorted personal growth. Development of a code of ethics is an issue which needs more exposure and discussion.

CURRENT TRAINING PROGRAM

Currently around one hundred patients a week at St. Elizabeths are benefiting from bibliotherapy. The librarian of the patients' library, a certified poetry therapist, conducts groups as well as the full time bibliotherapist and the trainees. The bibliotherapist has a newly established Federal Civil Service rating in the 601 series. In this case the bibliotherapist is performing a library service to patients. Whether bibliotherapists will also be hired as other adjunctive therapists outside of library services lies with the trend established by those who become trained in the field and in the way they present the need for those services to communities and institutions. It would seem that both trends would continue.

Several regular hospital staff have taken a basic twenty-hour didactic-experiential course to acquaint themselves with the general scope and goals of bibliotherapy and provide a small amount of personal experience in bibliotherapy. For those few staff members who may want to continue through the 440-hour program and become Certified Poetry Therapists (CPT's) opportunities are made to join the nonstipended trainee program and to carry on supervised bibliotherapy groups.

The three-hour credit course in bibliotherapy taught at the Catholic University of America's Graduate School of Librarianship has resulted in also establishing a semester's practicum experience in bibliotherapy group work in the hospital with some bibliotherapy and psychotherapy supervision. Plans now are to start with a new group of trainees each fall for the total 440-hour certification program described by the Association for Poetry Therapy. One person has already received her CPT and the present interns will be ready to present to the Association for certification this winter. At some time we hope to investigate the possibilities of grants to stipend trainees.

At the present most of the nonstipended trainees meet the requirements of the training program after their regular working day. Therefore they devote two and three evenings a week to the certification program. They are not able to join in the regular training program at St. Elizabeths which involves a nine or twelve-month long eight-hour a day training program. The hope is that in the future stipended bibliotherapy trainees would join in the core curriculum of the Overholser Division classes now held for students in many therapeutic fields. The core curriculum holds sessions in each of the following: clinical psychiatry, human growth and development, mental health delivery systems and both didactic and experiential sessions in hospital group work. These are significant learnings from which the bibliotherapy trainees would profit. As in the other training disciplines, trainees would also follow the specific work and training experiences of the bibliotherapy program.

SUMMARY AND CONCLUSIONS

Some practical matters relating to the value of course work versus the present Association for Poetry Therapy certification standards can be examined in the light of recent experiences. At the present time it seems that a worthwhile didactic-experiential course in bibliotherapy for three or six graduate credit hours could be readily developed for library schools or in other disciplines. A regular practicum experience for another three hours of credit involving group work with patients in a hospital setting is also valuable. But even a two-semester course and another semester practicum are not equivalent to the Association for Poetry Therapy certification.

Neither would a three-month, eight-hour-a-day program, such as colleges sponsor, for those in recreational or occupational therapy programs qualify. Nor would such a brief program of training for those already serving in institutions qualify. And a week-long-mini-course, such as taught at Denver University Library school in 1975, 1976 and 1977, or any of the brief workshops available offers no more than a taste of bibliotherapy. However worthwhile the various short-term programs may be, they do not begin to equate with the Certified Poetry Therapist program.

The standards, potentially amendable by the Association for Poetry Therapy, are purposefully high so that institutions for mental health, correctional institutions and drug and alcoholic programs can rely on well-trained staff to provide bibliotherapy or poetry therapy services. As Miss Kinney stated, this hospital background will also be "the most concentrated and valuable training" for those who may choose to work later in youth and children's programs, retirement homes or in public libraries and schools.[7]

Screening of applicants for the Association for Poetry Therapy certification program at St. Elizabeths began with the fall 1976 group. Screening interviews are held and evaluated. After three months is another evaluation to determine suitability and commitment to the program. Another interview session is set up between the bibliotherapist, the psychiatrist who leads the group supervision supervisory sessions weekly, and the trainee to check further progress toward certification at the end of the first half of the program. There is a final evaluation, as well, before certification is applied for.

As other training programs in bibliotherapy and poetry therapy continue to develop in and out of hospital settings, there will be need for continuing dialogue to sort out, evaluate and creatively deal with the many issues that are going to be raised as time goes on. For example, as more training programs develop, the dependency in training on a psychiatrist or psychologist (whether also trained as a bibliotherapist or not) will need to be clarified. Trained bibliotherapists may reject the medical model of oversight as have the other activities therapies such as occupational, recreational and dance therapy who monitor their own training programs.

Research and consultation of all kinds is essential to the growth of any field. For example, there has been little serious discussion about whether specific modes and measurements of effectiveness will have to be developed for bibliotherapy. For example, is it possible to measure bibliotherapy's effectiveness in bringing out potentiality? Will it be possible to measure the number and depth of healthy responses to literature versus appearance of delusional responses? What is the role of communication, of empathy, of evocativeness, of creativity, of trust, of morale building and of beauty in relation to bibliotherapy and how can these be tested? Furthermore, the relationships between bibliotherapy and the several schools of psychotherapy needs to be studied. Consultation might well result in a code of ethics or guidelines for bibliotherapists and poetry therapists, and concensus on the choice of a better generic term for the field might be the most popular need to fill.

At any rate, those of us who share enthusiasm for the whole field of bibliotherapy or for that special part, poetry therapy, are likely to agree with Dostoievsky: "The world will be saved by beauty."

Note: Arleen M. Hynes, CPT is the librarian in the Circulating Library at St. Elizabeths Hospital. This paper was presented at the Fourth World Poetry Therapy Conference and the annual meeting of the Association for Poetry Therapy, April 23-24, 1976 in New York City.

1. Burt, Lesta Norris. "Bibliotherapy: Effect of Group Reading and Discussion on Attitudes of Adult Inmates in Two Correctional Institutions." Doctoral thesis. (University of Wisconsin, 1972).

2. Sclabassi, Sharon Henderson. "Literature as a Therapeutic Tool: A Review of the Literature on Bibliotherapy." *American Journal of Psychotherapy* 28:70-77.

3. Morrison, Morris R. "Standards for Certification of Poetry Therapists and Related Matters; A Proposal." *Association of Hospital and Institution Libraries Quarterly* (Summer/Fall 1973).

4. Kinney, Margaret. "The Bibliotherapy Program: Requirements for Training," *Library Trends,* ed. by Ruth M. Tews (October, 1962).

5. Leedy, J. J. ed. *Poetry Therapy* (Philadelphia, Pa: J. B. Lippincott & Co., 1969); and *Poetry the Healer* (Philadelphia, Pa.: J. B. Lippincott & Co., 1973).

6. Kinney, Margaret. "The Bibliotherapy program . . ."

7. Ibid.

Appendix III B

Standards for Certification of Poetry Therapists and Related Matters: A Proposal

by Morris R. Morrison

Since poetry therapy as a recognized modality has been accepted by the healing professions as a valuable adjunct in the treatment of emotional dysfunction, it is the intent of this document to protect the public by setting standards of qualification, training, and experience for those who seek to engage in the profession of poetry therapist.

Teachers, librarians, counselors, and others not licensed by the state to practice therapy but who in the judgment of their various facilities have been authorized to adapt the uses of poetry therapy to their practice, must understand that theirs is an adjunctive role. Their understanding of the salutary and rehabilitative value of poetry does not represent a displacement of medical authority.

STANDARDS FOR THE CERTIFICATION OF THE POETRY THERAPIST

What Is Poetry Therapy? Poetry Therapy is the use of poetry in the treatment of emotional disorders. The trained poetry therapist serves as subordinate to the attending physician in a program designed to assist the patient to a greater understanding of himself and the world about him, resulting in a more effective adjustment to society and better mental and physical health. Periodic evaluations, it is understood, will be conducted by the acting psychiatrist and the staff to determine the effectiveness of the procedures employed by the therapist.

With Whom Is Poetry Therapy Used? Poetry Therapists customarily work with subjects attending an accredited facility for the treatment of mental disorders. Patients may range from the maladjusted and schizophrenic child to the disturbed adolescent to the various types of adult mental illnesses to geriatric cases, wherever behavioral modification is medically prescribed. Poetry may also be used in work with the mentally retarded, the cerebral palsied, the crippled, the blind, and those with multiple handicaps. Poetry therapy may be used in schools where students give evidence of emotional dysfunction. No program may be pursued unless it is monitored by a supervising psychiatrist, clinical psychologist, or mental health worker with comparable qualifications. Some poetry therapists may work in their own offices with patients referred by psychiatrists or other medical specialists who will continue to act as consultant to the therapist.

What Are the Opportunities for Poetry Therapists? The value of the arts in therapy continues to find greater recognition with each succeeding day. Already more than 600 hospitals and similar institutions employ music therapists. According to the National Association for Music Therapy "Undoubtedly there are many more who would like to have music therapy but there are not enough therapists." The demand exists throughout the United States and students from foreign countries are now coming to the United States for training in music therapy. More than half the states have Civil Service classifications which provide for music therapists.

What Are the Personal Qualifications for Poetry Therapists? Emotional stability is very important. The therapist, as a person, understanding himself as well as his fellow-man, is often as important as the modality he employs in treatment. There is no substitute for a genuine feeling and desire to help others. Patience, tact, understanding, and a healthy sense of humor are indispensable. The therapist must work well with other medical personnel without exaggerating his own importance in the therapeutic team.

What Educational Preparation Is Necessary for Poetry Therapists? A trainee in poetry therapy should have graduated from an accredited college with a degree in the humanities or the behavioral sciences. Equivalent credit may be granted for a combination of completed college courses and experience in a recognized institution. Recommended are studies in sociology, anthropology, psychology, art, music, and literature. There should be evidence of concentration in poetry covering the primitive, the classical, the post-renaissance cultures as well as the modern and avant-garde writing. The trainee must also provide evidence that he has been accepted into a mental health program as a volunteer or salaried employee under professional supervision.

What Is the Association for Poetry Therapy? Poetry therapy predates all current attempts to provide mental healing. Evidence exists of its use in preliterate times and in surviving primitive societies. The Greek philosopher, Gorgias, compared the effect of poetry on man's soul to the expulsion of evil humors from the body. Plato and Aristotle speculated on poetry as a healing modality. Freud referred to the poets as "valuable colleagues." "In the knowledge of the human heart," he wrote "they are far ahead of us common folk, because they draw on sources we have not yet made available to science." A considerable body of literature is available today on the structured use of bibliotherapy and poetry in public institutions, in schools, and in private practice in mental health programs. The publication of *Poetry Therapy* in 1969 by J. B. Lippincott and Company focused public attention on the work now being done in this area and its future promise. Shortly thereafter the Association for Poetry Therapy was officially incorporated in the State of New York to set standards for the certification of future poetry therapists, to serve as a center for mutual exchange in new developments in poetry therapy and to provide for annual conventions where papers devoted to recent research may be presented and workshops set up for the exploration of new techniques.

Who May Become Members of the Association for Poetry Therapy? There are two categories of membership. The first is reserved for psychiatrists, psychologists, social workers (MSW), nurses (RN), guidance counselors, registered rehabilitation counselors, occupational therapists, recreation therapists, educators, and librarians. The second category, that of associate member, includes professional poets and lay people not in the aforementioned groups, who are concerned with furthering the promotion of poetry therapy as a valuable resource with multiple applications both to the prevention and treatment of mental illness.

What Are the Requirements for Certification? Honoring the grandfather clause, validation is allowed to those certified *prior to February 1, 1973.* Hereafter, no applicant may be granted a certificate as poetry therapist unless he meets one of the following requirements: (1) He presents evidence of holding the degree of doctor of medicine or a doctorate in clinical psychology or has been licensed to practice psychotherapy in the State of New York. (2) He has completed two years of supervised training under approved auspices—one year as trainee in poetry therapy and an additional year as intern in poetry therapy and has completed the course work hereafter.

To obtain designation of trainee in poetry therapy the applicant (1) must present proof of graduation from an accredited college, (2) or achieve equivalence through other study programs and experience, and (3) must have been accepted as a volunteer or salaried employee in an educational, rehabilitation, or mental health facility where he will be trained in poetry therapy under the supervision of a psychiatrist or registered psychologist.

What Is the Role in Certification? The Association for Poetry Therapy, incorporated in the State of New York, will continue its policy of certifying qualified practitioners to pursue the vocation of poetry therapist according to the requirements set down by the standards committee. Anyone so certified may represent himself as a poetry therapist by adding the letters C.P.T. to his name.

As stated, all certifications granted before February 1, 1973 shall be deemed valid. After February 1, 1973 no certification shall be made except to those applicants who fulfilled the requirements set down in this document, which shall be attested to by the committee on certification. The committee shall be made up of three members appointed by the president of the Association for Poetry Therapy. It shall include one psychiatrist, one licensed psychologist, and a representative from the field of education.

After February 1, 1973 no person may represent himself as poetry therapist by adding the letters C.P.T. unless he has fulfilled all qualifications for certification, attested to by the signatures of the certification committee.

Fees The following fees shall be paid in connection with certification:

1. application for certification as poetry therapist: $15.00
2. application for designation as intern in poetry therapy: $10.00
3. application for designation as trainee in poetry therapy: $10.00
4. application for renewal of any foregoing certification: $10.00
5. all fees are nonrefundable and shall be deposited in the treasury of the association.

Privileged Communication No certified poetry therapist, intern, or trainee may disclose any information he may have acquired from persons consulting him in his professional capacity that was necessary to enable him to render services in his professional capacity to those persons except:

A. With the written consent of the client. In the case of death or disability, of his personal representative, other person authorized to sue, or the beneficiary of an insurance policy on his life, health, or physical condition;

B. That a certified poetry therapist shall not be required to treat as confidential a communication that reveals the contemplation of a crime or harmful act;

C. Where the person is a child under the age of sixteen and the information acquired by the therapist indicated that the child was the victim or subject of a crime, the therapist may be required to testify fully in relation thereto upon any examination, trial, or other proceeding in which the commission of such crime is a subject of inquiry.

D. Where the person waives the privilege by bringing charges against the therapist, intern, or trainee.

Separability Clause: If any section of this document, or any part thereof, be adjudged by any court of competent jurisdiction to be invalid, such judgment shall not effect, impair, or invalidate the remainder of any other section or part thereof.

Note: Morris R. Morrison is the executive director of the Association of Poetry Therapists (APT), chairman of the Committee on Standards and Certification.

Appendix III C

Job Descriptions for Bibliotherapists

1   Bibliotherapist I for County of Santa Clara, California

SALARY RANGE $901-1,096 Monthly

THE POSITION

Conducts bibliotherapy sessions with emotionally disturbed patients in a community rehabilitation facility; selects material for patient reading or group discussion; reads selected poems, plays, short stories and other material to patient groups; facilitates group discussion of the literature, observes and keeps notes on patient reactions to the material and to the group situation; consults with staff of community rehabilitation organizations such as mental health centers, board and care facilities and jails regarding status of current bibliotherapy participants, new patient referrals, and establishment of new bibliotherapy programs; assists in interpreting the bibliotherapy program to community groups and organizations through lectures and demonstrations; assists in preparation of program reports as needed; and performs other related duties as required.

APPLICATION REQUIREMENTS

Training and experience equivalent to graduation from an accredited college or university with a major in psychology or counseling, and some experience in working with groups of emotionally disturbed individuals.

Knowledge of: Usage of library reference materials; a wide variety of literature suitable for use for emotionally disturbed patients; techniques of group leadership and conflict resolution.

Ability to: Relate literature to individual and group needs; research and select literary material suitable for emotionally disturbed patients; lead groups in discussions of literary materials and relate such materials to personal experiences; evaluate patients' participation in a bibliotherapy program for use by professional and mental health personnel; speak and write effectively; maintain effective relationships with patients and professional personnel.

EXAMINATION

The examination will include one or more of the following parts: application review; written test; oral interview. If applications are received in such numbers that a competitive rating of education and experience is not possible from a review alone, those factors will be determined by a written test and/or oral interview. If both a written test and an oral interview are required, 50 percent of the total examination weight will be assigned to the written portion and 50 percent to the oral.

Applicants will be notified by mail when and where to appear for any written or oral examinations that are scheduled.

A minimum rating of 70 percent is required for each part of the examination. According to Merit System Rules, the 70 percent used to represent the minimum acceptable score on the written test need not be the arithmetical 70 percent, but may be adjusted, based on a consideration of the difficulty of the test, the degree of competition, and the needs of the service. Those eligibles scoring 80 percent or more on the examination will be certified to the department in which they are working before eligibles from other County departments.

As a condition of employment each employee in this class must sign a payroll deduction authorization form providing for deduction of union membership dues or a service fee. A 30 day cancellation period is provided.

Issued 12/4/74

2   Bibliotherapist II
for County of Santa Clara, California

SALARY RANGE $994-1,209 Monthly

THE POSITION

Conducts bibliotherapy sessions with emotionally disturbed patients in a community rehabilitation facility; selects and obtains materials for patient reading or group discussion; reads selected poems, plays, short stories and other material to patient groups; facilitates group discussion of the literature, observes and keeps notes on patient reactions to the material and to the group situation; consults with staff of community rehabilitation organizations such as mental health centers, board and care facilities and jails regarding status of current bibliotherapy participants, new patient referrals, and establishment of new bibliotherapy programs; primary responsibility for interpreting the bibliotherapy program to community groups and organizations through lectures and demonstrations and correspondence; trains and supervises Bibliotherapist I; prepares reports on the status of program as needed; supervises university work-study students in bibliotherapy uses and techniques; and performs other related duties as required.

APPLICATION REQUIREMENTS

Training and experience equivalent to graduation from an accredited college or university with a major in psychology or counseling and some experience in working with groups of emotionally disturbed individuals, including demonstrated ability to assume program responsibility.

Knowledge of: Usage of library reference materials; a wide variety of literature suitable for use for emotionally disturbed patients; techniques of group leadership and conflict resolution; effective supervisory and training practices.

Ability to: Administer a bibliotherapy program; relate literature to individual and group needs; research and select literary material suitable for emotionally disturbed patients; lead groups in discussions of literary materials and relate such materials to personal experiences; evaluate patients' participation in a bibliotherapy program for use by professional mental health personnel; speak and write effectively; maintain effective relationships with patients and professional personnel.

EXAMINATION

The examination will include one or more of the following parts: application review; written test; oral interview. If applications are received in such numbers that a competitive rating of education and experience is not possible from a review alone, those factors will be determined by a written test and/or an oral interview. If both a written test and an oral interview are required, 50 percent of the total examination weight will be assigned to the written portion and 50 percent to the oral.

Applicants will be notified by mail when and where to appear for any written or oral examinations that are scheduled.

A minimum rating of 70 percent is required for each part of the examination. According to Merit System Rules, the 70 percent used to represent the minimum acceptable score on the written test need not be the arithmetical 70 percent, but may be adjusted, based on a consideration of the difficulty of the test, the degree of competition, and the needs of the service. Those eligibles scoring 80 percent or more on the examination will be certified to the department in which they are working before eligibles from other County departments.

As a condition of employment each employee in this class must sign a payroll deduction authorization form providing for deduction of union membership dues or a service fee. A 30 day cancellation period is provided.

Issued 12/4/74

3　Bibliotherapist for U.S. Civil Service Commission

CLASSIFICATION RANGE: GS 7-11

Purpose

Conducts bibliotherapy with mentally ill and emotionally disturbed individuals in the various divisions of the Hospital and the Circulating Library.

Major Duties

Under the supervision of the Librarian in the Circulating Library, establishes and organizes bibliotherapy groups by locating groups of patients that may benefit from the experience. Contacts medical officers, nursing personnel and others concerned with patient care and communicates the content and nature of the bibliotherapy program. Secures patient referrals from the sources.

After evaluating the group, selects literature or other media material suitable for the group. Reads aloud or otherwise uses the material. Acts as facilitator and encourages discussion of the material used. Guides the discussion to bring out feelings and to achieve fruitful self-understanding by the members. Observes reactions and writes clinical notes for incorporation into the patient's chart.

Meets with the team to discuss objectives and progress for individual patients. Regularly consults with a psychiatrist or other professional for group supervision.

Performs other duties as necessary.

Controls and Responsibility

Work is performed under the supervision of the Librarian in the Circulating Library. Incumbent exercises independent judgment in the performance of the duties, seeking advice of the supervisor in non-routine situations or negative responses. Performance is evaluated in terms of effectiveness and overall results achieved.

Other Significant Facts

Bibliotherapist must possess genuine respect and concern for individuals, mature personality traits, understanding of communication processes, broad knowledge of literature and its relationship to personal experience and problems, media materials and a working knowledge of group dynamics. A rating as a Certified Poetry Therapist is desirable.

Filed September 15, 1976

Appendix III D

Synopsis of Certification (or Registration) Standards for Other Therapy Groups

ALL THE BELOW ARE CERTIFIED BY THE ASSOCIATION LISTED

1. National Association for Music Therapy, Inc.
   Registration of therapists begun in 1950.

   Baccalaureate Degrees in Music Therapy are available from 32 colleges in the United States. Coursework is required in Music Therapy (10 semester hours), Psychology (10-12), Sociology/Anthropology (6-8), Music (60), Education (30).

   An additional requirement is a 6 month period of practical training in an approved clinical facility under the direction of a registered Music Therapist. Master's Degrees are also available in Music Therapy.

2. National Therapeutic Recreation Society. (Part of the National Recreation and Park Association).

   Registration is available for Therapeutic Recreation Assistants, Therapeutic Recreation Technicians, Therapeutic Recreation Leaders, Therapeutic Recreation Specialists, and Master Therapeutic Recreation Specialists. The last 2 seem most applicable.

   Requirements for Therapeutic Recreation Specialist:

   Master's Degree from an accredited college with an emphasis in Therapeutic Recreation or Master's with a major in Recreation and 1 year experience or Baccalaureate with major in Therapeutic Recreation and 3 years experience or Baccalaureate in another field and 5 years experience.

   Requirements for Master Therapeutic Recreation Specialist:

   Master's Degree with major emphasis in Therapeutic Recreation and 2 years' experience *or* Master's in Recreation and 3 years' experience *or* Master's in another field and 4 years' experience *or* Baccalaureate in Therapeutic Recreation and 5 years' experience plus 6 credits of Graduate Education *or* Baccalaureate in another major and 7 years' experience and 18 credits of Graduate Education.

3.   American Occupational Therapy Association, Inc.

The Association recognizes both Certified occupational Therapist Assistants and Registered Occupational Therapists. The latter classification seems applicable.

Requirements for Registered Occupational Therapists:

A Baccalaureate in Occupational Therapy (which includes 6-16 credits of Biology and Physics, 6-14 credits of English, 3-12 credits of Psychology, and 3-8 credits of Psychology, and 3-8 credits of Sociology. Sometimes included are Art, Education and Speech). 6-9 months of field experience is also required.

50 schools in the United States offer Baccalaureates in O.T. or a Baccalaureate in another field plus O.T. Certification, which entails a college program of 45 semester credits (included are 6-18 credits of Biology or Physics, 6-12 of Psychology and 3-8 of sociology. Sometimes included are facility in 3 manual skills such as Drawing, Speech, etc.). In addition, 6-9 months of clinical experience is necessary. 6 schools in the United States offer this certification program. Master's Degrees are also available in O.T.

4.   Association for Poetry Therapy.

Certification of Poetry Therapists began in February, 1973. Certified Poetry Therapists are considered "subordinate to the attending physician".

Requirements to be designated a C.P.T. are:

1)   M.D. Degree *or* license to practice psychotherapy

2)   *Or* completion of 2 years of supervised training—one year as a trainee and one as an intern—under the guidance of a Psychiatrist or Psychologist. In order to be a trainee, one must be a college graduate and must have been accepted as a volunteer or employee of a facility where training and supervision are available.

Bibliography to Text

Agel, Jerome, ed. *The Radical Therapist* (New York: Ballantine Books, 1971).

———. *Rough Times* (New York: Ballantine Books, 1973).

Agnes, Sister Mary. "Bibliotherapy for Socially Maladjusted Children," *Catholic Educational Review* 44:8-15 (1946).

———. "The Influence of Reading On The Racial Attitudes of Adolescent Girls," *Catholic Educational Review* 45:415-420 (September 1947).

*Alexander, Rosa Horn and Stephen E. Buggie. "Bibliotherapy with Chronic Schizophrenics," *Journal of Rehabilitation* 33:26-27+ (November 1967).

Algermissen, Virginia. "Biomedical Librarians In A Patient Care Setting," *Bulletin of the Medical Library Assn.* 62:354-358 (October 1974).

Allport, G. W. "Attitudes," in C. Murchison, ed., *A Handbook of Clinical Psychology* (Worcester, Mass.: Clark University Press 1935).

*Alston, Edwin F. "Bibliotherapy and Psychotherapy," *Library Trends* 11:159-176 (October 1962).

Appel, Kenneth C. "Psychiatric Therapy," in J. Hunt, ed., *Personality and the Behavior Disorders*, vol. 2 (New York: Ronald Press, 1944).

Appelbaum, R., and others. *The Process of Group Communication* (Chicago: Science Research Associates, 1974).

Arbuthnot, May Hill, and Zena Sutherland. *Children and Books* 4th ed. (Glenview, Illinois: Scott, Foresman, and Co., 1972).

Axeline, Virginia M. *Dibs: In Search of Self* (Boston: Houghton-Mifflin, 1964).

Axelrod, Herman and Thomas R. Teti. "An Alternative to Bibliotherapy: Audiovisiotherapy" *Educational Technology* 16:36-38 (December 1976).

Ball, Ralph G. "Prescription: Books," *ALA Bulletin* 48:145-147 (March 1954).

Bandura, A., and R. H. Walters. *Social Learning and Personality Development* (New York: Holt, 1963).

Beatty, William K. "A Historical Review of Bibliotherapy," *Library Trends* 11:106-117 (October 1962).

___. "Proceedings of American Library Assn, Bibliotherapy Workshop, St. Louis, June 25-27, 1964," *A.H.I.L. Quarterly* 4:1-60 [entire issue] (Summer 1964).

Bem, D. J. "An Experimental Analysis of Self-Persuasion," *Journal of Experimental Social Psychology* 1:199-218 (1965).

Berelson, Bernard. "The Public Library, Book Reading, and Political Behavior," *Library Quarterly,* 15:299+ (1945).

Bergin, Allen E. "When Shrinks Hurt," *Psychology Today* 9:96-100+ (November 1975).

Berne, Eric. *Principles of Group Treatment* (New York: Oxford University Press, 1966).

Berry, Franklin. "Analysis of Processes In Bibliotherapy" Unpub. speech presented at the Fourth Bibliotherapy Round Table, Washington, D.C. (January 1977).

___. "A Comprehensive Bibliography of Bibliotherapy: A Prerequisite Step to a Conceptual Integration of the Field." Unpub. paper presented at the Fifth World Poetry Therapy Conference, New York (April 1977).

Bettelheim, Bruno. *The Uses of Enchantment,* (New York: Knopf, 1976).

Bettencourt, Bruce, and others. "Agnews State Hospital Patients' Library Bibliotherapy Project Final Report." (San Jose, California: Santa Clara County Library, March 1972).

Blackshear, Orilla T. "A Bibliotherapy Workshop," *Wisconsin Library Bulletin* 60:296-298 (September 1964).

Bowker Annual of Library and Book Trade Information (20th ed. New York: Bowker, 1975).

Brammer, L. M., and E. L. Shostrum. *Therapeutic Psychology* (Englewood Cliffs, New Jersey: Prentice-Hall, 1963).

Briggs, John F. "Adverse Effects From Bibliotherapy," *Hospital Progress* 45:123-125 (July 1964).

Brower, Daniel, M.D. "Bibliotherapy," in Daniel Brower and Lawrence Abt, eds., *Progress in Clinical Psychology,* 2nd ed. (New York: Grune and Stratton, 1956).

Brown, Eleanor Frances. *Bibliotherapy and Its Widening Applications* (Metuchen, New Jersey: Scarecrow, 1975).

Brown, Rosalie M. "Bibliotherapy as a Technique for Increasing Individuality Among Elderly Patients," *Hospital and Community Psychiatry* 28:347 (May 1977).

Bryan, Alice I. "Can There Be a Science of Bibliotherapy?," *Library Journal* 64:773-776 (October 15, 1939).

*___. "The Psychology of the Reader," *Library Journal* 64:7-12 (January 1, 1939).

Buck, Lucien, and Aaron Kramer. "Opening New Worlds to the Deaf and Disturbed," in Jack Leedy, ed., *Poetry the Healer* (Philadelphia: Lippincott, 1973).

Burt, Lesta Norris. "Bibliotherapy: Effect of Group Reading and Discussion on the Attitudes of Adult Inmates in Two Correctional Institutions" (Ph.D. dissertation, University of Wisconsin, 1972).

Calder, Bobby J., and Michael Ross. *Attitudes and Behavior* (Morristown, New Jersey: General Learning Press, 1973).

Cantrell, Clyde H., "Sadie P. Delaney: Bibliotherapist and Librarian," *Southeastern Librarian* 6:105-109 (Fall 1956).

Carlsen, George Robert. "A Study of the Effect of Reading Literature About the Negro on the Racial Attitudes of a Group of Eleventh Grade Students In Northern Schools" (Ph.D. dissertation, University of Minnesota, 1948).

Cartwright, Dorwin, and Alvin Zander. *Group Dynamics: Research and Theory* (New York: Harper and Row, 1968).

Casey, Genevieve. "Hospital and Institution Libraries," *ALA Bulletin* 55:822 (September 1961).

____, ed. *Libraries in the Therapeutic Society* (Chicago: Assn. of Hospital and Institution Libraries, 1971).

Chesler, Phyllis. *Women and Madness* (New York: Avon, 1973).

Cianciolo, Patricia Jean. "Children's Literature Can Affect Coping Behavior," *Personnel and Guidance Journal* 43:897-903 (1965).

____. "What Can the Illustrations Offer?," in Virginia M. Reid, *Reading Ladders for Human Relations*, 5th ed. (Washington, DC: American Council on Education, 1972).

Combs, A., and others. *Helping Relationships: Basic Concepts for the Helping Professions* (Boston: Allyn and Bacon, 1971).

Coville, W. J. "Bibliotherapy: Some Practical Considerations," *Hospital Progress* 41:138-142 (April/May 1960).

Delaney, Sadie P. "Bibliotherapy for Patients in a Drug Antabuse Clinic," *Hospital Book Guide* 16:140-141 (October 1955).

*____. "The Place of Bibliotherapy in a Hospital," *Library Journal* 63:305-308 (April 15, 1938).

Dolan, Rosemary, and others. *Bibliotherapy in Hospitals: An Annotated Bibliography 1900-1952* (Washington, DC: U. S. Veterans Administration, 1958).

____. *We Call It Bibliotherapy* (Washington, DC: U. S. Veterans Administration, 1967).

Dorland's Illustrated Medical Dictionary. 19th ed. (Philadelphia: Saunders, 1941).

Driver, Helen I. *Counseling and Learning Through Small Group Discussions* (Madison, Wisconsin: Monona Publications, 1958).

Edgar, Kenneth F., and Richard Hazley. "A Curriculum Proposal for Training Poetry Therapists," in Jack Leedy, ed., *Poetry Therapy* (Philadelphia: Lippincott, 1969).

——. "Validation of Poetry Therapy as a Group Therapy Technique," in Jack Leedy, ed. *Poetry Therapy* (Philadelphia: Lippincott, 1969).

Fader, Daniel. *Hooked On Books* (New York: G. P. Putnam, 1966).

——. *The New Hooked on Books* (New York: Berkeley Pub. 1976).

Fairbanks, Lucy F. "Activity Therapy," *AHIL Quarterly* 4:11 (Summer 1964).

Farrow, Vernon L. "Bibliotherapy: An Annotated Bibliography," *Curriculum Bulletin*, School of Education, University of Oregon (May 1963).

Festinger, Leon. *A Theory of Cognitive Dissonance* (Evanston, Illinois: Row, Peterson, 1957).

*Fierman, Louis B. and E. Y. Fierman. "Bibliotherapy in Psychiatry," in Dunton and Licht, eds., *Occupational Therapy: Principles and Practice*, 2nd ed. (Springfield, Illinois: Charles C. Thomas Pub., 1957).

Fierman, Louis B. "Psychiatry," *AHIL Quarterly* 4:12-14 (Summer 1964).

Figurel, Allen, ed. *Reading and Realism* (Newark, Delaware: International Reading Assn., 1969).

Fisher, Frank L. "Influence of Reading and Discussion on Attitudes of Fifth Graders Toward American Indians," *Journal of Educational Research* 62:130-134 (November 1968).

Floch, Maurice. "Bibliotherapy and the Library," *Bookmark* 18:57-59 (December 1958).

Floch, Maurice and Genevieve Casey. "The Library Goes to Prison," *ALA Bulletin* 49:126-128 (March 1955).

Frank, Jerome David. *Group Methods in Therapy*. Public Affairs Pamphlet no. 284 (New York, 1959).

Gagnon, Salomon, M.D. "Is Reading Therapy?," *Diseases of the Nervous System* 3:206-212 (July 1942).

Gardner, Richard A. "Mutual Storytelling as a Technique in Child Psychotherapy and Psychoanalysis," in J. Masserman, ed., *Science and Psychoanalysis*, vol. 14. (New York: Grune and Stratton, 1969).

Gilson, Preston, and Jamie Al-Saman. "Bibliotherapy in Oklahoma," *Oklahoma Librarian* 22:12+ (July 1972).

Goldenson, Robert M., ed. *The Encyclopedia of Human Behavior* (Garden City, New York: Doubleday and Co., 1970).

Goldsmith, S. "The Fable as a Medium for Character Education," *Elementary English Review* 16:223-224 (1939).

*Gottschalk, Louis A. "Bibliotherapy as an Adjunct in Psychiatry," *American Journal of Psychiatry* 104:632-637 (April 1948).

Graham, Mary B. "Motivation of Reading Among Neuropsychiatric Patients," *U.S. Veterans Bureau Medical Bulletin* 6:1088-1090 (1930).

Green, Elizabeth and S. I. Scwab. "The Therapeutic Use of a Hospital Library," *The Hospital Social Services Quarterly* 1:147-157 (August 1919).

Griffin, Julius, "Summary of Bibliotherapy Lectures Presented to the Professional Staff of Patton State Hospital During July and August 1959" (Encino, California: Griffin Clinic, 1959).

Griffith, Leah Ann, "The Agnews State Hospital Bibliotherapy Program," *News Notes of California Libraries* 66:400-404 (Summer 1971).

Groff, Patrick J. "Biography: The Bad or the Bountiful?," *Top of The News* 29:210-217 (April 1973).

Halleck, Seymour L. *Politics of Therapy* (New York: Science House, 1971).

Haines, Helen E. *Living with Books: The Art of Book Selection.* 2nd ed. (New York: Columbia University, 1950).

Hannigan, Margaret C. "The Librarian in Bibliotherapy: Pharmacist or Bibliotherapist?" *Library Trends* 11:184-199 (October 1962).

——. "Survey of Hospital Library Activities in Reading Guidance and Bibliotherapy," *ALA Hospital Book Guide* 17:65-66 (April 1956).

*Hannigan, Margaret and William Henderson. "Narcotic Addicts Take Up Reading," *Bookmark* 22:281-284 (July 1963).

*Harrower, Molly. *The Therapy of Poetry* (Springfield, Illinois: Charles C. Thomas Pub., 1972).

——. "The Therapy of Poetry," in Jules H. Masserman, ed., *Current Psychiatric Therapies* (New York: Grune and Stratton, 1974).

Hartman, Esther A. "Imaginative Literature as a Projective Technique: A Study in Bibliotherapy" (Ph.D. dissertation, Stanford University, 1951).

Havighurst, Robert J. *Developmental Tasks and Education* (New York: Longmans, Green, and Co., 1950).

Heminghaus, Earl George. "The Effect of Bibliotherapy on the Attitudes and Personal and Social Adjustments of a Group of Elementary School Children" (Ph.D. dissertation, Washington University, 1954).

Hinseth, Lois. "Contract Considerations in the Practice of Bibliotherapy," *HRLS Quarterly* 1:21-22 (October 1975).

Hirsch, Lore. "Bibliotherapy with Neuropsychiatric Patients: Individual and Group Therapy," *Hospital Book Guide* 17:87-93 (May 1956).

____. "Book Service to Patients," *Wilson Library Bulletin* 27:634-635 (April 1953).

____. "How a Doctor Uses Books," *Library Journal* 75:2046-2049 (December 1950).

Holland, Norman N. *The Dynamics of Literary Response* (New York: Norton & Co., 1968).

____. *Five Readers Reading* (New Haven: Yale University Press, 1975).

Horn, Thomas D. *Reading for the Disadvantaged* (New York: Harcourt, Brace and World, 1970).

Huey, Edmund Burke. *The Psychology and Pedagogy of Reading* (New York: Macmillan, 1908).

*Huntting, Inez. "The Role of the Occupational Therapist As Related to Bibliotherapy," *Library Trends* 11:207-216 (October 1962).

Hynes, Arleen. "Bibliotherapy At St. Elizabeths Hospital," *HRLS Quarterly* 1:18-19 (October 1975).

*____. "Bibliotherapy in the Circulating Library at St. Elizabeths Hospital," *Libri* 25:144-150 (December 1975).

____. "Bibliotherapy Training Program at St. Elizabeths Hospital" paper presented at the fourth annual Association for Poetry Therapy conference, New York, April 24, 1976.

Ireland, G. O. "Bibliotherapy: The Use of Books as a Form of Treatment in a Neuropsychiatric Hospital," *U.S. Veterans Bureau Medical Bulletin* 5:972-974 (June 1929).

*Jackson, Evalene P. "Bibliotherapy and Reading Guidance: A Tentative Approach to Theory," *Library Trends* 11:118-126 (October 1962).

____. "Effects Of Reading Upon Attitudes Toward Negroes," *Library Quarterly* 14:47-54 (January 1944).

____. "The Therapeutic Value of Books," *Modern Hospital* 25:50-51 (July 1925).

Jones, E. K. "Library Work Among the Insane," *ALA Bulletin* 6:320-324 (July 1912).

Jones, Ernest, ed. *The Collected Papers of Sigmund Freud.* vol. 2 (New York: Basic Books, 1959).

Jones, Perrine. "Hospital Libraries: Today and Tomorrow," *Bulletin of the Medical Library Assn.* 32:467-478 (1944).

Junier, Artemisia J. "Bibliotherapy: Projects and Studies With the Mentally Ill Patient," *Library Trends* 11:136-146 (October 1962).

____. "A Subject Index to the Literature of Bibliotherapy 1900-1958" (M. S. Thesis, Atlanta University, 1959).

Kantrowitz, Viola. "Bibliotherapy with Retarded Readers," *Journal of Reading* 11:205:212 (December 1967).

Kaufman, F. W., and W. J. Taylor. "Literature as Adjustment," *Journal of Abnormal and Social Psychology* 21:229-234 (September 1936).

Kemp, C. Gratton. *Small Groups and Self-Renewal* (New York: Seabury Press, 1971).

Kinney, Margaret M. "The Bibliotherapy Program: Requirements for Training," *Library Trends* 11:127-135 (October 1962).

____. "The Patients Library in a Psychiatric Setting," *AHIL Quarterly* 6:12-17 (Winter 1966).

Kircher, Clara J. "Bibliotherapy and the Catholic School Library," in Brother David Martin, ed., *Catholic Library Practice* (Portland, Oregon:University of Portland Press, 1950).

____. *Character Formation Through Books* 2nd ed. (Washington, D.C.: Catholic University Press, 1945).

Klapper, Joseph T. "The Comparative Effects of the Various Media," in Wilbur Schramm, ed., *The Process and Effects of Mass Communication* (Urbana, Illinois, University of Illinois Press, 1954).

Knight, Douglas M., and E. Shepley Norse. *Libraries at Large* (New York: Bowker, 1969).

Koch, Kenneth. *Wishes, Lies, and Dreams: Teaching Children to Write Poetry* (New York: Chelsea House Pub., 1970).

Koch, Kenneth. *I Never Told Anybody: Teaching Poetry In A Nursing Home* (New York: Random House, 1977).

Koestler, Arthur. *The Act of Creation* (New York: Macmillan, 1964).

Kujoth, Jean S. *Libraries, Readers, and Book Selection* (Metuchen, New Jersey: Scarecrow Press, 1969).

Kusterbeck, Patricia V., "Commentary on Bibliotherapy," *Special Libraries* 66:543-544 (November 1975).

Lack, Clara, and Bruce Bettencourt. "Bibliotherapy in the Community," *News Notes of California Libraries* 67:372 (Fall 1973).

____. "Group Bibliotherapy," *HRLSD Quarterly* 1:19-20 (October 1975).

Laing, R. D. *The Divided Self* (London: Penguin, 1965).

____. *The Self and Others* (London: Penguin, 1971).

Lawler, Justus G. "Poetry Therapy?" *Psychiatry* 35:227-237 (August 1972).

Lazarsfeld, Sofie. "The Use of Fiction in Psychotherapy," *American Journal of Psychotherapy* 3:26-33 (January 1949).

Leedy, Jack J. *Poetry Therapy* (Philadelphia: Lippincott, 1969).

___. *Poetry the Healer* (Philadelphia: Lippincott, 1973).

*Lejeune, Archie L. "Bibliocounseling as a Guidance Technique," *Catholic Library World* 41:156-164 (November 1969).

Lenrow, Elbert. *Readers' Guide to Prose Fiction* (New York: Appleton-Century-Crofts, 1940).

Lerner, Arthur. "Poetry as Therapy," *American Psychological Monitor* 6:4-5 (August 1975).

___. "Poetry Therapy," *American Journal of Nursing.* 73:1336 (August 1973).

Leventhal, Howard. "Attitudes: Their Nature, Growth and Change," in Charlan Nemeth, ed., *Social Psychology: Classic and Contemporary Integrations* (Chicago: Rand McNally, 1974).

Lewin, Kurt. *A Dynamic Theory of Personality* (New York: McGraw-Hill, 1935).

___. *Field Theory in Social Science* (New York: Harper, 1951).

Lind, J. E. "The Mental Patient and the Library," *Bookman* 65:138-141 (1927).

Lindahl, H. M., and K. Koch. "Bibliotherapy in the Middle Grades," *Elementary English* 29:390-396 (1952).

Loevinger, Lee. "The Ambiguous Mirror: The Reflective-Projective Theory of Broadcasting and Mass Communication," in Francis and Ludmila Voelker, eds., *Mass Media: Forces in Our Society* (New York: Harcourt Brace, 1972).

Lorang, Sister Mary C. *Burning Ice: The Moral and Emotional Effects of Reading* (New York: Scribners, 1968).

___. "The Effect of Reading on Moral Conduct and Emotional Experience" (Ph.D. Dissertation, Catholic University, 1945).

Lucioli, Clara C. "Bibliotherapeutic Aspects of Public Library Services to Patients in Hospitals and Institutions," in Margaret E. Monroe, ed., *Reading Guidance and Bibliotherapy in Public, Hospital, and Institution Libraries* (Madison, Wisconsin: University of Wisconsin Library School, 1971).

Luft, Joseph. *Group Process: An Introduction to Group Dynamics.* 2nd ed. (Palo Alto, California: Mayfield Pub. Co., 1970).

Lyman, Helen. *Library Materials in Service to the New Reader* (Chicago: American Library Association, 1973).

Malkiewicz, Joseph E. "Stories Can Be Springboards," *The Instructor* 79:133+ (April 1970).

Marshall, Gail. "Make Way for Children," *Elementary School Journal* 76:157-160 (December 1975).

———. "Stories for Children and Children's Stories." *Elementary School Journal* 76:157-160 (December 1975).

Maslow, Abraham H. *Motivation and Personality* (New York: Harper, 1954).

Mason, Mary Frank. "What Shall the Patient Read?," *The Modern Hospital* 66:74-77 (February 1946).

Matters, Gloria. "Bibliotherapy in a Sixth Grade" (Ph.D. dissertation, Pennsylvania State Univeristy, 1961).

Maxfield, David K. *Counselor Librarianship* University of Illinois Library School Occasional Papers no. 38 (Urbana, Illinois: University of Illinois, March 1954).

Mayden, P. "What Shall the Psychiatric Patient Read?," *American Journal of Nursing* 52:192 (1952).

McClaskey, Harris, "Bibliotherapy with Emotionally Disturbed Patients: An Experimental Study" (Ph.D. Dissertation, University of Washington, 1970).

McDaniel, Walton B. II. "Bibliotherapy: Some Historical and Contemporary Aspects," *ALA Bulletin* 50:584-589 (October 1956).

McDowell, David J. "Bibliotherapy in a Patients' Library," *Bulletin of the Medical Library Association* 59:450-457 (July 1971).

McFarland, J. H. "A Method of Bibliotherapy," *American Journal of Occupational Therapy* 6:66-73+ (March/April 1952).

McKinney, Fred. "Explorations in Bibliotherapy: Personal Involvement in Short Stories and Cases," *Psychotherapy: Theory Research, and Practice* 12:110-117 (Spring 1975).

Meckel, H. C. "An Exploratory Study of the Responses of Adolescent Pupils to Situations in a Novel" (Ph.D. dissertation, University of Chicago, 1947).

*Medlicott, R. W. "Bibliotherapy," *New Zealand Libraries* 38:205-209 (August 1975).

Menninger, Karl A., M.D. *The Human Mind* 2nd ed. (New York: Knopf, 1937).

*———. "Reading as Therapy," *ALA Bulletin* 55:316+ (April 1961).

Menninger, William C., M.D. "Bibliotherapy," *Bulletin of the Menninger Clinic* 1:263-274 (November 1937).

Mereness, Dorothy. "Bibliotherapy: Its Use in Nursing Therapy," *Library Trends* 11:199-206 (October 1962).

*Miller, A. M. "The Reading Matter of Patients," *International Library Review* 4:373-377 (1972).

Monroe, Margaret E. *Library Adult Education* (Metuchen, New Jersey: Scarecrow, 1963).

____. "Services in Hospital and Institution Libraries," in Genevieve Casey, *Libraries in the Therapeutic Society* (Chicago: Association of Hospital and Institutional Libraries, 1971).

____, ed. *Reading Guidance and Bibliotherapy in Public, Hospital, and Institution Libraries* (Madison, Wisconsin: University of Wisconsin Library School, 1971).

____. "What Makes a Good Book Collection?," *Maryland Libraries* 30: 6-11 (Spring 1964).

Monroe, Margaret E. and Rhea J. Rubin. "Bibliotherapy: Trends in the United States," *Libri* 25:156-162 (1975).

*Moody, Mildred T. "Bibliotherapy for Chronic Illnesses," *Hospital Progress* 45:62-63 (January 1964).

____. "Bibliotherapy: Modern Concepts In General Hospitals and Other Institutions," *Library Trends* 11:147-158 (October 1962).

Moody, Mildred T. and Hilda K. Limper, eds. *Bibliotherapy: Methods and Materials* (Chicago: American Library Association, 1971).

Morrison, Morris R. "Standards for Certification of Poetry Therapists and Related Matters: A Proposal," *AHIL Quarterly* 12:33-34 (1973).

Moses, Harold A. "Counseling with Physically Handicapped High School Students" (Ph.D. dissertation, University of Missouri, 1965).

National Society for the Study of Education. *Adult Reading* (Chicago: University of Chicago, 1956).

Oathout, Melvin C. "Books and Mental Patients," *Library Journal* 79:405-410 (March 1954).

Ohlsen, M. *Guidance Services in the Modern School* (New York: Harcourt Brace, 1964).

Opler, Pauline. "The Origins and Trends of Bibliotherapy as a Device in American Mental Hospital Libraries" (M.S. Thesis, San Jose State College, 1969).

Otto, Herbert A. *Group Methods to Actualize Human Potential* (Beverly Hills, California: Holistic Press, 1973).

Panken, Judge Jacob. "Psychotherapeutic Value of Books in the Treatment and Prevention of Juvenile Delinquency," *American Journal of Psychopathology* 1:71-86 (January 1947).

Pearson, John S. "Bibliotherapy and the Clinical Psychologist," *Library Trends* 11:177-183 (October 1962).

Peller, Lili E. "Daydreams and Children's Favorite Books," in Judy Rosenblith and Wesley Allensmith, eds., *The Causes of Behavior* (Boston: Allyn and Bacon, 1962).

Penland, Patrick R. *Communications Management Of Human Resources to Librarians* (Pittsburgh, Pennsylvania: University of Pittsburgh, 1971).

——. *Leadership Development for Librarians* (Pittsburgh, Pennsylvania: University of Pittsburgh, 1971).

Penland, Patrick R. and Sarah F. Fine. *Group Dynamics and Individual Development* (New York: Marcel Dekker, Inc., 1974).

Perrine, Charles J. "A Correctional Institution's Library Services," *Wilson Library Bulletin* 30:249-252 (November 1955).

Peterson, Stan. "Harnessing Book Power Through Biblioguidance," *Idaho Librarian* 27:64-66 (April 1975).

Pfeiffer, J. William, and John E. Jones. *A Handbook of Structured Experiences for Human Relations Training* (La Jolla, California: University Associates, 1974).

Plank, Robert. "Science Fiction," *American Journal of Ortho-Psychiatry* 30:799-810 (1960).

Pomeroy, Elizabeth. "Bibliotherapy: A Study in Results of Hospital Library Service," *Medical Bulletin of the Veterans Administration* 13:360-364 (April 1937).

Pomeroy, Esther B. "Aims of Bibliotherapy in a Tuberculosis Sanitoria," *Library Journal* 65:687-689 (September 1940).

Porterfield, Austin L. *Mirror for Adjustment: Therapy in Home, School, and Society Through Seeing Yourself and Others in Books* (Fort Worth, Texas: Leo Potishman Foundation, Texas Christian University 1967).

Powell, J. W., and others. "Group Reading and Group Therapy," *Psychiatry* 15:33-51 (February 1952).

Powers, Audrey and Rhea Rubin. "Bibliotherapy," *Booklegger* 3:20-24 (Summer 1976).

Progoff, Ira. *At A Journal Workshop: The Basic Text and Guide for Using the Intensive Journal* (New York: Didalogue House, 1975).

Purves, Alan C. and Rippere, Victoria. *Elements of Writing About A Literary Work: A Study of Response to Literature* (Urbana, Illinois: National Council of Teachers of English, 1968).

Purves, Alan C. and Beach, Richard. *Literature and the Reader: Research in Response to Literature, Reading Interests, and the Teaching of Literature* (Urbana, Illinois: National Council of Teachers of English, 1972).

Quint, Mary D. "The Mental Hospital Library," *Mental Hygiene* 28:263-272 (1944).

Raimey, Victor C., ed. *Training in Clinical Psychology* (New York: Prentice-Hall, 1950).

Reid, Virginia M., and others. *Reading Ladders for Human Relations.* 5th ed. (Washington, DC: American Council on Education, 1972).

Riccio, A. "The Status of the Autobiography," *Peabody Journal of Education* 36:32-37 (1958).

Robinson, Helen M. and Samuel Weintraub. "Research Related to Children's Interests and Developmental Values of Reading," *Library Trends* 22:81-108 (October 1973).

Robinson, S. Sue, and Jean K. Mowbray. "Why Poetry?," in Jack Leedy, ed. *Poetry Therapy* (Philadelphia: Lippincott, 1969).

Rogers, Carl R. "The Necessary and Sufficient Conditions of Therapeutic Personality Change," *Journal of Consulting Psychology* 21:95-103 (April 1957).

____. *On Becoming a Person* (Boston: Houghton-Mifflin, 1961).

____. *Person to Person: The Problem of Being Human* (New York: Pocket Books, 1971).

Roman, M. *Reaching Delinquents Through Reading* (Springfield, Illinois: Charles C. Thomas, Pub., 1957).

Rome, Howard P. "Whence, Whither, and Why: Psychiatry Circa 1964," *AHIL Quarterly* 4:31-40 (Summer 1964).

*Rongione, Louise A. "Bibliotherapy: Its Nature and Uses," *Catholic Library World* 43:497-498 (May/June 1972).

____. "Science Fiction: The Psychological Aspects of Science Fiction Can Contribute Much to Bibliotherapy,"*Catholic Library World* 36:96-97 (October 1964).

Rosenblatt, Louise M. *Literature As Exploration* (New York: Appleton-Century-Crofts, 1938).

Rosenblith, Judy and Wesley Allensmith. *The Causes of Behavior* (Boston: Allyn and Bacon, 1962).

Rothstein, Samuel. *The Development of Reference Services Through Academic Traditions, Public Library Practice, and Special Librarianship.* Association of College and Research Libraries Monograph no. 14 (Chicago: A.C.R.L., 1955).

Rovin, R. "Identification Patterns of High School Students with Literary Characters," *The School Counselor* 14:144-148 (January 1967).

Rubin, Rhea J., ed. "Bibliotherapy" *HRLS Quarterly* 1:1-27 [entire issue] (October 1975).

____. "Service to the Ex-Advantaged," *Catholic Library World* 45:438-442 (April 1974).

____. *U.S. Prison Library Services and Their Theoretical Bases.* University of Illinois Library School Occasional Papers no. 110 (Urbana, Illinois: University of Illinois, December 1973).

Ruitenbeek, Hendrik M. *The New Group Therapies* (New York: Avon, 1970).

____. *Psychoanalysis and Literature* (New York: Dutton, 1964).

*Russell, David H. and Caroline Shrodes. "Contributions of Research in Bibliotherapy to the Liberal Arts Program Part I," *School Review* 58:335-342 (September 1950).

____. "Contributions of Research in Bibliotherapy to the Liberal Arts Program Part II," *School Review* 58:411-420 (October 1950).

Ryan, M. J. "Bibliotherapy and Psychiatry: Changing Concepts 1937-1957," *Special Libraries* 48:197-199 (May/June 1957).

Sample, Hazel, *Pitfalls of Readers of Fiction* (Chicago: National Council of Teachers of English, 1940).

Schauffler, R. H., *The Poetry Cure* (New York: Dodd, 1931).

Schloss, Gilbert. *Psychopoetry: A New Approach to Self-Awareness Through Poetry Therapy* (New York: Grossett and Dunlap, 1976).

Schneck, Jerome, M.D. "Bibliotherapy and Hospital Library Activities for Neuropsychiatric Patients: A Review of the Literature with Comments on Trends," *Psychiatry* 8:207-228 (May 1945).

Schneider, Daniel E. *The Psychoanalyst and the Artist* (New York: Mentor, 1962).

Schramm, Wilbur. *The Process and Effects of Mass Communication* (Urbana, Illinois: University of Illinois Press, 1954).

____. "Why Adults Read?," in National Society for the Study of Education, *Adult Reading* (Chicago: University of Chicago Press, 1956).

Shiryon, Michael. "From Bibliotherapy to Literatherapy: The Next Twenty-Five Years." Speech presented at the California State Psychological Association Convention, Oakland, California, January 26, 1973.

____. "Group Literatherapy: A Bibliotherapeutic Approach." Speech presented at the 13th annual Golden Gate Group Psychotherapy Society Conference, San Francisco, California, June 20, 1970.

Shrodes, Caroline. "Bibliotherapy: A Theoretical and Clinical-Experimental Study" (Ph.D. Dissertation, University of California, 1949).

*____. "Literatherapy: Theory and Application," Speech at the Annual Meeting of the Western Psychological Assoc., 1973.

*Simsova, Sylva. ed. *Nicholas Rubakin and Bibliopsychology* (Hamden, Connecticut: Archon Books, 1968).

Smith, N. B. "Personal and Social Values of Reading," *Elementary English* 25:490-500 (1948).

——. "Some Effects of Reading on Children," *Elementary English* 25:271-278 (1948).

Squire, James R., ed. *Response to Literature* (Urbana, Illinois: National Council of Teachers of English, 1968).

Starbuck, Edwin D. *A Guide to Literature for Character Training.* vol. 1 (New York: Macmillan Co., 1928).

——. *A Guide to Literature for Character Training.* vol. 2 (New York: Macmillan Co., 1930).

Stone, Alan A. and Sue S. Stone, eds. *The Abnormal Personality Through Literature* (Englewood Cliffs, New Jersey: Prentice-Hall, 1966).

Stone, Walter. "Adult Education and the Public Library," *Library Journal* 88:437-454 (April 1953).

Strang, Ruth. *Explorations in Reading Patterns* (Chicago: University of Chicago Press, 1942).

*Sweeney, Daniel. "Bibliotherapy and the Elderly," Speech presented at the East Coast Bibliotherapy Round Table, Washington DC, January 11, 1976.

Szasz, Thomas S. *The Myth of Mental Illness* (New York: Dell, 1967).

Termand, Lewis M. and Lima, Margaret. *Children's Reading: A Guide for Parents and Teachers* (New York: D. Appleton Co., 1926).

Tews, Ruth M. ed. "Bibliotherapy," *Library Trends* 11:97-228 [entire issue] (October 1962).

——. "Bibliotherapy," in Allen Kent and Harold Lancour, eds., *Encyclopedia of Library and Information Science* (New York: Marcel Dekker, 1969).

——. "The Patients' Library," in Thomas E. Keys, *Applied Medical Practice* (Springfield, Illinois: Charles C. Thomas, Pub., 1958).

——. "The Role of the Librarian in Bibliotherapy." Speech presented at the University of Wisconsin library school, July 1968.

*——. "The Role of the Librarian on the Interdisciplinary Team," in Margaret Monroe, ed., *Reading Guidance and Bibliotherapy* (Madison, Wisconsin: University of Wisconsin Library School, 1971).

Tews, Ruth M. and Mildred Moody. "The Practice of Bibliotherapy," in *Institutional Library Service: A Plan for the State of Illinois* (Chicago: American Library Association, 1970).

Tsimpoukis, Constantinos J. "Bibliocounseling: Theory and Research Implications and Applications in Counseling and Guidance" (Ph.D. dissertation, University of Wisconsin, 1968).

Tyson, Robert. "The Validation of Mental Hygiene Literature," *Journal of Clinical Psychology* 4:304+ (July 1948).

Underwood, Benton J. *Experimental Psychology.* 2nd ed. (New York: Appleton-Century-Crofts, 1966).

Van der Post, Laurens. *Jung and the Story of Our Time* (New York: Pantheon, 1975).

Vernor, P. E. *Creativity* (London: Penguin, 1970).

Voelker, Francis and Ludmila. *Mass Media: Forces in Our Society* (New York: Harcourt Brace, 1972).

Waples, Douglas; Bernard Berelson; and Franklyn Bradshaw. *What Reading Does to People* (Chicago: University of Chicago Press, 1940).

Weimerskirch, Philip J. "Benjamin Rush and John Mimson Galt II — Pioneers of Bibliotherapy in America," *Bulletin of the Medical Library Association* 53:510-526 (1965).

Weiss, Carol H. *Evaluation Research: Methods of Assessing Program Effectiveness* (Englewood Cliffs, New Jersey: Prentice-Hall, 1972).

Western, Leone Noble. *The Goldkey to Writing Life Histories, Memoirs, or Autobiographies* (Lummi Island, Washington: The author, 1975).

Whipple, Charles M. "The Effect of Short Term Bibliotherapy On the Personality and Academic Achievement of Reformatory Inmate Students" (Ph.D. dissertation, University of Oklahoma, 1968).

Whipple, Gertrude. "Practical Problems of School Book Selection for Disadvantaged Pupils," in J. Allen Figurel, ed., *Reading and Realism* (Newark, Delaware: International Reading Association, 1969).

Wilson, J. Watson. "The Treatment of an Attitudinal Pathosis by Bibliotherapy: A Case Study," *Journal of Clinical Psychology* 7:345-351 (October 1951).

Wineman, David. "The Effects of the Institution on the Person," in Genevieve Casey. *Libraries in the Therapeutic Society,* pp. 1-10 (Chicago: AHIL, 1971).

Witty, Paul A. "Meeting Developmental Needs Through Reading," *Education* 84:451-458 (1964).

——. "Reading to Meet Emotional Needs," *Elementary English* 29:75-84 (1952).

Wolman, B. B. *Handbook of Clinical Psychology* (New York: McGraw-Hill, 1965).

Zaccaria, Joseph S. and Harold A. Moses. *Facilitating Human Development Through Reading: The Use of Bibliotherapy in Teaching and Counseling* (Champaign, Illinois: Stipes Pub. Co., 1968).

Zentner, T. R. *The Effects of Bibliotherapy on Depressed Behavior In Prison Inmates* (M.A. thesis, University of Montana, 1972).

Zimbardo, Philip and Ebbe E. Ebbesen. *Influencing Attitudes and Changing Behavior: A Basic Introduction to Relevant Methodology, Theory and Applications* (Reading, Massachusetts: Addison-Wesley, 1970).

*Articles can be found in *Bibliotherapy Sourcebook,* by Rhea J. Rubin (Phoenix, Arizona: The Oryx Press, 1978).

Index

Compiled by Susan Stein